A Whaler at Twilight

A WHALER AT TWILIGHT

*A True Account of Whaling and Redemption
in the South Pacific*

ALEXANDER R. BRASH AND
ROBERT W. ARMSTRONG

FOREWORD BY TOM KIERNAN, PRESIDENT AND
CEO OF AMERICAN RIVERS

LYONS
PRESS

Essex, Connecticut

An imprint of Globe Pequot, the trade division of
The Rowman & Littlefield Publishing Group, Inc.
4501 Forbes Blvd., Ste. 200
Lanham, MD 20706
www.rowman.com

Distributed by NATIONAL BOOK NETWORK

British Library Cataloguing in Publication Information available

Library of Congress Cataloging-in-Publication Data

Names: Armstrong, Robert W., 1828-1905 author. | Armstrong, Robert W., 1828-1905.
  Autobiography. | Brash, Alexander, 1958- author.
Title: A whaler at twilight : a true account of whaling and redemption in the South Pacific /
  Alexander R. Brash and Robert W. Armstrong.
Other titles: True account of whaling and redemption in the South Pacific
Description: Essex, Connecticut : Lyons Press, [2023] | Includes bibliographical references and
  index.
Identifiers: LCCN 2022060946 (print) | LCCN 2022060947 (ebook) | ISBN 9781493074761
  (cloth) | ISBN 9781493074778 (epub)
Subjects: LCSH: Armstrong, Robert W., 1828-1905—Travel. | Whalers (Persons)—
  Massachusetts—New Bedford—Biography. | Whaling—South Pacific Ocean—History—19th
  century. | Armstong family. | Baltimore (Md.)—Biography.
Classification: LCC G545 .A76 2023 (print) | LCC G545 (ebook) | DDC 910.4/5 [B]—dc23/
  eng/20230315
LC record available at https://lccn.loc.gov/2022060946
LC ebook record available at https://lccn.loc.gov/2022060947

Contents

To the whalers and sailors who didn't make it back around Cape Horn;

To the cetaceans, tubenoses, and all the other creatures of our planet's cerulean seas;

And to Robert Gelston Armstrong, Monuments Man.

'Is it he?' quoth one, 'Is this the man?
By him who died on cross,
With his cruel bow he laid full low
The harmless Albatross.

The spirit who bideth by himself
In the land of mist and snow,
He loved the bird that loved the man
Who shot him with his bow.'

The other was a softer voice,
As soft as honey-dew:
Quoth he, 'The man hath penance done,
And penance more will do.'

THE RIME OF THE ANCIENT MARINER
BY SAMUEL TAYLOR COLERIDGE[1]

FOREWORD

An autobiographical duet? I'd never heard of such a thing. Even Google seems confused. And yet this conundrum of a description is a wonderful beginning to the voyage of discovery, enjoyment, and human development found in *A Whaler at Twilight*.

This shouldn't surprise me, as I have known Alex now for twenty years. He's a superbly knowledgeable conservationist yet also a passionate historian, as he demonstrated by leading the work of the National Parks Conservation Association throughout the Northeast. He's whip smart, sensitive, and astute while also at times courageously bold. His great-great-grandfather Rob Armstrong, whose personal writings are the second voice in this duet, was equally talented, though tortured through much of his life as an orphan and alcoholic.

Using these two protagonists, Alex beautifully weaves together this autobiographical duet into a single story about life on Earth. As a species, humans are complicated, as are both authors. It is the two different perspectives of the natural world of these two individuals that becomes a central theme of this tale. As Alex's great-great-grandfather explains in his portion of this wonderful story, whales were an exciting kill that brought riches of resources to companies and people. We harvested whales because we could and felt this was our right and our destiny. Yet, Alex's poignant and mystical interaction with a whale was very different in a world that is now on the verge of ecological collapse.

It is this evolution of our relationship with the natural world that is a fundamental through-line of this story that binds Alex with his ancestor. And it is this through-line that also speaks to us as readers. Where is this through-line pointing for life on Earth? For those of us who care about the environment and the future of our only planet, what does our future look like? Can whales survive even after we realize that they are more than blubber to be boiled for oil? Will we survive as a species and as a planet?

So, while this is a wonderfully personal story, it is also a devastatingly impactful connection that calls for reflection by the reader on how to conserve our national systems and creatures while understanding the complexity of the human species as transparently shared by Alex and Rob. And, as seen through the alcoholic eyes of Rob Armstrong, how can we as flawed humans effectively work to protect an interconnected natural world upon which we depend?

But this book is not just an environmental treatise. It includes a fascinating exploration of American history, and it highlights the importance of historical preservation, of museums, and of places like the New Bedford National Historical Site and Whaling Museum that retain the wisdom of the past ages so that the present generation, like Alex, can explore their own heritage. Finally, this book also brings in the learnings of a morally tortured man in Rob Armstrong, who finds his savior in God. As Rob eloquently said in the final strains of this duet, "I have had victory over the enemy of my soul, where I used to only meet defeat. I have consecrated myself with all that I am, and have, to Him. He has come into my poor heart in the power of his Holy Spirit, and he now abides there."

A Whaler at Twilight is a deep story worth reading slowly and considering seriously.

Tom Kiernan

President and CEO, American Rivers

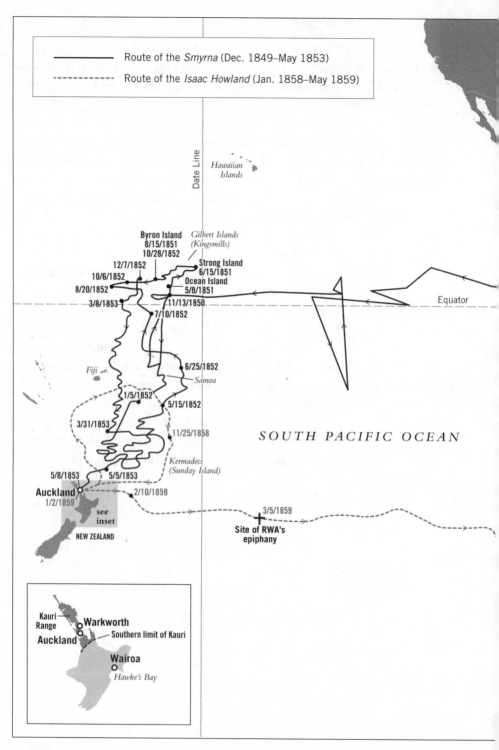

A simplified map of R. W. Armstrong's voyages. Courtesy of Melissa Baker, Lyons Press. Based on RWA's own map (circa 1885), a photo of which can be found in the color insert.

New Bedford
Baltimore

6/25/1859
12/27/1849

6/19/1859

ATLANTIC
OCEAN

WEST INDIES

VENEZUELA

COLOMBIA

BRITISH GUIANA

SURINAM

FRENCH
GUIANA

5/22/1859

5/15/1859

7/15/1850

Galápagos
Islands

ECUADOR

DISPUTED
AREA

Santé

6/24/1850

PERU

BRAZIL

BOLIVIA

2/19/1850

Abrolhos
Banks

5/30/1850

PARAGUAY

ARGENTINA

CHILE

URUGUAY

Montevideo

3/6/1850

4/25/1859

3/30/1859

4/4/1859

Amundsen's Sea

Falkland
Islands

Cape
Horn

3/30/1850

4/18/1859

4/12/1850

4/13/1859

Elephant
Island

South Shetland Islands
and Antarctica region

PART I

"THAR SHE BLOWS"

The Manuscript and Background

CHAPTER I

Lost, But Now Am Found

THE HORIZON WAS MARKED ONLY BY THE UNDULATION OF THE DESUL-tory swells. Then there was a whisper of white, far off; a whale's blow. Our ship turned to the site, but the seas were empty when we got there. For quite some time we drifted in silence. The morning's warm air over the cool ocean waters off Cape Cod in late May had created a heavy fog that hovered just over the sea. The sunlight slipping through the haze reflected tantalizing off the waves and created a numinous silvery sheen with a blinding effect. Dazzled by the glare, I stared into the dark waters, then gasped.

A great eye, smoky gray and opaque, the size of a dinner plate, stared at me as it ascended from the ocean's depths. It was curious, not a hint of malevolence. When its rostrum broke the surface, the scores of ivory-colored barnacles peppering its head resolved themselves, and elicited a moment of deep sympathy. The rising mass created a swirling eddy, and from the murky waters its two great white-edged flippers materialized, each fifteen feet long and also barnacle-encrusted. This humpback whale, near enough to touch, was my first great cetacean so close at hand. Its was mesmerizing both for its colossal size and for immediately imparting an impression of curiosity.

The whale's gaze took in our ship and the people lining the rails. The eye flickered, distracted, then it tracked the movements of a photographer shifting along the rail for a better shot. Then its gaze came back to me, probing; I felt it questioning my intent. There was a connection then, as one would nod to a close friend across a crowded room, and a powerful wash of affinity enveloped me. Then, with a slow blink, the whites of its eye showing, and perhaps satisfied with my innocence, the whale lowered its massive head, raised its flukes high in the air, and slid silently back into the deep.

It was May 1985 and I had come to Cape Cod to trade my expertise as a birder for the chance to go offshore to the Stellwagen Bank to see pelagic seabirds. Pairing up with a graduate student from Rhode Island studying cetaceans and practiced in leading whale watch trips, I had agreed to help him lead a trip to see Cape Cod's whales and birds. So, as my spring semester at Yale's School of the Environment concluded, we set off one Friday afternoon for Provincetown in several cars with roughly twenty patrons. My task was to lead a bird trip through the woods at the tip of Cape Cod on Saturday morning and then identify what oceanic birds we saw when we headed offshore to Stellwagen Bank that afternoon and again on Sunday morning. He was in charge of the whale watching.

Provincetown wasn't yet the thriving LGBT town it has become, nor was traffic to Cape Cod nearly as horrific as it is now. Commercial fishermen, many still speaking Portuguese, lived there year-round, and in the colder months they dominated the town's culture. It was only toward summer that families from Boston and New York would arrive en masse to fill their seasonal cottages. There were few, if any, of today's beautiful B&Bs, and most of what are now elegantly renovated Victorians were then dilapidated windblown structures. Their stately decorative moldings barely hung on, and their busted shutters slapped in the wind as their once colorful shingles faded to cryptic pastels. Our group stayed in a beaten-down motel on the outskirts, and we walked to town for a late dinner on that chilly Friday night. The restaurant did not have the snappy snow peas or the spinach salad I am sure they serve now, but offered only a bluefish fillet smothered in a tomato sauce with a baked potato on the side.

The next morning, in a heavy fog, I led the group around Blackwater Pond in the picturesque Beech Forest of Cape Cod National Seashore. We then hiked out to Race Point, by the Old Harbor Life Saving Station, hoping to spot seabirds that might have strayed inshore in the still vaporous gloom. Near noon, as it cleared, we drove down to the wharves and took one of the Dolphin Fleet's ships offshore. We cruised around the sandy tip of Cape Cod and then turned north to cross Race Point Channel. Six miles to the north a broad undersea plateau rises to within sixty feet of the surface . . . Stellwagen Bank.

When the *Dolphin V*, our eighty-five-foot converted party fishing boat, was still but a mile north of Cape Cod, we saw our first whales. A pod of finbacks sped east in the channel. Their singularly tall and elongated blow patterns and white jaws are distinctive. Their speed is astounding; usually cruising at twenty mph, they can sprint at thirty mph, faster than Jamaican sprinter Usain Bolt. We barely caught a glimpse of them as they plunged by. After another half hour of slow cruising, we arrived at Stellwagen Bank, and in just a few minutes we stumbled onto the misty encounter above. It changed my perspective forever. The humpback's apparent perceptivity stirred sympathies within, and the experience elicited a greater appreciation for the acuity of whales. Over the course of that afternoon we saw many more whales, mostly humpbacks, but a few rights as well. One of the rights came as close to the ship as the first humpback, and even the captain of the ship left the bridge to watch in awe. He dryly observed, "Dang, that's as close as I've ever seen one of 'em." We watched fifty-foot humpbacks breach, their colossal bodies almost completely leaving the sea before slapping back down with a thunderclap. Is breaching a romantic clamor, a means to shake off parasites, or something else? I wondered. We also watched a trio of whales hunt cooperatively. After working together to corral some fish by blowing bubbles around them, they took turns lunging to the surface in their midst with their mouths agape. Each time one of the feeding whales surfaced, one could see thousands of sand eels streaming from the sides of its mouth. As the whale slowly closed its jaws and contracted its ventral pleats, hundreds of screaming and fighting gulls rushed in to grab the escaping fish. It was sheer pandemonium, life on the edge; a raucous and chaotic feeding frenzy. The next morning we repeated the trip, enjoying similar views.

The trip to Stellwagen Bank opened my eyes to many facets of a whale's life, some I probably did not explicitly recognize at the time.

Before then, I hadn't really thought much about their intelligence or mammalian empathy, and certainly not that they might have a "culture." Defined as the cognitive ability to acquire and transfer knowledge through observation and communication, culture is the conscious passing of information within a population instead of a genetic transfer. We had watched humpback whales dive below schools of sand eels, then swim in a spiral beneath them, slowly releasing air to encircle them in a curtain of bubbles. I did not know this was a learned behavior. Subsequently, marine scientists documented that at the time of my visit to Stellwagen Bank, bubble curtains were a new behavior, and one that was just beginning to spread.[1] Humpbacks were also just learning that if they used their tail fluke to smash the rising school of sand eels consolidated by the bubbles, this further disoriented them and made it easier for the whale rising from below to swallow more in one bite. These cooperative behaviors were first observed in the area in the mid-1980s, but shortly after they began to be passed along more broadly and are now employed by most of the humpbacks found in the Western Atlantic.

Not then, but now it is fairly common knowledge that other whale species have cultures defined by distinct dietary preferences, foraging behaviors, communication, and kin care. For example, besides the humpback's feeding techniques, killer whales are well known for population-specific prey selection. Some killer whale groups specialize in salmon, others in marine mammals, and some in sharks and rays. Similarly, sperm whales pass along an array of behaviors related to childcare, and in some groups, only closely related females will guard and suckle young, while in other groups a broader array of kin will share these tasks.[2] Bottlenose dolphins are known to pass along insights in tool use. Perhaps most beguiling, humpback societies are delineated by their complex songs. Males craft songs that are a set of notes woven into melodic rhythms. Sometimes a song lasts for only a few minutes, but more typically a half hour or more. Not to cast pedagogic aspersion among whale species, but while the simpler songs of blue and fin whales appear to persist unchanged within a population for decades, the more complicated humpback songs evolve rather rapidly in time. A recent study of humpback songs in the South

Pacific showed new songs were passed from whales off Eastern Australia to groups around French Polynesia in just two years.[3]

This breadth of cetacean culture certainly elevates them amid their mammalian peers, and drifting off to sleep back home in New Haven that Sunday night, it occurred to me that elements of whales' culture are older than the dawn of man. So, when I called home the next day to tell my parents about the trip, I was astounded when my mother said, "You know, Alex, we have a whaler in our family history."

More than surprised, I was aghast. This seemed so anachronistic. Busy with my own life that day, and for years after, I brushed off the remark, and she let the matter drop.

A decade passed. I had the pleasure to work for a brilliant conservationist, Tom Lovejoy, at the World Wildlife Fund in Washington, D.C., then shifted to a PhD program in community ecology at Rutgers University, and next found myself at New York City's Parks Department. One day my mother again brought up the subject of the whaler.

"You know, there's a map," she said.

"That's great, Mom," I replied.

She pressed on, asserting there were more tangibles. Not only a map, but a manuscript, she said. "He's your ancestor," she noted with a "harrumph."

A bit vague on the details, Mom said nothing about where this manuscript was, only that the "whaler" had written about his time at sea. It still seemed abstract to me. I imagined this manuscript was, at best, a lengthy, illegible letter. More years went by. My father died, and in the aftermath, my mother spent considerable time digging into the family's genealogy. Mom has always been interested in our ancestors. She loves to observe that "one fought in the Revolution, and another was a female Paul Revere." We also have a Jamaican slave in the past on my father's side, and Mom struggled for years to resolve our kinship with an early Dutch and Native American set of ancestors. She would always follow her geneaological comments by saying she wasn't a fan of those "uppity groups" like the Daughters of the Revolution. "We're swamp Yankees and should be proud of it," she'd add.

Meanwhile, I forged ahead on my road in life. I was married with two kids and living in a small apartment in Manhattan and now serving as the chief of the park rangers for the city. My job was 24/7. Responsible for all the uniformed officers in the agency, I managed security at the city's parks, beaches, and pools and at large special events like rock concerts and papal visits. Bad days meant responding to a bloodied crime scene in a playground, while a good day was releasing screech owls in Central Park with Isabella Rosellini. But, like most mothers, mine is an indomitable person. And, like most children, I've always felt I owe her. I am not exactly sure the nature of the debt, its size, its depth, or its temporal boundaries, but owe I do. She gave nearly every hour of every day to raise me, and she poured out pure, unconditional love. Such fathomless love is a great blessing and wonderful thing, but also sometimes a burden. Families are complicated stuff. Anyway, over these latter years I promised her, again and again, that I would read the whaler's manuscript and assume responsibility for the family's history, but I must admit, secretly I found her research self-indulgent and irrelevant to my busy world.

In due course, after serving under four mayors, I left NYC Parks to be a regional director for a wonderful nonprofit, the National Parks Conservation Association (NPCA). Oddly, this job came with a desk at Bloomberg LLP. One of Mike's partners, Tom Secunda, while gruff as a grizzly, has a heart of gold and loves our national parks, and so I went to work in the firm's black glass building at 59th Street. I spent most of my days sitting at a small, impersonal "workspace" surrounded by thousands of others in the organization's famous, but sterile, open office floor plan. While I pondered potential new parks, budget cuts, congressional relationships, donor preferences, and other matters, those around me shouted and hollered as they sold the wizard's machines. Most days I left home before light and returned after dark. After a decade at NPCA I left to run the beleaguered Connecticut Audubon Society for several years. Tripling its endowment, adding some significant nature preserves, and refocusing its educational and conservation efforts, it was also a stewpot of conflicted interests, and so I retired.

Through these years, my mother's pursuits seemed not only trifling, but reflective of an Old World, claustrophobic, aristocratic view of life. Probably beginning with my adolescent rebellion, but ramping up during my years of public service, I had long embraced an ethical indifference to my past. I felt that we are who we are, and we make of our lives what we can. Cloaked with the sentiments of Horatio Alger and Ayn Rand, I espoused an Americanized view of family history as opposed to a more classic European embrace of class and society. In my world, one was judged in peer-reviewed journals, or by the success of tasks completed, parks created, events safely managed, and by operating numbers as reported to City Hall or to headquarters in Washington, D.C. However, as in most things, with time's passing the tide changed and my perspective shifted. The righteous stark contrasts I had embraced in my youth gave way to a grayer milieu. So upon my retirement, after taking several months to do nothing but relax, read, and fish a bit, at last I felt compelled to add structure to my now open-ended future. I began to assemble a purposeful bucket list. Not the usual one, detailing pipe dreams about where I wanted to go and what I might want to do, but rather one that delineated those requisite tasks I felt obligated to complete. In particular, I focused on multigenerational projects that needed to be finished while family elders were still capable. One of these tasks was to digitize, catalog, and archive our family photographs, incorporating my mother's and my paternal aunt's collections, too. Another was to review my mother's genealogical work and ensure its preservation for posterity. Simultaneously, and perhaps not coincidentally, my sentiments on family history shifted. My previously held, vaguely nihilistic, views waned and were replaced with considerably more interest in our heritage. Youthful sentiments of black and white faded to an older person's palette of gray.

My mother, now in her early nineties, was luckily still in great shape, though she would say "my knees creak," and her macular degeneration required stronger lenses every few years. Anyway, we began meeting more frequently as I assembled the family's photos. Together we went through several shoeboxes of sepia-toned black-and-white photos from her side of the family. She also helped me with piles of photographs I found strewn on the floor of the closet in my aunt's apartment on my father's side, even a pair of daguerreotypes. Mom and I had fun together, pausing often to recollect or simply surmise. I encouraged her to identify as many of the distant relations in the photographs as she could, for I knew the window of opportunity was closing. Then, when the photographs were all digitized and chronologically archived, I had them stored on hard drives, with an extra copy placed in a safe-deposit box. Naturally, the story of the "whaler" reemerged in this endeavor. My mother again urged me to "read what I have." So, at last, thirty-two years after I had first heard of the whaler, I acquiesced and one spring day asked to read his tale. Not cracking a smile, she then slowly pulled herself up from her armchair and somewhat painfully went back to her bedroom's closet. After a few minutes she called out, "Alex, you come do this. Pull that trunk out from back there."

Tucked in the back of her closet, stashed under her venerable collection of dresses and skirts, was a large black leather trunk. Bound with brass hinges and corners, the dried leather was cracked, scuffed, and dinged up from years of wear. Inside the trunk was the treasure trove of her world before marriage; her family's relics, mementos, and artifacts. Her baby shoes, white satin with pink ribbons and tiny as could be, lay on top. Beneath were her father's World War I paraphernalia, complete with a compass, an architect's triangle, maps, and posters. In one corner at the bottom of the trunk were two large red leather albums. Instead of photos, these contained newspaper clippings, letters, and programs that my mother's father, G. Franklin Ludington, had collected. Her father, the whaler's grandson, was fortunately quite the collector. Within the pages of the two red albums he had glued items ranging from his elementary school report cards to letters from the War Department. There was also an array of love letters from girlfriends when he was in law school; surprisingly a considerable number and all tenderly written.

In another corner of the trunk, beneath a handful of small lead toy soldiers and a miniature train set, was a manila folder. Inside was a thick sheath of startling black pages against which bright white lettering lept out.[4] The manuscript's pages were akin to the dark purple mimeographed pages from my grade school days, the ones that stained my fingertips. It turned out that in 1937 my grandfather used a newfangled photostatic machine in his office to make a complete copy of the whaler's handwritten manuscript. Bright and clear in its antipodal presentation, the white script against the black pages made for easy reading. There was also a map of the South Pacific in the same white-on-black presentation. I was now firmly sucked into my mother's vortex, and for the next three months, I spent each morning painstakingly reading and transcribing the whaler's manuscript. I read his handwriting slowly, parceling out scrawled words, clearly enunciating each one into my laptop's microphone. Spring turned to summer. My wife and children thought I had gone daft. They frequently pointed out all the chores that needed to be done around the house. But they didn't feel my filial debt and the legacy the endeavor represented. I understood their distaste for my compulsion but navigated it with my best equanimity. At last, the manuscript was completed, and the whaler's story came to life.

Weeks rolled into months, and months into a couple of years, and between other life happenings, I read and reread the whaler's tale. I lightly edited his account and then, curiosity aroused, I researched its underpinnings. I investigated the whaler's friends and acquaintances, the nomenclature of distant South Pacific islands, whaling techniques, and even towns along the Peruvian coast. I contemplated certain assertions about events he witnessed, ships on the voyage, mutinies, and the inhabitants of various islands. Fortunately, as an alumnus of Yale's School of the Environment, the university had blessed me with access to JSTOR, the online academic research library. Between JSTOR, Google, and various other online libraries, I delved far and wide, pursuing family connections, newspaper clippings, numerous arcane reference materials on whaling, the South Pacific, Baltimore, and other threads that presented themselves. With Ancestry.com I researched and tracked the whaler's side of my family. I added background and context to his tale; then, no longer able to contain my curiosity, I followed a bit in his footsteps.

My inquisitiveness piqued by reading about distant lands and great adventures, I roused myself from the glowing screen of my laptop and decided it was time to venture out to experience what facets of my ancestor's life I could. First, I visited Baltimore to walk its streets. I stood in front of long-gone addresses of where my family lived and worked. I wandered all around the Inner Harbor, focused on the remaining structures from the whaler's era. With the USS *Constellation* in the background, I sat on the seawall and watched people stroll by. I mentally replaced their modern apparel with period garb and pushed them back in time. I breathed in the smells, walked the wharves, and tried to envision the city's past.

I then expanded my efforts and visited New Bedford, Massachusetts, the whaling capital of the world in the nineteenth century. There, I had my mind blown by an incredible stroke of fortuitous circumstance, and in a way that rebounded directly into my mother's work on our family history. My first intention was simply to see New Bedford, visit the national park site, and walk the town's historic district. I wanted to see the old buildings, especially those that still had period features, such as gingerbread trimmings, widow's walks, or windows of crown glass. I thought simply breathing in the salty air of Buzzards Bay and feeling the cobblestone streets underfoot would be enough. But, not wishing to miss an opportunity, I also called ahead to inquire about visiting the New Bedford Whaling Museum and their library, thinking I might as well combine some additional research with my visit. My call was rather stuffily answered by a man who asked me to state my purpose. Taken aback, I replied that I was researching an old manuscript and looking for background on several of the whaling ships named therein. The person answering the phone turned out to be the librarian, Mark Procknik, and after describing my interests, his attitude quickly warmed. "Indeed," he chirped, "we have various lists and logs for some of the ships you mention." He welcomed me to stop in, and we agreed on a date. So on a brisk, bright October morning, the type of day that has the last sailboats on Long Island Sound scurrying to their winter quarters, I drove north to Massachusetts.

Like so many New England towns, New Bedford is caught between its past, present, and some undetermined future. After taking I-95 and then heading east on I-195, one exits to drive south into town on Route 18. The historic town of New Bedford is to the right, while a great fleet of modern fishing boats is docked on the left by Fish Island. Modern, meaning they are of this century, but in fact the ships are all old and weathered. When I went, there were close to a hundred trawlers and draggers, each daubed with long rivulets of rust weeping from under their portholes and steel spars. In the older part of the city, William and Union Streets bracket Johnny Cake Hill and Acushnet Avenue. The blocks around the New Bedford Whaling Museum are crowded with iconic buildings, from the Seamens' Bethel Church and the "Landing" to the shops on Water Street. Farther inland an array of vestigial Victorian houses stand side by side, testament to the wealth that ship owners and captains once brought to the city. Beyond lies the vaster surrounding area of weather-beaten homes, rusting cars, and squalid bars, complete with fake-brick asphalt siding. The largest stain on the town's history, the infamous Big Dan's Tavern in the North End, is long gone, but its social heirs remain.

I walked the neighborhood for a while before entering the grandiose Georgian redbrick museum with its octagonal cupola perched on top. Past several huge whale skeletons hanging from the steel rafters, I climbed the stairs to find hallways filled with lances, harpoons, and scrimshawed teeth. I made my way along a somnolent carpeted corridor lined with portraits of dark-jacketed and scowling sea captains. At the end was a set of heavy glass doors, gates to the library. They whispered open at my touch. The main reading room consisted of a half-dozen heavy oak tables surrounded by uncomfortable wooden chairs on a thick, cream-colored rug, and around the room's perimeter were ship models in glass cases, one strikingly made entirely from ivory. In one corner stood an anachronistic, dusty gray 1970s-era microfiche machine. At the back of the room were several tall shelves filled with index books and a long desk, behind which the librarian waited. Mark greeted me in hushed tones and asked more specifically what I was looking for. I told him of my ancestor's manuscript, naming him for the first time: Robert W. Armstrong.

"Ah, we know of Robert Armstrong quite well," he said. "In fact, we have his logbooks."[5]

I was stunned. My first thought was that it must be a different Armstrong. Surely it wasn't that uncommon a name? Without seeming to notice my shocked expression, Mark led me around the room, showing me how the various indexes worked. "This one's for newspapers, that one's for logbooks, and we have another for port records," he said, and explained the library's system for requesting a document, microfiche, or book. He then pointed me toward a table where I might settle in. As I sat down and began pulling out my papers, Mark looked pointedly at the pen in my hand. "Sorry, you're not allowed to use a pen in the room," he said, "or even have it out on the desk."

"Not even on my own papers?" I asked.

"No, sorry," Mark said, adding that only #2 pencils were allowed, and he nodded toward a cup full of them on the librarian's counter. He suggested I start by browsing the indexes to find out which nineteenth-century newspapers, books, or logbooks I might want to peruse regarding the various whaling ships I had mentioned.

With barely a nod, he then disappeared into the reference section of the library, or the stacks, on his way to get Armstrong's logbooks. Meanwhile, I pulled out my notes chronologically listing certain proper names I had identified in the whaler's text. Shortly, I moved over to a row of black leather-bound indexes and squatted on a very uncomfortable plastic stool to begin looking for my ancestor's whaling ships, the *Smyrna* and the *Isaac Howland*.

After fifteen minutes or so, Mark silently appeared and tapped me on the shoulder. He motioned for me to join him back at my table, and there, wearing white cotton gloves, he laid out two logbooks that were indeed from my great-great-grandfather's time. Neither was the whaling ship's actual logbook as kept by the ships' captains, but they were clearly Armstrong's accounts. The first book was the size of a twentieth-century desk diary, each page roughly six by nine inches. I read through it for a while, rapt, and carefully examined some scribbled notations as well as two letters tucked inside. I soon realized it was itself a copy of one of Armstrong's logs. Then I turned to the second book. This one was clearly his book, with his handwriting and marks. Tall and narrow, it was bound in cardboard and covered with a stained, pale cotton cloth. Whether the stains were blood or coffee, they gave the book an inauspicious appearance. Printed as an accountant's book, its pages were horizontally lined but also had several vertically marked columns on the right side of each page for tallying. Portions of the book had been used upon Armstrong's return to note customer accounts and sales in his Baltimore store. In other sections he had ignored these vertical lines and simply kept a diary covering his time upon first returning to Baltimore in 1859. I spent the rest of the afternoon laboriously photographing each page with my phone for later analysis and then reading several relevant newspaper articles on microfiche.

When I returned home, the two different books and their origins continued to fascinate me. In particular, the odd copied version intrigued me so much that I spent several days simply staring at old photographs and squinting at the appalling chicken-scratch while contemplating ancient family dynamics. In the end, I discovered that, upon Armstrong's passing, his children split up his historical legacy, and three of the siblings took various documents as personal mementos. My great-grandmother, the eldest child, took his autobiographical manuscript; the youngest daughter, Jenny, took one logbook; and the youngest son, Gelston, took the other logbook. Decades later, Jenny was still interested enough in her father's adventures that she borrowed Gelston's logbook. She then made her own handwritten copy before she returned it. Many years later, in 2006, the year before she died, Jenny's daughter-in-law, Mary McNeely Free, thoughtfully gave the two books to the New Bedford Whaling Museum. I can only bless her appreciation of history and belief in what to her then were distant and intangible family connections.

Back at home I returned to working on the manuscript, buoyed by the idea that others had also appreciated Armstrong's account of his time at sea. The first step, after fully reviewing the two logbooks, was to sparingly add some of their content to fill out his entries, selectively incorporating a few sections where it seemed appropriate. Surrounded by related texts and parallel stories, I then decided it would enhance his tale if I broadened his story by including some of the historical background that would fill in some blanks and provide context. I enlarged my probe to a larger arc of the people, places, and ships' names he listed. I found several historical accounts that augment his tale, including the logbook for the whaling ship he took home, the *Isaac Howland*. Written by the ship's captain, Reuben Hobbs, the logbook was at the Nantucket Whaling Museum. The museum was just in the process of digitizing their collection, and their staff, Sara David, archive intern, and Amelia Holmes, the archivist, kindly moved it up the schedule so I could review it. I then returned to the black leather trunk in my mother's closet and there found a few more hidden treasures. Nestled in the bottom was a Bible Armstrong had purchased on October 7, 1855, in Auckland, New Zealand.[6] His inscription inside the front cover beckoned with a graceful cursive lettering: "*In te, Domine speravi*," translated as "I put my trust in you, Lord." Notes in the page margins portrayed his ecclesiastical interests. I also found a small memorial booklet prepared for the funeral service of his uncle, Thomas Armstrong. This helped clarify family history. Lastly, tucked in among other effects, I found a note left to Armstrong from his wife, and from this learned that she affectionately referred to him as "Rob," so that's the name I've used throughout the rest of this tale.

After three years of research, a larger and clearer story emerged. His account of the four and three-quarter years he spent on two whaling ships in the South Pacific and the four and a half years he spent logging in New Zealand is not just an incredible adventure story, but also a unique glimpse into a turbulent moment of populism and imperialism in American history. Beginning with his earliest days in Baltimore, his story is a timeless tale in the heart of American history about a human being who struggles with his personal demons, as we all do, and seeks to find purpose. Somewhere along the way, I too became ensnared and then enraptured by his epic adventure, his moral labyrinth, and his travels along—what might be termed—his own yellow-brick road.

In these subsequent pages, our duet continues with two chapters covering a short history of whaling and how the whaler's family came to Baltimore. The whaler's tale follows, intact. His original autobiographical text[7] was first gently edited for grammar, clarity, and cohesion. Next, his text was augmented at intervals with some additional detail, segments from his logbooks or from Captain Hobbs's logbook from the *Isaac Howland*. Then for verisimilitude and color, several of his chosen poems and lists, taken from his logbooks, were added. A few dates and current geographic names were also inserted along the way to help with temporal and geospatial tracking, and one paragraph (on the *Ann Alexander*) was moved in order to bring his recollections in line with fact. This expanded tale is then followed by several chapters exploring in greater depth the historic milieu of his experience. Finally, we conclude with a couple of chapters that probe his faith—the heart of the matter, our personal connection, the fate of our oceans, and illumine his life's twilight.

Chapter 2

A Primer in Whaling

Whales are a product of millions of years of evolution: the tricky biological mechanism whereby sex creates a constant re-mingling of genes, producing diverse individuals, each a unique answer to their world's conditions. These "answers" are then winnowed down to those most successful by the process of natural selection. Winning designs ratchet forward through time while losers go extinct. Sometimes, though, the conditions overwhelm almost all designs, and evolution shifts from the gradual to the abrupt. One such event was the Chicxulub meteor, which smote the Yucatán sixty-six million years ago. Tidal waves, fire, and smoke—repercussions of its impact—darkened and cooled the earth, apparently wiping out most of the dinosaurs and bringing about the rise of mammals.[1] From shrewlike ancestors, warm-blooded, live-bearing, hairy little creatures gradually diversified to fill an abundance of empty ecological niches left by the vanquished reptiles.

Roughly eight million years after the impact, whales split from their earthbound ancestors, the hooved ungulates such as cows, sheep, hippos, and deer, and began their journey back into the seas.[2] At first, they likely spent their time in shallow rivers and estuaries, probably feeding on planktivorous fish. Even forty-seven million years ago, whale ancestors still had all four limbs, their tail was dorsoventrally orientated, and they came out of the water to give birth on land. They looked like giant, short-tailed crocodiles lurking in the mangroves, but with hooves instead of claws and fur instead of scales.[3]

Ten million years later, in the Eocene, an early whale was adapted to living in saltwater. It was characterized by a now horizontally flattened tail that looked like a modern fluke, disconnected tiny hind limbs of no real importance, large forelimbs with "hands" whose fingers were melded together to form fins, and an elongated body. Like a seal today, this creature was no longer capable of living on land.[4] Over the next few millions of years, whale flukes continued to enlarge, their nostrils migrated to the top of their heads, and baleen evolved inside the mouths of one lineage so they could become filter-feeders. The toothed whale group—sperm whales, killer whales, and porpoises—split off just before this last trend, about thirty-five million years ago. The baleen whales then continued to branch out in their own great evolutionary tree. Today, the bowhead and right whales are viewed as one group, from which the gray, blue, and sei whales split off twenty-three million years ago, while the fin whales and humpbacks form a third group. Finally, the diminutive minke whales split off just nineteen million years ago into their own family.[5]

Over this arc of evolution, the great whales navigated the seas, evolved in their ecological niches, and delineated their geographical realms. While they faced predators and pathogens and endured stochastic events like El Niño, they were peacefully oblivious to the little monkeys scampering in the trees. But the monkeys evolved in parallel. Some turned into primates, and some primates evolved into Anthropocenes. For comparison, "Lucy," the hominid, was wandering around just 3.5 million years ago. Finally though, a population of Anthroprocenes evolved into hominids who learned to hunt quite effectively.

No doubt far back in prehistory, humans scavenged and hunted marine mammals from shore. Archaeological finds indicate that indigenous people with access to the ocean have eaten or used marine mammals' skins and bones for thousands of years, particularly pursuing seals, walruses, and smaller inshore whale types such as belugas and narwhals.[6] The earliest such archaeological finds from this era include whalebone use, toggling harpoons, and boat parts made of whale skin. Scant evidence portrays a possible whaling tradition beginning to arise in the Bering Sea region and then slowly spreading to the Eastern Arctic. The expansion of shore-bound whaling activities to more regular offshore chases after great whales became evident around three thousand years ago as indigenous natives in northern Japan, Siberia, and Alaska went to sea to chase down nearshore bowhead, gray, and right whales. Using sealskin kayaks and tiny harpoons, they set off in their frail craft after the great beasts, eager for the meat and bone, but imperiled by weather and angered leviathans.

In one of the first documented accounts about European involvement, Thorfinn Karlsefne, a Norseman, mentions his people trying to eat a beached whale found on Cape Cod in 1008.[7] It was so awful that they all got sick and angrily threw the remains back in the sea. However, by the twelfth century, Norsemen were killing, harvesting, and consuming whales with great relish off Greenland.[8] No doubt fresh kills were healthier than rotted remains. The Basques were the first Europeans to harvest whales on a commercial basis. They supplied Europe with whale meat and oil from the Bay of Biscay beginning in the fourteenth century. Whale tongue was a highly sought epicurean delight for royal feasts.

After having exterminated the Atlantic gray whale, also known as the scragg whale, in the Eastern Atlantic by the 1580s, the Basques began crossing the Atlantic to pursue western right whales off the St. Lawrence River in Canada. The Dutch and English, with their greater experience in sailing and managing fleets, soon followed, and they quickly brought Basques on board as their skilled harpooners and lancers. The industry then expanded northward into the Arctic. By the summer of 1680, more than 188 whaling ships were gathered in the harbor at the town of Smeerenburg on the north shore of Spitzbergen.[9]

By the time of European colonization, the Native Americans of the New England coast had also advanced beyond scavenging for whales to actively hunting them offshore. There is a vague account of this from Florida in 1590, but it was more clearly witnessed by an unnamed English visitor to Nantucket in 1605. He reported that natives went "in company of their king with a multitude of their boats [to] strike a *powdawe* (indigenous term for a whale) with a bone made in fashion of a harping iron fastened to a rope, which they make great and strong of the bark of trees."[10] However, for the European colonists, whaling remained a scavenging effort until the 1660s, largely practiced on Cape Cod and

Long Island, and to a lesser extent along the Delaware, Virginia, and North Carolina shores. Credited with being the first professional whaler, James Lopar was hired to move to Nantucket from Cape Cod in 1672 and teach residents the art of whaling. His salary was one-third the proceeds of any whale brought in.[11]

As with elephants, rhinos, and bison, soon whales were valued for more than their meat. It turned out that whale oil was better than bayberry candles; it was easier to light, lasted longer, and burned brighter. In an increasingly industrialized society, whale oil was also valuable as a lubricant. Economically driven, Nantucket's considerable expertise in fishing evolved and shifted toward whaling. By 1715, there were half a dozen thirty- to forty-ton whaling vessels in the port, most with Native Americans as harpooners.[12] This initial racial mutualism was key, for it paved the way for the industries' future dealings with South Pacific islanders, freed slaves, and others who ultimately crewed its ships. Whaling was, from the beginning, a more egalitarian community than most.

Nantucket's industry continued to expand, and in 1726, eighty-six whales were taken over the course of the year, though all still close to shore. They were then towed to the beach to be flensed, or cut up, and boiled down. The economic success of this small fleet soon brought more entrepreneurs to the effort, and by 1730 the fleet had expanded to 25 small sloops. There were 80 ships by 1756, and in 1775 Nantucket's fleet surpassed 150 ships, bringing home 30,000 barrels of oil. That year also marked the moment the first ship crossed the equator to scout southern seas. The captain, fittingly named Uriah Bunker, returned home to accolades on the day of the battle of Lexington and Concord.

The American Revolution proved disastrous for the nascent whaling industry. The British navy took what they could, capturing or burning more than 134 of Nantucket's fleet. Roughly 1,200 crew were impressed by the British or lost at sea. Among the 800 families on Nantucket, there were at least 202 widows in the late 1770s. The whaling industry, once the backbone of the island's economy, simply died. A number of long-established whaling families, such as the Macys, broke up and left the island to seek employment elsewhere. There was no relief until after Cornwallis surrendered.

The whaling industry revived somewhat in the next decade and then began to prosper again—until the War of 1812. Again, British depredations stripped the sailors' ranks and caused the loss of many ships. The Nantucket fleet, which had regrown to 116 ships by 1812, was reduced to only 23 tattered hulks by 1815, listlessly rotting in the harbor. However, with the conclusion of the war and a surge of whalers onto the Pacific Ocean, the industry blossomed into its "Golden Years." This era truly began in 1818, the year that Captain George Gardner supposedly first sailed a whaler, the *Globe* of Nantucket, west around Cape Horn.[13] By 1833, the American whaling fleet was mostly split between New Bedford and Nantucket and consisted of 392 ships crewed by 10,000 seamen. In 1844 the fleet had grown to 644 ships employing just more than 17,500 sailors. The heyday was roughly in 1847, two years before Rob sailed, when the fleet had grown to 722 ships. Of those, 254 whaling ships called New Bedford home, 75 hailed from Nantucket, 70 from New London, 62 from Sag Harbor, New York, and the rest from 30 other ports.

During Rob's time at sea, New Bedford's dominance continued to grow, and just before his return, New Bedford's fleet peaked at 329 ships in 1857, employing 20,000 sailors. They accounted for 60 percent of the $20 million in capital invested in whaling. During these years, the markets also peaked. Sperm whale oil, which had been worth $0.73 per gallon in 1842, rose to $1.08 in 1849, the year Rob headed out. It crested at $1.77 in 1855 and dropped to $1.36 per gallon by the time he returned in 1859. As the price of oil continued to decrease in the late 1850s, several additional factors also portended the decline of the industry. Least surprising was that under a ruthless siege of the oceans it became harder and harder to locate whales. The financial returns thus declined as ships had to stay at sea longer and venture farther afield to find whales. Whalers then had to push dangerously deeper into polar ice packs.

In one of the greatest economic losses associated with the industry, virtually the entire Arctic whaling fleet was destroyed in the Bering Strait in the fall of 1871. An early fall freeze captured and crushed thirty-three ships. While the crews all managed to miraculously escape and make their way south that year on foot, the financial loss was immense. During the same period, it also became more difficult to find crews for the ships and more expensive to outfit them. The Gold Rushes of the 1850s, and subsequently the Civil War, depleted the manpower available to crew the ships, and since both historical events required lots of supplies, competition for equipment and food drove up outfitting costs.

One clear result was that in the post–Civil War years, ships sailed with increasingly diverse crews. Ships typically had a greater numbers of "beachcombers," sailors who had deserted at some point to remain on a South Pacific island, as well as African Americans, native islanders, or *kanakas*, and a mix of others. As the Gold Rush, Civil War, and westward expansion all absorbed so many fit men, the crews of the 1860s and 1870s shifted to being generally less educated and less experienced. Thus, it's easy to see why whaling toward the end of the nineteenth century was beset by financial woes associated with rising costs, decreasing returns, and scant human resources.

Even with these issues, though, bigger external forces were responsible for finally slamming the door shut on whaling's heyday: the discovery of petroleum and the development of a refinery process. By 1906, the grand whaling fleet of the United States had effectively diminished to just forty-two vessels, and the last wooden ship washed up on the rocks at Cuttyhunk, Massachusetts, in 1924. Whaling's second act, while brief, was one of steel, speed, exploding lances, and the near-final decimation of the greatest leviathans.

During Rob's time, whalers focused on only a few of the roughly fourteen larger whale species. Initially, from the Colonial period until the early 1800s, American whalers chiefly sought the right, humpback, and sperm whales.[14] The Atlantic's population of the gray whale, the scragg whale, as noted had already been driven to extinction by the Basques more than a hundred years before. The cantankerous gray whale off the coast of California and its equally isolated population off Japan and Korea were already rare and had the bad habit of charging whaleboats when harpooned. The other speedy baleen whales, such as the blue or sulphur-bottomed whale, fin whales, and the smaller sei and minke whales, remained elusive until the still-distant future. The sail-powered nineteenth-century whaling ships, with their whaleboats propelled by blistered palms and bent backs, were simply no match for them. The last great whale, the bowhead whale, was a high Arctic species and heretofore had been fairly hidden except to indigenous hunters. Living north of the Bering Strait, it was only recognized and targeted beginning in the late 1850s.

Distressingly, whaling became truly untethered in the twentieth century.[15] With oil fields opening across the nation, sperm whales lost their economic interest and baleen whales were again the target, but this time for their "whale bone" and meat. "Whale bone" was actually the baleen plates in their mouths, which were used in human goods where plastics or spring steel are employed today. Now sustained hunting shifted back to "inshore" species and brought the near annihilation of right and bowhead whales. Hunting for the remaining great baleen whales ratcheted up with high-powered harpoon guns and factory ships. In the final push, the blue, fin, and sei whales that had swum too fast for Rob's ships were now the quarry of modern high-speed diesel-engine boats. Coupled with ice-breaking steel hulls, the specter of death now penetrated the great whales' last refugia, the polar regions. Following a brief respite, as the world waged war in the 1940s, the gears of commerce shifted higher again in the 1950s and 1960s. In the last throes, an ethnocentric Asian, Russian, and Norwegian predilection for whale meat led to the decimation of the remaining populations of the humpback, blue, and fin whales.

This final era of whaling heralded the ultimate "tragedy of the commons." Coined by ecologist Garrett Hardin in 1968, the phrase reflects the historical concern for overgrazing by a few egocentric livestock owners in early New England's "common" pastures. More pointedly, it describes the result of selfish individuals who seek to gain disproportionate benefits by depleting a public resource at the expense of others. Indeed, by the mid-twentieth century, there was no material need or economic rationale for taking whales. Rather, it was done by a number of nations to protect and project their self-identity.[16]

Surprisingly, some still regaled in the macho aspects of the hunt. Ironically, even as late as 1954, famed explorer Roy Chapman Andrews, at that time the director of the American Museum of Natural History, exalted at the opportunity to hunt whales, declaring that each kill "was always tremendously exciting."[17] Best known for finding fossil dinosaur eggs in the Gobi Desert, he was the "scientist" aboard the ship off Alaska that brought back the great blue whale that hangs in the museum to this day. Fortunately, other scientists intervened, such as Scott McVay, a board member of the World Wildlife Fund I met early in my career.[18] As it became clear by the 1960s that several whale species were headed to extinction, the bureaucratic International Whaling Commission (IWC) finally moved to begin curtailing the take. Created in the 1930s but put on hold through World War II, the IWC reemerged as a nominal force in 1946. However, the commission was racked by politics and disinformation, and it wasn't until 1964, when Scott McVay and other scientists, and not politicians, finally managed to set the quotas, that limits were placed on the slaughter. It was almost too late. The blue whale population was reduced to barely a few thousand. Even then, while most nations ended their whaling efforts, a few continued, and the Soviet Union and Japan tripled their harvests through the late 1960s until a full moratorium was at last imposed.

CHAPTER 3

Reivers in Baltimore

THE ARMSTRONGS ARRIVED IN BALTIMORE AT THE DAWN OF THE NINE-
teenth century, still questing for a home of their own in the wake of their
Scottish clan's diaspora three hundred years previously. With the curiosity one inevitably has about ancestors, and naturally trying to envision
the genetic stock of Rob's traits, I dug into his roots with limited success.
It is said the Armstrongs began with Macbeth. In 1040, Earl Macbeth,
a powerful but discontent nobleman, slew Scotland's King Duncan and
chased his son Malcom to England. Siward Fairbairn, a Dane whose
daughter was married to King Duncan, was then asked by King Edward
the Confessor to help his father-in-law. Soon he rode north with Malcom to confront Macbeth. Malcom's horse was killed in battle and
the young king surrounded, but luckily Siward Fairbairn immediately
grasped Malcom by his thigh and set him upon another horse, and
together they persevered to victory. For this assistance at such a critical
moment, King Edward rewarded him lands on the border, and to perpet-
uate the memory he gave him the appellation of "Armstrong."[1] In fact,
we really only know that the Armstrongs originated in the backwater of
the forests near Ousby, about fifteen miles south of Scotland.[2] Beginning
in the thirteenth century, the clan shifted north and thrived for hundreds
of years by "reiving" in what then were known as the "Debatable Lands."
Their hallmark, not an honorable one, was to slip back across the border
and plunder the English countryside. Over time the Armstrongs became
the largest and toughest of the "reiving" clans. However, with James VI's
ascension in 1603 astride both the Scottish and English thrones, the

king vowed to clean up and pacify the borderlands. With swift action and two armies at his call, he had the Armstrongs' castles torn down and the remaining clan members hunted down and executed. Hundreds were killed, while many others fled to northern Ireland. The last clan chief, who was holed up in the hills, was dragged out of his lair and hanged in Edinburgh in 1610.[3]

In any event, after two hundred years, the family emerges from the ancestral mists on a gravestone in Baltimore, in an emigration record, and in a small printed booklet entitled *Discourse at his Funeral*.[4] From this and other records,[5] we know that William and Jane Armstrong were both born around 1760 and emigrated in 1799 from Sligo, Ireland. It remains unclear so far from whom this first William is exactly descended. However, an earlier William Armstrong, who was a grandson of John Armstrong of Gilnockie, notably left Scotland as the borderlands were being "cleansed" and settled in Fermanagh, Ireland, which neighbors Sligo. He is credited with "founding a large family with numerous branches."[6] We do know though that William and Jane married and came to the United States on a packet from Liverpool, and they had three sons: Thomas, who was born in 1790, Robert in 1793, and William in 1796. By 1800 William, the father, is listed in the Baltimore Directory as a grocer on Caroline Street, and shortly after he moves to Stall #5 on the County Wharf. He dies in 1805, leaving his wife to raise their fifteen-, twelve-, and nine-year-old sons. It must not have been easy. One odd facet of the tale is that while Jane lives to a ripe eighty-one years of age, dying in 1841, her grandson makes no mention of her in his account, nor could I find her mentioned in any records from Baltimore.

The three brothers' start was clearly a Dickensian one, a view ultimately reflected on their parents' grave. William and Jane's marker in Baltimore, half-buried and edged with moss, is chiseled with the sad epitaph, "the weary wheels of life at last stood still." Apparently soon after his father's death, the oldest son, Thomas, apprenticed as a grocery store clerk. He appears to have done well enough so that he is listed in the city's business directory in 1810 on his own, and no less, in his father's old stall on the County Wharf. The site, at the base of Calvert Street, is now known as Harbor Place. Thomas's hard work and diligence paid off, and by 1815 he has become an independent merchant. This was achieved, perhaps, with additional cachet from his role in helping to defeat the English assault on Baltimore in 1814. Fresh from burning Washington, D.C., in August that year, British troops had turned their attention to Baltimore and its fleet of marauding privateers. Thomas is listed as having served as a private under Captain John Montgomery in the Baltimore Union Artillery, famous for having stood its ground on the night of September 12. With just half a dozen four-pounder guns in their unit, they, along with several other units, faced nine thousand redcoats advancing up Long Log Lane. Repulsing them, they saved Baltimore,[7] and all those who served that day and night were forever honored as Baltimore's "Old Defenders." Thomas went on to grow his business into what ultimately became one of Baltimore's largest retail stores. Called a "millinery" store, more than selling hats, it was "a leading house in white goods, linens, laces, feathers, and straw goods."[8] Initially located at 21 West Pratt Street, the store moved to 175 Baltimore Street, and at last, it settled in two adjacent buildings at 237 and 239 West Baltimore Street, where it remained for decades. The site is now the Royal Farms Arena. Caught up in the Panic of 1837 and some poor business decisions, Thomas took on significant debt and was forced to take in one of his managers, Robinson Cator, as a partner in 1847. Together the partners eventually grew the business, which thereafter was called Armstrong & Cator. At its peak in the 1870s, the store had 115 clerks and salespeople, plus 60 fashion experts, serving customers from Pennsylvania south to the Carolinas and west to Missouri and Texas.

While Thomas was still running his business on the County Wharf, a second brother emerged in the business community, Robert G. Armstrong. He, too, began his career in the dry goods business but within a few years shifted to selling and publishing books. He pursued this career and first formed Armstrong & Plaskitt Booksellers in 1822 or so, then later he partnered with a John Berry to form Armstrong & Berry in 1838. His stores were always on the same stretch of Baltimore Street, where the downtown Holiday Inn now stands.

Of the youngest brother, William, born around 1796, less is known. He initially emerges in the records working with his oldest brother,

Thomas, around 1826. At first they sold dry goods together, but within two years they split. William did not nearly do so well in his business, but he was at least able to expand from a stall on the wharf to his own store at 41 Baltimore Street by 1831. The site, a subway entrance now, is opposite the Lord Baltimore Hotel. An advertisement in the *Baltimore Sun* in his day notes, "Wm. Armstrong is offering calicoes, ginghams, fresh muslins, crape, silk shawls, gloves, French net, Irish linen, needle-worked collars, and brown and white sheeting."

The three brothers—Thomas, Robert, and William—worked hard through the 1840s, growing their respective businesses and building their families. Thomas ultimately married twice but remained childless, and thus it was Thomas who became a key player in Rob's life, both early and even more so later when he took him in. Robert, the bookseller, married Achsah Gwinn and they had two children, Rebecca and Dorsey. Meanwhile the youngest brother, William, married a "Rebecca C.," and in December 1828, they had one child, Robert W. Armstrong, whose tale this is.

The Baltimore these Armstrongs inhabited and Rob grew up in was populated with a tumultuous crowd that epitomized the new America. The American Revolution was as far in the past to his generation as the Vietnam War is to us today, and the grip on the nation's governance by the heroes of the Revolution had long been relinquished. Elected the year Rob was born, the nation's first populist president, Andrew Jackson, was loud, abrasive, and acquisitive, not dissimilar to a recent one. Jackson and his protégés, Martin Van Buren and James Polk, reset the nation's agenda and aggressively advanced their bellicose views. One of the last of the old guard, Thomas Jefferson, thought Andrew Jackson despotic and "a dangerous man." A current historian, Alan Taylor, reframed Jackson as simply a president who "vowed to punish the nation's enemies and push the survivors farther away."[9]

Jackson unleashed American expansionism, and from the Appalachians west, indigenous Americans were purposefully exposed to smallpox and other diseases, brutally harassed, driven from their villages, summarily slaughtered, and essentially dispossessed of their lands. In the time of Rob's youth, the Seminoles lost Florida, the Cherokees lost

Georgia, and the Cree nation faded in the state of Alabama. The vast array of tribes throughout the upper Midwest and Far West were also great tragedies of despair, and under the populists' manifest destiny, a ruthless combination of American soldiers and swarming settlers clawed away the territories of the indigenous nations as well as those formerly held by Spain, Mexico, and Britain. By 1849 the nation had grown from the boundaries set after Jefferson's Louisiana Purchase in 1803 to include Florida, Texas, the Rocky Mountain states, California, and Oregon. It was now a new and sprawling nation coast to coast, unsteady on its feet but with burgeoning imperialist tendencies. The Pacific Ocean was on the horizon.

Baltimore itself, originally marked off by sixty plots in 1732, had remained a pastoral little village for several decades.[10] By 1752, there was only a small brewery on Hanover Street, a tobacco inspection house, St. Paul's Church, Kaminsky's Tavern on German Street, and two brick houses. However, with its position at the head of the Chesapeake Bay, essentially the northernmost ice-free harbor, and the addition of several large wharves in the 1780s,[11] Baltimore soon became the key trading link between ships plying the Atlantic Ocean and the nation's interior. Baltimore leapt forward again as the city's commercial interests sought to compete with the newly opened Erie Canal in New York. In 1827, the year before Rob was born, the city's merchants and bankers banded together to fund the nation's first railroad. The Baltimore & Ohio Railroad ultimately stretched from the harbor west across the state to Harper's Ferry, where it connected wagonloads of Midwestern grain with ships waiting to cross the Atlantic. By 1852, the railroad reached the Ohio Valley and leveraged open the vast agricultural heartland of the Mississippi River Valley.

Rob's Baltimore was resolving itself, shifting from a quaint English village to a diverse cosmopolitan city. Once separate, the historical villages of Fell's Point, Cole's Harbor, and Jones' Town slowly merged to form Baltimore. Neighborhoods shifted with an influx of immigrants, and Jones' Town became "Limerick" with its Irish. French refugees escaping the previous century's revolution, as well as newer French immigrants from Canada's eviction of the Acadians, lived primarily around South

Charles Street. A census in 1860 covering the neighborhood northeast of the docks showed residents to be mostly German, with smaller numbers from England and Hungary.[12] These new citizens were listed as grocers, mariners, bakers, seamstresses, upholsterers, druggists, servants, dry goods dealers, cabinetmakers, laborers, potters, and even a "huckster." A little to the west, closer to the Pratt Street docks and the businesses along Light Street, the residents were more directly linked with the city's maritime industry. Here were the sailmakers, caulkers, machinists, ship carpenters, master coopers, mariners, boatbuilders, booking agents, and draymen, along with a solid sprinkling of washerwomen and servants.

Along the city's streets, financially secure working-class families lived in a mixture of clapboard houses and new brick town houses. Backyard gardens provided herbs and vegetables for the table. Up Hanover Street, where the bankers and merchants resided, blue-stone sidewalks and elevated boardwalks bordered gracious cobblestone streets. Inside an upper middle-class house in Baltimore, the ceilings were low and the rooms were dimly lit by small windows with greenish glass set in lead frames. The dining rooms gleamed with mahogany and oak furniture polished with wax and cork. Elegant sideboards were set with Jamaican rum, cognac, and Madeira. Poorer homes were planked shacks with dirt floors. Piles of straw served as beds. Muddy during the rains, they were deathly cold in the winter.

Rob lived with his parents in a house at the corner of Lexington and Charles Street, now the site of the Charles Center, and spent most of his time playing in the streets around the Inner Harbor. Stretching away from the intersection of Light and Pratt Streets, his youthful realm ranged from the Lexington Market east to Calvert Street, and back south to the Inner Harbor, or the "Basin" as it was called. Baltimore's wharves and docks were a major nexus for the young nation's burgeoning trade, and enormous brick warehouses fronted each dock or wharf. Stacks of wooden crates, hogsheads, and barrels were piled in long rows along the curb, sometimes four or five layers high. Each wharf had half a dozen schooners tied up, lashed side to side, and the Outer Harbor was packed with hundreds more anchored in each cove and bay. As quickly as the ships were unloaded, they were filled again with sheaves of tobacco, bushels of corn or soybeans, bales of raw cotton, and other raw materials before heading back across the Atlantic.

"Hicks," backwoods Appalachian Scotch-Irish, rode into town each day to feed the teeming masses with an array of chickens, wild turkeys, rabbit, quail, and venison for sale. Before returning to the mountains, they thronged the taverns and streets. Just one generation past Daniel Boone and Davy Crockett, these mountaineers still lived in log homes, wore simple buckskins, and tread the dirt roads in moccasins. The Golden Horse tavern on the corner of Franklin and Howard Streets, the White Swan on Eutaw, and the Black Bear on Saratoga Street—with a live bear chained outside—all catered to this raucous crowd. Closer to the harbor, the Fountain Inn on Light Street drew Eastern shoremen in their boots and thick canvas aprons. Meanwhile, the Three Tuns Tavern and the Rising Sun on High Street were swarmed by the horse dealers, wagoneers, and cattlemen coming from the yards and stables on the western edge of town. The Methodist Church Rob attended on Light Street was a splendid two-story brick edifice with great arched windows along the front. Nearby, the Baltimore College of Dentistry, the first of its kind, was formed from two brownstones on Lexington Street. Roughly forty feet wide and three stories tall, it was particularly noticeable, with second-story windows more than twelve feet high. These were necessary to allow a good amount of light inside for the tricky work of tooth extraction and dental repair.

Baltimore also had establishments inherent to the human tragedy marked by the Middle Passage. Most of the slave trade in the city took place among a dozen pens and yards in the streets just northeast of Fell's Point, where the "Guineamen," or slave ships, landed. A hulking brick building on the corner of Pratt and Howard Streets with bars on the windows served as a slave pen managed by Hope Slatter. A Georgia-born trader, Slatter specialized in sending, as some said, the most "independent-minded" slaves to the New Orleans market.[13] When Rob was a child, Frederick Douglass lived with his owners, the Aulds, only two blocks from Fell's Point at the intersection of Alliceanna and South Durham. Douglass was "often aroused [late in the night] by the dead

33

heavy footsteps, and the piteous cries of the chain gangs that passed our door."[14]

Most of his youthful days Rob and his friends rumbled in the streets, no doubt running errands and delivering groceries, but also rolling hoops, playing catch, or flicking marbles. As they ran along the crowded ways, they were immersed in the cacophony of clanging of ships' bells, the booming cracks of sails snapping in the wind, and the loud ringing from wagons' great iron wheels rolling along the cobblestones. Near the docks and along Baltimore Street the drovers shouted at their beasts and snapped their whips as they struggled to get their teams underway. These weren't fancy horses around the docks—not the trotters and high-steppers attached to the buggies and landaus up the hill—but mostly huge workhorses, such as Percherons or Clydesdales. It should have been a great place and wonderful time to grow up in, exciting and fresh; a new nation on the cusp of its being.

However, there oozed a darker side of Baltimore in these times; alcohol and a culture of inebriation. Indeed, one of Baltimore's most famous sons, Edgar Allan Poe, died from it. When Poe returned to Baltimore in October 1849, his arrival coincided with federal elections. After joining a friend for a drink in a bar, Poe apparently became the victim of *cooping*, wherein political operatives grab an already drunk voter, ratchet him up a notch or two to insensibility, and then drag him to several polling sites to vote for their candidate. On October 7th, two days after the elections, Poe was found "lying on a bench . . . on Light street . . . in a stupor"; he died later that day.[15] As we will see, Rob was luckier, but only barely. For just as Poe lay on the streets of Baltimore, Rob was on his horse carousing along the roads of South Carolina, the drunken dentist. The shadow of alcohol that gripped him so early in life grew such that soon enough he could no longer control his cravings nor keep his head up. At which point the claws of shame and remorse pulled him into a decade of wandering in the wilderness, the heart of this tale.

Part II

The Whaler's Tale

In His Words

CHAPTER 4

Early Years

O pale, pale now, those rosy lips,
I aft hae kiss'd sae fondly!
And clos'd for aye, the sparkling glance
That dwalt on me sae kindly!
And mouldering now in silent dust,
That heart that lo'ed me dearly!
But still within my bosom's core
Shall live my Highland Mary.[1]

There are two pictures hung up in the chambers of my memory that stand out vividly and distinctly after more than sixty years, and to which I always return that with thankfulness and delight. The first is that of a sweet-faced woman, delicate and frail, leading by the hand a little boy of three years into a low ceiling, back, second-story room, and kneeling with him by the side of the old-fashion curtained four-poster bed, while she poured out her soul to the heavenly father in behalf of her child and her loved ones, and taught him to join with her in repeating "our father, who art in heaven."

The companion picture presents to my view a tall, spare-looking man, standing erect with an intelligent countenance glowing with holy joy, and by his side the same sweet-faced woman with the child's hand clasped in hers. Other members of the household are there too, a little table, and the family Bible still open upon it. In the room, the echo of the familiar hymn . . . "Further, I stretch my hands to thee" . . . is just ceasing, as they all reverently bow before God around the family altar.

Many years have passed since then, and my father and mother have long since joined in song with the blood-washed and redeemed in His upper sanctuary. However, many times, in many lands, and under widely differing circumstances, the memory of those happy holy childhood hours has returned. My memory of those times comforts me in sorrow, rebukes me in the hours of sin, and incites me to a closer holy walk with God in hope of a blessed reunion with my loved ones gone before. My mother died when I was about six years old, and my recollection of her includes but a few pictures. One of those is of the holy joy of her death-bed, and of the return of my father, who not anticipating that she was so near her end, was away from home on business. It seems as though it was but yesterday, that he caught me up in his arms at the head of the stairs and, with breaking heart, cried "Oh my poor boy I did not think to return and find you motherless."

Several years before my father died, his failing health compelled him to relinquish his business. However, as long as he was able to enjoy outdoor exercise, I was his companion in his daily walks, and on one of these occasions, as he halted for rest at a relative's house she brought him a glass of wine. In that day it was the custom, even in many Methodist families, to keep the decanter of brandy and the bottle of wine upon the sideboard, and to offer them to friends who came in. I had never known my father to take wine prior to this, but being almost exhausted from his walk he drank part of the glass, and while he was doing so, our friend poured out another glass, which she handed to me. My father remonstrated with her, but meanwhile I swallowed the wine. Her act had been meant in love, but she had erred in judgment. As that first glass of wine went tingling through my veins, and mounted up into my head, a love for the cursed stuff was born in me, which in after years led me deep into sin, and but for God's grace came near hopelessly wrecking my life. My father had been an earnest worker at the church, and especially in our Methodist Sunday school, to which I had been carried from the time I was three years old. The influence around me was such that from very early I became the subject of religious impressions. When I was nine I went forward to the altar, and during the progress of a revival in the old Light Street, professed conversion, and united with the church on probation. My father's death on August 22nd, 1844, when I was sixteen, of course brought a great change to my life. My uncle and aunt with whom we had been living had never had any children, and while she was always very kind and disposed to "spoil" her orphaned nephew, my uncle was severe, strict, and with a certain coldness of manner. In my youthful days he seemed almost unkind. I had reason however, in after years to believe that his heart was in the right place.

In my seventeenth year I joined with some ten or twelve young men, all of them older than I was, belonging to the Charles Street Methodist Episcopal Church, in the formation of a new mission. A mission for the seamen and the people who lived in the locality known as "the Basin," around Baltimore's Light and Pratt Street wharves. We first occupied a sail loft on Light Street, and our mission was christened the Sailors' City Bethel. Here our God revered the labors of his servants, and many souls we happily converted to Him, most of them seamen. Quite a number of them were drunkards, who were reclaimed by the power of divine grace, and later led sober useful lives. After about twelve months the room became too small for those who desired to attend, and with the aid of friends, an old ship, the *William Penn*, was purchased. Converted into a comfortable chapel, it was moored in the corner of the basin where Light and Lee Streets meet. Here the blessing of God rested upon the labors of his young servants, and many a sailor was converted and went out with the love of God in his heart to the ends of the earth. Several of these young man afterward entered in the ministry, and some of them have gone home to heaven. I recall the names of Rev. Samuel Kramer, Alfred Cookman, Charles J. Thompson, Adam Wallace, all three of whom shortly joined the Philadelphia conference, and of Thomas Dryden and his brother Robert, John Landstreet and others whose names I cannot now remember. To my regret, even at this time, I had formed an acquaintance with some other young men whose influence over me was only evil. Sadly, my own heart was not slow to respond to the temptations which beset youth. No longer having loving parental oversight and their restraint, which had blessed my boyish days, my downward progress was very rapid. My uncles, Robert and Thomas, who were generous to me (for my father died leaving me nothing in the way of money) were desirous that I should engage in some business, and after a good deal of discussion it was at length determined that I should study dentistry. The Baltimore College of Dental Surgery had been established a few years previously through the efforts of Dr. Chapin A. Harris, the first of its kind in the nation. In his day, he was the recognized head of his profession in the country, and as the doctor was a personal friend of my uncles, it was arranged that I should become a student in that institution. After a course of two years I graduated with the degree of D.D.S.

Dentistry was at that time beginning to take its rank as one of the learned professions, and presented as fair an opening and prospects for success as any a young man might desire. The very attractive future which it held out drew to the college young men from all parts of the country, and from every walk of life. Some of them were of such sterling character they would honor any position in life, while others had souls already honeycombed with vice, and were companions who would only degrade and injure those who chose to associate with them. I was about to say "unfortunately," but it was as much my fault as my misfortune. I soon became intimate with some of the latter class, and though I kept up with my studies, for I thoroughly enjoyed them, the accursed taste for drink won. Hitherto I had only been able to gratify my taste occasionally and in secret, but I was soon led to yield to their invitations to the saloons, and to convivial parties in their private rooms, where the impure song and lewd jest blended with oaths, and the air was filled with the smoke of tobacco. This was all regarded as fun, and enjoyment, but with such companions and instructors my course tended downward very rapidly. Of course, it was not possible to conceal entirely my manner of life from my uncles and their families, and it must have caused them great pain and considerable shame. I recall their expostulations and entreaties, which in my folly and ingratitude, I regarded as impertinent intermeddling in my private affairs. The college course ended at length, and as I had been invited by a fellow graduate, a man of better character and of more principle than some of those with whom I had been keeping company, I consented to unite my fortune with his. I would assist him in his practice, for he had been practicing dentistry for several years before he came to the college. So, entering into partnership with him, we left Baltimore in March of 1847 for Paris, Kentucky.

At that time Cumberland, Maryland, was the western terminus of the Baltimore and Ohio Railroad. We reached that city about nightfall, and after supper at the hotel, travelers for the west were seated for a ride of eighteen hours, in a succession of five or six stagecoaches. The night was very cold, and in crossing the Allegheny Mountains the snow was in places three or four feet in depth. Our ride was not made any more pleasant by the report we heard before leaving Cumberland, that on the previous night one of the stage drivers had frozen to death up on his driver's box. We reached Wheeling, West Virginia, in good time the next day, and that evening found ourselves on one of the Ohio River steamers on our way toward Cincinnati. Soon thereafter we reached our destination, Paris, the county town of Bourbon County, Kentucky. I was very much pleased with the appearance of the place and the kindly manner by which I was received by my partner's friends. His office had been refitted and neatly furnished prior to our arrival, and I found that though but five or six years older than myself, he was regarded with high esteem by his fellow townsmen. So I began to congratulate myself on my good fortune in securing his friendship and on the favorable prospects that opened up before me.

In our many conversations before leaving Baltimore, Dr. John Jackson Adair, that was his name, had faithfully warned me of the necessity of quitting my bibulous habits, of which also I was fully aware. I had promised myself and him that I would be very abstemious, and this was indeed my earnest determination. I soon found however that Paris was a very poor place to carry out that pledge, for everybody drank there. Bourbon County, of which Paris is the county town, had given its name to a peculiar brand of whiskey which is made there in large quantities. At the time I speak of, I think it would have been difficult to find many persons of either sex, young or old, who were not at least entitled to be called moderate drinkers. For a time, I was abstemious enough to excite the attention and the remarks of some of my friends, and devoted myself to the practice of my profession, in which I took great pleasure. I was beginning to regard myself as being completely reformed.

One warm evening however, in the early summer, a number of gentlemen who boarded in the same house as I were sitting in chairs on the sidewalk of the Main Street. This was also the turnpike between Covington on the Ohio River and the city of Lexington. Our attention was suddenly drawn by a cloud of dust up the road. We saw a runaway team rapidly approaching; the horse dashing along with tremendous speed, dragging a buggy in which were seated two young man, who had evidently lost control over their steed. Jumping up as they drew toward us, we made an effort to check the horse. This caused him to swerve suddenly, the buggy was overturned, and the men thrown out. One of them was able to get up with a little assistance, but the other was badly hurt, and we carried him in to our boardinghouse and summoned a physician. It was several weeks before he was able to be carried to his home, and during that time, we all took turns in nursing and caring for him in conjunction with some members of his family who came to stay with him. He was the son of a planter in comfortable circumstances, whose plantation was about eight miles out on the Lexington Road. Upon his recovery to health, all of the borders at our house were invited to his birthday party, as he had turned eighteen shortly after his accident.

On this occasion a barrel of Old Bourbon whiskey, which according to a custom of that part of the country had been put away in the cellar at his birth to be kept until he came of age, was broached. All, or nearly all, of the large company who were present indulged so freely that the party soon became a bacchanalian orgy. This proved too much for my weak resolution and my strong inclination for the accursed stuff. I do not remember how long the party lasted or how I got home, but from that time my path steadily deteriorated, in spite of the councils of my partner and the advice of the better class of my friends. Finding that I was injuring the business of my friend, and without a hope of redeeming my own prospects and character, soon enough I consented to a dissolution of the partnership. In the early summer I left Paris and returned to Baltimore.

Mortified at my conduct, I came back to a very different moral atmosphere in my uncle's house, and having brought little money with me, I was constrained to act differently. Although my nearest and most intimate friends could not but be aware of my past conduct, they did everything they possibly could for me, and so for some months I kept myself quite sober. Luckily, my professional relations with the faculty of the dental college were such that their influence was employed on my behalf to obtain another position, and I hoped that with different surroundings I might be able to redeem my tarnished reputation and recover my professional standing. So, in the spring of 1849, I was admitted to a partnership with Dr. Kemp S. Dargan of Winnsboro, South Carolina. He had built up for himself a large and lucrative practice in that city and the surrounding country. As he was now advancing in years, the country practice was becoming too much of a burden upon him. Furnishing me with a horse and buggy, it became my duty to travel the neighboring districts, making appointments in advance, and attending to such business as might offer, while the old doctor took care of the office practice in Winnsboro. I found the work very pleasant, the roads very fine, the country beautiful, and the planters, as this was before the rebellion, wealthy and exceedingly hospitable. When I returned to Winnsboro from riding the circuit to see patients, I was received as a member of Dr. Dargan's own family. For a while everything seemed encouraging and prosperous, but it was too good to last. Although compelling myself to outwardly appear sober and maintain a proper decorum, the devil was still in my soul. My thirst for drink was only kept hidden, but not destroyed. At first my indulgence was occasional, and in the secrecy of my own room. Soon I allowed myself greater liberty when on my rides through the country. It was through my reckless driving on these occasions, when half crazy with liquor, that an intimation of my habits was conveyed to my partner. Dr. Dargan was an old-school Presbyterian, of the rigid sort, and on my return to the office he took occasion to let me know very plainly, yet with great kindness, what he thought of my behavior, and intimated that the next offense would necessitate a separation between us.

I was terribly mortified, and sorry, and had the good sense to be grateful for his kind intentions toward me and to acknowledge the justice of all he had said. Unfortunately knowing the force of the appetite within me, I had little confidence in my ability to resist the temptation to drink. I gave him my promise to abstain entirely from liquor, but it was a losing fight that I was engaged in. Though entirely conscious that my reputation, life, nay my soul itself was at stake, I refused to look to the strong for help. I knew that Christ could save and keep me, but I would not submit, and vainly strove again under my own strength, or rather weakness, to resist the irresistible force of the thirst that enslaved me. The result is quickly told. In November I left Charleston, South Carolina, on a steamer for New York City. I might have gone back to Baltimore, for there were those there who still loved me. They would again have endeavored to cover over my shame and conceal my disgrace from the world. There was still a door of hope open to me, but in my pride, I would not enter. On reaching New York, I went to one of the best hotels and began to drink harder than ever, until my money was gone. Next I sold my dental instruments, my watch, and everything I possessed. When all was gone, in December 1849, I sold myself to a whaling agent and found myself, I hardly knew how, in New Bedford, Massachusetts, bound for a whaling voyage on the barque *Smyrna*, under Captain Rodolphus H. Tobey. Not having the money to buy liquor with, I necessarily sobered up before the *Smyrna* sailed and took occasion to write to my two uncles in Baltimore, who had shown me such unwavering and undeserved kindness. These proved to be the only letters they received from me until my return home, nine and a half years later.

I had just passed my twenty-first birthday and had never done a real hard day's work in all my life. I had always enjoyed the best of everything, both to eat and to wear, and even yet, I hardly comprehended how very different my future life was to be. I was aware that coarse food and hard living with the dangers, perils and hardships of a seafaring life were before me, and that the men with whom I was henceforth to live with in the most intimate companionship were, many of them, lawbreakers and notable for the very low level of their intellectual and moral character. Yet knowing these things, I kept back my letters from the mail until sailing time, so as to afford no opportunity to my uncles to make an effort to bring me back home, and to a life in which I could only see present and future disgrace.

CHAPTER 5

Before the Mast

ON DECEMBER 27, 1849, WE SET SAIL FROM NEW BEDFORD ON A WHAL-
ing voyage bound for the South Pacific, expecting to return to America in three and a half, or four years. Our ship's company consisted of
twenty-three men including the officers; Captain Rodolphus H. Tobey,
1st Mate Seth A. Gifford, 2nd Mate Philip Caulk, 3rd Mate Charles
Lockwood, Boatsteerers Gilbert Marsh, who was colored, and Payne
Winney (or Winerie), and Jack Frost; Steward Charles Moore, Cook
Isaac Ford, Blacksmith Elias Stemland, Cooper John Rogers (or Rowe);
and as crew, Stanley Craft, George L. Spooner, Seth W. Walker, Charles
Ben Smith, John Smith, John Smith (another), William (Bill) Grosvenor,
Luther Wardell, F. Tom Burns, E. F. Mosher, R. W. Armstrong, and Peter
Puuch (or Funk), a Spaniard. More than one half of those before the mast
were greenhands and had never been to sea. Of those, quite a number of
them had never even seen a ship before coming to New Bedford.

The night before we sailed it snowed quite heavily, and on the morning of our departure everything about us had a cold and cheerless look.
Before we were well clear of the harbor some of us were already wishing
that we were back on the land. The wind was fair however, and before long
the pilot wished us a successful voyage and bid us goodbye, and we were
out on the broad Atlantic. The motion of the vessel made all of us "greenhands" sick. Then as the wind increased and soon came from dead ahead,
the old barque began to pitch in the great green seas. Soon we could not
even stand up on the deck, and our malady grew worse. By that night the
wind was blowing a gale, and as it became necessary to reef the top sails,

we were all ordered aloft to assist in that duty. Going aloft however was a very serious matter for us. I hardly know how we managed to climb to the top in the storm and darkness, with the wind almost blowing us away, and the rigging coated with ice. The rolling and pitching was of such a fearful manner to us then. Some of the greenhands got no farther at that time, for the howling of the wind as it shrieked through the cordage, and the noise made by the "slatting" of the sail just above our ears, filled them with such terror as to render them indifferent to the oaths of the officers and the taunts and jeers of the experienced sailors. Finally, those of us up on the topsail yard, with the aid of the petty officers, succeeded after a while in reducing sail. We then slowly, and carefully, managed to follow the officers down the rigging and were glad enough to get our feet once more on deck. By this time our watch was up, wet to the skin and nearly frozen, some of us were also very seasick. We were glad enough to then climb down into the small, badly lit, and horribly smelling, forecastle, which for many a long month would be our home.

Changing our wet clothing we got into our berths, only to find that the deck boards above us, which had been exposed to the rays of the summer sun while the vessel lying at the wharf in New Bedford, had shrunk and leaked so badly, that our bedding was wet. Our beds were pools of water waiting for us to get into. The old sailors, however, assured us that we would soon get accustomed to it, and that it being salt water, we wouldn't catch a cold. Being completely exhausted, we were soon fast asleep. It took a while though, for to our unaccustomed ears the sound of the rushing of the water, against the bows as the ship plunged into the big seas, was quite terrifying.

I had hardly lost consciousness when I was roused by a tremendous banging upon the forecastle scuttle, and the mate's cry of "Starboard Watch, Ahoy. Eight Bells, below there, do you hear the news?" This told us that our four hours of rest was over, and that it was our turn for duty on the deck again. Very sleepily and unwillingly, we donned our wet clothing and managed, in spite of the pitching of the old barque, to climb up and take a look at the weather. We found what sailors call a "heavy sea on," with whitecaps cresting the waves, and, as far as one could see huge waves, called billows by the sailors, rolling on and on, threatening to engulf us. Our vessel, under close-reefed topsails, struggled to climb up and over the seas, and at last surmounting them, plunged down the other side, deep into the trough of the waves as though she was going to the depths of "old ocean." All the while, the gale shrieked through the rigging with a wild and mournful melody.

No tongue or pen can fittingly describe the appearances of "old ocean" in such a storm, and there is perhaps hardly anything else in all the wide world so well adapted to give one so vivid a conception of the power and majesty of Him, who holds the waves in the hollow of his hand. However, familiarity soon smooths away the feeling of awe and fear which such a sight produces in one who first gazes on the wide expanse of waters when roused to great fury by the lashings of such a storm. On the first day, the excitement of putting to sea, and the terrible nausea that came upon us, robbed us of all desire for food. However, after just a few hours of sleep, and the appetizing "whet" of the salt air, some of us were ready for breakfast. When eight bells was struck again the next morning, we rushed below to get our tin crockery, a plate and a spoon, though the smell from the forecastle was almost too much for us. Breakfast was then passed down to us in the hold; a black greasy dirty-looking tin pot, or "kid" as it is called, with a piece of pork in it on which the fat was about two or three inches in thickness, and a large tin pan, filled with ship biscuit, that had been soaked in water. The biscuit was covered with the fat slush which our cook, Isaac Ford, known as the "Doctor," had skimmed from the pot in which the pork had been boiled and then put into oven and baked. This the sailors know as "lobscouse." Finally, we also got a dirty-looking black bucket filled with something that was dignified by the name of coffee. All this was too much for a fellow like me, who before this time could only touch the white meat of chicken or turkey and could not endure fat meat of any kind, and who had been accustomed to white tablecloths and clean dishes. So leaving the "savory viands" for those whose appetites were stronger, I rushed up on deck for fresh air until the breakfast had been eaten and the remains of the food cleared away. When going below again I jumped into my bunk and tried to bury my sorrows with sleep. It was only after I had been pretty badly starved for about four days, and after becoming used to the motions and smells of the ship, that I was able to eat the food provided. However, after I had lost my "dainty tooth" as the fellows called it, I could do as well as the others when eight bells struck.

On a Sunday morning, the gale having moderated and the sea being somewhat smoother, we were finally able to bring our anchors in over the rails. While engaged in this work, one of our boatsteerers, a tall young fellow we called Winnie, Payne Winney, was sitting out on the stock of the anchor trying to pull a "lanyard," a small piece of tarred rope, through a "dead-eye" to lash the anchor down. When the lanyard broke, Winnie lost his balance and fell overboard. "Man Overboard!" was the cry, and rousing the watch below who came rushing on deck, the headsails were thrown back, and the progress of the ship, which had been going ahead at about eight knots an hour, was immediately checked. One of the whale-boats was quickly lowered, a boat's crew jumped in, and in a very short time Winnie, whom we had left nearly half a mile astern, was picked up and brought onboard. The sails were filled again and on we went.

The weather came on stormy again, and the winds being from ahead, it was nearly three weeks before we finally got south of the Gulf Stream and into the smoother seas and warmer weather. The *Smyrna* is a fine vessel, but she has two faults; she has a small leaky forecastle and is very wet forward. On February 8, we first crossed the equator, and as is tradition, "Old Neptune" came on board. His antics afforded an occasion of great jollity to the officers and the old salts, but we greenhands, called polly-wogs for the occasion, did not find quite so much enjoyment in his visit, and we were rather glad when the Sea King went back over the ship's side that night. As soon as we had crossed the Gulf Stream and sailed into fine weather, the ship's company was divided into three boat crews. During daylight hours the men took regular terms of duty of two hours each at the fore and main mastheads to keep a lookout for whales. Frequently blackfish, a small whale also known as a pilot whale, were seen. The boats were often lowered in chase of them, especially so as to give the men practice in the use of their oars and also to obtain oil for our lamps. We sometimes saw larger whales, but they were at too great a distance, or the circumstances were unfavorable for lowering. Also, as Captain Tobey was desirous of getting around Cape Horn into the Pacific Ocean as quickly as possible, and having struck the Southeast trade winds, we carried a lot of sail and tried to make a quick passage. One day, however, when not very far from the Cape Verde Islands, we got into a school of small cow whales and lowered our boats in chase. We were unsuccessful, however, as the whales were very shy, and we only got a very small calf. The 1st mate struck her in the hope that he would be able to secure her mother also, but without success. We towed the calf to the ship and got about five barrels (bbl.) of oil from her, but the oil was thick and would not burn, and our catch was valueless.

I wrote to Uncle Tommy today, on Valentine's Day, 1850. Our course was SW, and we spent the day setting up rigging and spinning yarns into rope. At ten o'clock that night the cook sang out "Sail Ho," and the ship that had been in sight all day turned out to be quite close under our lee bow. Hidden by our sails, we had nearly run her down. So we hauled back our sails to gam with [speak with] the ship *James Stewart* of New Bedford, bound for California. On March 7, we were on the Abrolhos Bank, the edge being about one hundred miles off the coast of Espirit de Santos, Brazil, noted as one of the best feeding grounds of the sperm whale in the Atlantic Ocean. For about a week, the winds were quite high and the seas very rough. The lookouts at the masthead had seen whales, blackfish and grampus, another small whale, on different occasions, but we had not been able to lower the boats for them. This morning though, a brisk northwest breeze was blowing and the ocean was comparatively smooth. The morning watch was getting some provisions out of the hold when from the masthead there came the well-known cry "There she blows." This was followed by the quick response of the officer of the watch, "Where away?" The reply from aloft, "Two points on the lee bow, Sir. A large sperm whale." By this time the captain had reached the deck and was on his way up the rigging, his spyglass in hand. Soon came the command "Call the watch below and let the cook give the men their breakfast."

Meanwhile the watch on deck was getting their boat in readiness to lower, and an excitement pervaded officers and men that I had not previously witnessed. The whale had gone down shortly after the captain had reached the masthead, and the time had been carefully noted, for a large whale will generally stay down for about an hour. The men aloft had been charged to keep a sharp look out, and with breakfast over, and the boats all in readiness to lower. Just at eight bells came the expected cry "There she blows." This was followed by the orders, "Stand by your boats," then "Lower away." Next, "Jump in, boys," "Out oars," and "Pull away." All three boats were off in chase.

The whale was now about a mile off, to leeward, so packing the oars the boats' sails were set. Admonishing the men not to make the slightest noise, as a whale hears very well, we sailed downwind rapidly to the whale, who had no idea that his enemies were so close upon him. The 1st mate's boat was in the lead, and soon his boatsteerer, Jack Frost, jumped up in the bow and, watching for his opportunity, plunged two harpoons, one after the other, deep into the hump of the unsuspecting whale. Instantly the whale lashed the water with his enormous flukes, throwing a great column of whitewater high in the air. Plunging beneath the waves, his huge tail rising above the boat, then the whale disappeared from sight, as one of the men cried "There goes flukes!" The sails of all the boats were quickly taken down, and the 1st mate went to the bow of his boat to pick up his lance, while the boatsteerer took the 1st mate's place in the stern. Taking a turn with the line around the loggerhead, the wooden post in the whaleboat, the line ran out with great velocity as the whale sounded. The boatsteerer endeavored, carefully, by putting some strain on the line, to try to check the speed of the whale. Calling from time to time to the after oarsmen to wet the hot line, for it was smoking with the speed with which it was being carried out. The other boats, noting from the motion of the 1st mate's boat the direction the whale seemed to be going, bent to their oars and hoped to be near enough when he next came to the surface to put their harpoons in him also.

Still, however, the old bull continued to sound, and the line continued to run out, until it became evident that the whale would take it all. A signal was then made to the other boats, for they were too far off to be of any use. All that could be done now was to tie a "drag," a piece of board about a foot square so arranged as to offer the greatest resistance to the water, to the end of the line and let it go. Soon the whale again rose to the surface with such velocity that half of his body was out of the water and set his course directly to windward with tremendous speed, going "eyes out" as sailors say. There was nothing else to do but to chase him, and the men bent to their oars with a measured stroke that meant business. The old bull meant business too. Sometimes he would stop still and lash waves until they foamed again as he vainly endeavored to get rid of the irons that were so deeply embedded in his body. At these times the boats would gain on him and the men were encouraged with the hope that with a few more strokes they would be able to get fast to him again. Then the old fellow would start off again, and soon leave the boats way behind. Meanwhile the wind picked up and began to blow half a gale, and the sea grew more and more rough, causing the men to labor greatly at the oars. Soon the waves were breaking over their boats and drenching the men to the skin. They kept up the chase however, until about five o'clock, when it became clear to everyone that there was no longer a chance to take that whale. Exhausted, yet still reluctantly, the boats were turned about, and setting their sails the whaleboats started for the ship now many miles away and barely to be seen. As it grew dark, lanterns were hung at the masthead of the ship, and soon we tired and disappointed men got on board. Nearly famished, we were glad to get our suppers, and those who were not then on watch, turned in to their bunks for rest and sleep.

As my story is an autobiography, and not an account of a whaling voyage, I will say some, but not too much, hereafter regarding the number of times when we saw whales, lowered our boats in chase of them, or the details of the process of turning whale blubber into oil. There have been many books published giving an account of a whaleman's life, which are both interesting and instructive, but it is my intention, however, to omit most things of this nature, instead covering only such events as have a direct relation to the purpose of this history.

CHAPTER 6

'Round the Horn

LEAVING THE ABROLHOS BANK, OUR BARQUE HEADED ON A south-southwest course which, with the favoring trade winds, brought us in less than a month into the neighborhood of Cape Horn. Along the way, on March 10th, we spoke with the ship *Largorda* of New Bedford. She was forty-three months out, but bound for home. The weather was generally favorable, though at times the winds were very high and the seas quite rough. Every clear night, we noticed the Magellanic Clouds and the constellation of the Southern Cross rising higher and higher, and the air was steadily becoming colder as we passed 42° and sailed ever southward. Thousands of new and strange birds were around the ship; the Great Southern Albatross, other albatrosses we called "mollymawks" and "stinkpots," large petrels, and flocks of the smaller petrels called "Mother Carey's Chickens" followed in the wake of the ship. They skipped from wave to wave for many hundreds of miles without ever seeming to rest even for a moment.

Commencing this day of March 17th, we were in a dead calm. Towards morning a fair breeze sprang up, and we saw two sails, and many penguins, or "Johnny Woggins," in sight, as well as great quantities of kelp floating past. The waters seemed alive with dolphins, skipjacks, and albacore, with flying fish endeavoring to escape from these, their natural enemies, both in the air and in the water. They frequently flew on board and afforded us a very agreeable change from "salt horse" and fat pork. Quite often some of us would get out on the end of the flying jibboom during our fore-noon watch below, our time off, and with a long and

stout fishing line, baited with a piece of ivory, or glittering tin, catch albacore or skipjack. We could catch enough in a short time to furnish a meal
for all hands. Sometimes when a school of porpoise would come under
the bows, a boatsteerer, or one of the mates, would get out the martingale
guys, the ropes from the bowsprit back to the hull, and secure himself
well with the end of a rope. For when the old barque made a plunge, he
was liable to be carried under the water. He would then with a harpoon,
or "iron" as we call it, spear one of them. Then when a running noose, or
"bowline," was put over the flukes of the fish, a half-dozen of us would
seize hold of the rope and haul him on deck where, after admiring its
beauty, he was turned over to the cook and steward to appear again in the
form of porpoise steaks and fish balls. The lower jaw became the trophy
of the officer who had caught the fish and was prized not alone for the
beauty of the teeth, but for the oil which was extracted from the bone by
exposure to the sun. On this oil quite a high price is set by watchmakers
and jewelers. Our course southbound was marked by squally weather,
occasionally a sail was sighted, and there were visits by the usual albatross.

One morning, April 3, when at daylight the lookouts went to the
masthead, the cry of "Land Ho" rang in our ears. As the wind was
favorable, the captain ordered the ship to be steered directly toward it,
and under fair winds and light rain we drew near it in a few hours' sail.
Our eyes were greeted by one of the most magnificent views it has ever
fallen to my lot to behold, Cape St. John on Staten Island. This is the
most southeastern island off Tierra del Fuego. Rising sheer out of the
ocean to a height of about eight hundred or a thousand feet, covered
with ice and snow, it glitters and sparkles in the rays of the midday sun
and reflects from thousands of spires of ice, covering the prismatic hues
of the rainbow. The great waves of Old Ocean dashed in a line of snow-
white foam at its base, ever and anon throwing the spray in milk-white
clouds high in the air, while below the blue waves rolled on, forming one
of the grandest spectacles one can well imagine. With Staten Island out
of sight astern, we sailed in the long peculiar swell of the Pacific Ocean
under light winds and rain.

Leaving the glorious view, and the beautiful weather behind us,
we were soon tossed about in the severe and bitterly cold weather, for

which these seas are proverbial. One gale passed over us on April 5th at latitude 56° 15ʹ, another the next day coming up from the south, so we shortened sail at night and all hands were called out to splice the main brace. The gale continued throughout the following week. Finally, a few days later, April 12th, was a comparatively fair day, and we continued heading southwest by west. We crossed with, and spoke to, or "gammed" with the barque *Lagrange* of Fairhaven, under Captain Dexter. They were fifty-two months out and bound for home with 400 bbls. of sperm whale oil and 1,100 bbls. of right whale oil. They were last at Oahu and reported three whaleships as having burnt up when there, one of them being the *Tobacco Planter*. The *Lagrange* carried home only one of her original crew, the rest being all kanakas, island natives, and Portuguese, with just two Americans. One of her boatsteerers is returning to the States after an absence of sixteen years!

Soon we had made a sufficient southing to clear the southern point of the continent and were met by the long and heavy swells peculiar to the Pacific Ocean. We were not, however, to get so quickly "around the Horn." The winds which had hitherto been so propitious, now turned dead in our teeth, and we were compelled to beat against them under shortened sail, and often forced to "lay to" under close-reefed fore topsail and fore topmast staysail. When the gale built to cyclonic proportions, we would drift back eastward, ever watching the tremendous waves, far exceeding anything I had ever witnessed in the Atlantic gales through which we had previously passed, and which again and again threatened to engulf us. The *Smyrna*, however, was a staunch ship and rode over the big waves as gracefully as a seabird. After a little while our sense of fear gave way to a rapturous awe with which we came to contemplate the grandeur of the scene. One day when the storm was at its height, two immense sperm whales came almost alongside and played about the ship for several hours. We would very much have liked to have caught them and put their oil in our empty casks in our hold. Old whalers on board thought they would have turned out more than 100 bbls. apiece, but they were safe from molestation by us, and perhaps they knew it, for it would have been madness to lower our whaleboats in such a sea. Indeed, had we caught them, it would also have been almost impossible to "cut them in" and save their oil anyway.

When the gale had blown itself out, we caught an easterly breeze and after three weeks of hard buffeting westward we were at length enabled to turn our ship to the north. As we got into finer weather and smoother seas, we shook the reefs out of our topsails, and setting the topgallant sails and flying jib we kept our course north along the west coast of Patagonia. We were too far off from the land though to get more than a distant view from the masthead of some great mountain peaks. We spent a few days working on the ship. We sent up the fore royal yard, got the anchor on the bows, got the deck pot on deck, and got out the fluke chains from the fore hold. On Wednesday, May 8th, we spoke with the *Phocion*, Captain Nichols, of New Bedford. She was five months out, with 230 bbls. of sperm oil. We then saw the Island of Massa Tierra at daybreak on May 17th, passed it that night, and during the day mended the windlass, and rattled down the mizzen topmast rigging. A few days later off the island of Fuego, the mates went in toward shore in the afternoon and caught some large fish.

Among our crew there was a young man named Seth W. Walker, a clerk hailing from Boston, but whose birth place was Portsmouth, New Hampshire. He was about twenty-seven years old and had served as a volunteer during the Mexican War. During the war he was taken down with the diarrhea that proved fatal to many of our soldiers. Walker, however, recovered and returned home, where he afterwards married and worked in some fancy goods business in Boston. The amount of mercury he had taken to affect his cure, however, undermined his constitution and was a possible cause of his coming on a whaling voyage. There was still on another cause, but he would not converse on the subject, though occasionally he would make some chance allusion to his wife and children, whom he appeared to love very dearly. We were not long at sea before he became a general favorite. He was intelligent, with some considerable education, generous and unselfish, and faithful to his duty to a fault.

Men who have never been engaged in manual labor will have soft hands, and when first put to work in handling and hauling upon the rigging, especially in cold weather when the hemp ropes becomes stiff and rigid as steel wires, soon find their hands covered with blisters, and so tender and sore that it becomes absolute agony to take hold of, and haul upon, a rope. In such cases, and until the hands heal and become protected by a thicker and less sensitive cuticle, there are but few men who would not spare themselves to some extent and permit their horny-handed shipmates to do a greater share of their work. Walker, again and again, in spite of the remonstrances of the men, and even against the orders of the petty officers, would at a command, catch hold with the others and haul with all his strength, while the blood would gush from his torn and painful hands.

The stormy Cape Horn weather was too much for our shipmate, and one day he failed to "turn to" when his watch was called on deck. He grew rapidly worse. The captain took him into his own cabin, watched over him like a father, and did all he could for him. The officers and men strove to show him all possible attention, but soon his mind became affected, and he babbled of wife and loved ones. Growing feebler, his life ebbed away, and on June 3, the poor fellow breathed his last. When the captain had found that he was seriously ill, he set our course for Talcahuano, about halfway up the coast of Chile near Concepcion, hoping there to obtain proper medical aid and treatment for him. Sadly, the course of the disease was too rapid, and Walker died before we sighted the land, and so the captain decided to bury him at sea. The main yard with swung aback and the vessel lay like a log on the water, while Walker's body was prepared. Then, dressed in his best suit of "shore clothes," he was sewn up in heavy canvas with a bag of sand weighing about twenty pounds securely lashed to his feet. The gangway plank was taken out, the body covered with the American flag was then laid on a plank, one end of which extended out from the side of the ship. At six bells, in the dog watch, all hands were summoned. The captain read burial service from the Church of England, and when he came to the words "we commit his body to the deep," the end of the plank was elevated. The body of our shipmate slid off, plunging feet foremost into the depths of the Old Ocean, there to remain until the sea gives up its dead. The main yard was then braced forward, and the ship swept away on its course for the coast of Peru. The next day at noon all hands were called aft, and Walker's belongings were brought on deck, where the captain auctioned each of them off to the highest bidder.

The following day, June 5, we caught our first view of the spectacular Andes, although the coast of Chile was still eighty or a hundred miles away. The great mountain peaks seem to tower almost up to mid heaven, and we kept them in view day after day for nearly three weeks. Swept along by the trade winds, we ran up the coast of Chile and Peru, until on June 24, 1850, nearly six months out from New Bedford, we made our first port. We came to anchor in the harbor of Santé, a small town in Peru, north of Lima. The town itself is not visible from the anchorage as it lies about three miles inland and is of very little commercial importance. Its principal business is confined to supplying fresh provisions to the occasional whaling ship that comes in here to restock and recruit after a long cruise at sea. There are probably a half-dozen wretched-looking hovels or shanties on the hot, sunny, sandy beach, and our first close view of them and of the "cholos," as the natives call themselves, certainly failed to give me any confidence in their cleanliness.

As soon as our anchor was down, hoists and tackles were raised over the fore and main hatchways, and about twenty large empty water casks were hoisted onto the deck. There they were examined by the cooper, John Rogers. He fitted them with "beckets," or loops of rope, through which a towrope was passed, and the casks were thrown overboard. Tied together they were known as a "raft." Two of the whaleboats were then manned, and taking a raft in tow, they proceeded to the mouth of a small freshwater stream some two or three miles away. Here the casks were filled with sweet fresh water, which was a great improvement on that we had been drinking for some months past. The lively songs of the men as they bent their oars made the harbor ring again, and after being pent up on shipboard for six months, the idea of a run on shore made "Jack," a general name for all sailors, merry as a cricket.

Having filled the casks, they were then rolled into the water deep enough to float them, attached to the towrope, and the raft was towed back to the ship. This was, however, an entirely different matter from bringing the light empty casks on shore, for the full casks, sinking until their tops are barely above the surface of the water, offer such resistance that it becomes very hard and slow work to tow them to the ship. When alongside at last, they were hooked onto, and hoisted onto the deck to the merry tunes of some nautical song, and by means of a hose the water was then run down into the hold into other casks, which the cooper has meanwhile examined and prepared. This work had taken the whole day, and the men who have not been engaged in it had been working in the rigging, scraping the masts, slushing them down, painting, repairing, and getting everything in order for the next leg of our cruise. Indeed, at daybreak on the second day, when we got sufficient water up on deck, we used it to heel the ship over for the purposes of painting her bottom.

The next day another watch takes the raft ashore, and so the routine of work goes on in harbor, day by day, until four or five rafts of water, half a dozen boatloads of firewood, and such fresh vegetables as can be obtained are gotten on board. Sweet potatoes, yams, onions, etc. in large quantities, with oranges, limes, lemons, a few chickens, a pig or two, a side of beef, and such other eatables as may be had, were then stowed away so as to keep as long as possible after we get out on the blue water again. On June 30th we painted the ship's bends, and Pete ran away. We also sold four barrels of blackfish oil and shipped a chola, named Andrew, a ram, a rooster, and a puppy. While lying in port, we live entirely on fresh provisions, for on these long voyages the danger of scurvy from the continued use of salt meats becomes very great, and it is to the interest of the captain to give us fresh food as long as it will keep.

After the work of stocking, provisioning, and repairing the ship has progressed quite far, the crew, one watch at a time, are given several days of liberty ashore. We each got a little spending money from the captain; $1.00 liberty money, which comes to $1.32 in the States. This is then duly charged against the men on the ship's books. The starboard watch, or 1st mate's watch, to which I belonged, had the first day's liberty. Donning our best "bib and tucker," we were pulled ashore in the ship's boats. Waiting for us on the beach we found a number of the wild and dirty-looking cholas, with horses and mules to hire. The bridles and high pommeled saddles of the beasts were gaily decked with ribbons and tinsel, and the men were vociferous and earnest in their endeavors to rent these animals to us. As none of us understood Peruvian Spanish, it was somewhat difficult to arrange a trade with them, but soon however, we were all mounted, and off we galloped to the town over a rough sandy road under the burning tropical sun, for Santé is but a few degrees from the equator.

There were probably a hundred houses in the town. All looked very much alike; one story in height, built of adobe or sunburnt bricks laid in a clumsy manner within a sort of timber frame, and then plastered with mud. The only building of note in the place is the "cathedral" as we called it, notable mainly for its size, and distinguished from the other houses by having an outer coat of lime, or rough stucco. Being neatly whitewashed it looks well. We did not go inside, though from the open door we could see the lighted candles on the high altar. The natives were very much addicted to cockfighting, the priest setting the example, and it was no unusual thing to see gamecocks tied on the plaza in front of the church, while the owner was within at his prayers. We were the objects of considerable attention for the natives, who, however, seemed peaceably disposed. They were anything but attractive in their appearance, and the houses into which we entered appeared to have little or no furniture, although there was no lack either of children or fleas. Finding very little to amuse us, we were not very sorry to get back to the beach at an early hour, where we found the men waiting for their beasts. Each watch had three days' liberty on shore. On our second liberty, I got 75 cents liberty money, which comes to 99 cents in the States. We rowed back in to Santé, and that night we witnessed a dance, a fandango, and then got into a "muss." Finally, we went back on board, tired, hungry, and glad that we had not to live in such a place as Santé. After two weeks stay here we were very well pleased to heave up anchor and put to sea again.

Although I had been deprived of any form of liquor for six months, with the exception of one or two occasions when we first got into bad weather in the Gulf Stream and again in the bitter stormy weather off Cape Horn, when liquor was served out to us, I found the accursed thirst revive when I could get the opportunity to gratify it in Santé. While there was "pulque," a sour, distasteful drink made from agave of which the cholas are very fond, it was not at all palatable, so I drank but little of it. They also had a "firewater," properly so called, named "aguardiente," made from sugarcane, for which all my liberty money was spent. I again became conscious of the strength of the chains which bound my soul. I wish to say that I make this confession, and those of a similar tenor which I may hereafter have occasion to make, solely so that I may exalt the Divine power and grace which, only many years later, broke me asunder from the fetters of the evil habits in which I had been enslaved and made me a free man under Christ Jesus. At the same time, I must also say that I had formed a habit of using the most terrible profanities, and blasphemies, so much so that I have been more than once rebuked by others, even some who were themselves as addicted to the same habit. Indeed, during all the time during which I was absent from home, until within four months of my return, I was fighting against the God, who, I fully believe, was there for me in answer to the prayers of my pious father and mother, both long since gone to heaven. I believe the Spirit was following me day and night, over many thousands of miles, and during many months and long years, seeking to win me back to my lost allegiance to Him. Sadly, I madly and blindly continued to resist His gracious influences, and turned a deaf ear to all His entreaties, until I wondered at last at the long suffering and forbearance of my God, who would not let me go until I at last surrendered to his love and grace. After Santé, I had chills, fevers, and dizziness lasting for several days.

On July 14th, 1850, I was still sick with chills and dizziness, but we saw finbacks and then the spars of a ship, which turned out to be the *Mary Frances* of Warren, Rhode Island, under Captain Smith. She was seventeen months out, with 600 bbls. of sperm oil. We gammed with her, and the crew spoke hard of her officers. That night, four days after leaving the coast of Peru, we were among the Galapagos Islands, meeting many whalers and saw many whales as well as great multitudes of sea-fowls, boobies, gannets, and pelicans, all of which reside there for breeding purposes. We made Charles Island, on the 17th, and went in to find the barque *John A. Robb*, under Captain Winpenny of Fairhaven, lying at anchor. We lay off, then during the afternoon while the captain went ashore in the waist boat, a boats' crew came over from the *Robb* and we had a short gam. The captain and officers were highly spoken of, and she is said to be an extremely fast ship. She was eight and a half months out, with 130 bbls. of oil in her hold. Our captain later came back aboard with a young man named George C. Ambrose, a German, whom he had found on the island and shipped for a 165th lay. Ambrose had run off from the barque *Persia*. He had been ashore for a month and was truly glad to get off. We then stood out and sailed westward. The islands are evidently of volcanic origin, and on Albemarle Island counted twelve perfectly formed and distinct craters, doubtless there are many more. Later, George was placed in 2nd Mate Caulk's boat, and I was switched to the 3rd mate's boat.

We continued to cruise the islands, raising several sails, among them was the *Ocean*, under Captain Driggs of New Bedford. She was twelve months out and had 500 bbls. of oil. We gammed with her. The men speak highly of the officers, and they told us that she is a fine sailer, and her last port was Tombiz. The next day we spoke with the *Balaena* of New Bedford, under Captain Dexter. She was ten months out and had 600 bbls. of oil. A few days later, in the morning, there were six sails in sight. We gammed with one, the *Minerva* under Captain Smyth Childs of New Bedford. She was twenty-two months out and had 350 bbls. of sperm oil. Later that day when the mate went fishing, he caught a number of rock cod, and a young Johnny Woggin, a penguin. That night we gammed with the *Balaena* of New Bedford. Captain Dexter said they were ten months out and that at the last port, Jalcahuana, seven of the crew ran away. As we headed away from the Galapagos on July 31st, we bore down on another sail, and spoke with her. She was the *Callao* of New Bedford, under Captain Sisson. She had 350 bbls. of oil, of which 150 bbls. had been obtained from the wreck of the *Lafayette* on Albemarle. Her captain and officers were not well spoken of by the crew. We then spent the next leg of our cruise on what is known as the "offshore ground." We enjoyed generally pleasant weather but had not very great success in taking oil.

CHAPTER 7

Along the Line

IN AUGUST WE HEADED WEST, CRUISING THE LINE; EACH DAY IN FAIR weather. On August 7th we saw turtles, dolphins, and in the afternoon the eclipse of the sun. During this time we saw the *Niger* under Captain Gray of New Bedford. She was twenty-six months out and had 1,300 bbls. of oil. On August 29th we spoke to the *Alfred Tyler*, under Captain Luce, who was twenty-two months out and had only 250 bbls. of oil. The *Tyler* hadn't had a whale alongside in thirteen months! Then we spoke with the *Jasper*, under Captain Roach of New Bedford, which was seven months out and had just 30 bbls., and on October 1st, we gammed with the *Sharon* under Captain Bonney of Fairhaven. She was twenty months out and had 1,050 bbls. of sperm oil. During this time we also broke out some lumber from below and built a house over the ship's wheel. On September 12th, I noted that heading south southwest with the wind, we were making ten knots, and that it was the anniversary of the battle of North Point, Baltimore, from the War of 1812.

A few days later on September 21st, we raised a sail on the lee quarter, which proved to be the barque *Alfred Tyler*, under Captain Luce of Nantucket. She hadn't done anything since we last gammed with her, though she has herself gammed with the *Java*, *Hercules*, and *Phoran*. I saw a California paper dated June 15th containing an account of a great conflagration at San Francisco, this being their third in six months. The losses totaled five million dollars.

The next day at 8 a.m. we raised a school of small sperm whales. We lowered and rowed until noon. The 1st mate's boat fastened to a whale and got him. The 3rd mate's boat fastened to three whales, the first of which was lost by the parting of the short warp. The line to the second got fouled of the 1st mate's line and so they had to cut it. The third whale carried off the remainder of their line, and worse their boat was stove in on the bow. Luckily, the 2nd mate's boat harpooned and got fast to, and saved, the first of the three whales that the 3rd mate fastened to. Both whales were towed alongside and cut in. The next day was a delightful day, which we spent cutting in, then mincing and boiling, or "trying out," the whales. We raised a sail, exchanged signals, then wore ship around 2 a.m. as we came alongside the *Jasper* of New Bedford, seven months out and with just 30 bbls. of oil. We got some recent papers and letters from her. The next day we continued mincing and trying out, and the *Jasper* got one of our dead whales about four miles off. A few days later as we were heading NNE we raised whitewater off the lee bow. We kept off and then tacked around, to find it was just porpoises all around. One night we passed a ship at 2 a.m. trying out. On October 1st, another fine day, we saw more porpoises all around, then raised a sail two points on the weather bow. Later that night, we overhauled aback the main yard and had a gam with the *Sharon* under Captain Bonney of Fairhaven, twenty months out and with 1,050 bbls. of sperm oil.

Saturday, October 5th, started as a fine day with the wind out of the northeast. We raised more porpoises, and then the dog went into fits, and so it was killed and thrown overboard. We broke out some fresh stores of beef and pork. The next day there were more porpoises around, and we raised a large diamond fish. Some days later, during the night, someone threw the "samp" overboard and the Old Man became enraged. Later that day the mate struck a blackfish off the martingdale guys and we got him in. There were also plenty of albacore around. We had butter duff and blackfish liver for dinner today! On October 8th were heading SSE at latitude 1°0 42⊠, longitude 13˚ 41⊠, raised a finback, and killed it.

One morning in mid-November, the captain lectured us on the whaling signals. When whales are up the signal flags will be up. When down, they will be down. When the whale is two points off the bow, there will be one signal on the forward mast, if four points, then two signals. If the whale is two points abeam, then one signal on the mainmast, then two, and so forth. If the whales are to leeward, the ship will head to them and haul down the jib. If a boat is stoved in and needs assistance, then the colors will be at half mast, and the signals as above. If two signals are at the mizzen peak, then one boat should return, and if there are three signals, then all boats should return. At night a light will be set at all times, if more lights are set, it means all boats should come in. Another day, the captain spoke to the 3rd mate about his not attending to duty. The 1st mate joined in on the captain's side and there was a good deal of ill feelings manifested and strong words passed on either side. The captain ordered the 3rd mate below to his cabin, however he was still on duty through the day. In the early afternoon, the pigeon went overboard, so we hauled in the mainsail and lowered a boat for him. We saved him, and when the boat came back on board we let out the sails and and headed on south-southeast. We passed one of the Phoenix Islands, Rawaki Island, during the night, as we are bound on this leg of the cruise to Samoa in the Navigator Islands.

Several months later on December 3, we were at anchor in Upolu, second largest of the Samoan, or Navigator, islands. The *Gratitude*, under Captain Wilcox and bound home, and an English fore-topsail schooner, the *Flash* of Sydney, lay nearby in the harbor. I cannot find language to adequately express the wonderful beauty of these islands in the sea. Their luxurious tropical foliage rising gracefully from the very edge of the ocean and covering the slopes of the hills with a rich, deep green, they form a picture once seen never easily forgotten. Our barque lay at anchor in very deep water, but so clear that we could readily see the coral reefs far below us and watch fish of many colors swimming in and out among them.

We found the Samoans fine-looking men, naturally fierce and warlike, but many of them evidencing in their conduct a great change that had come over them as a result of the labors of the faithful missionaries, who had taken their lives in their hands so that they might win these islands in the sea for Christ. There were at that time many natives who had not accepted the gospel but were still following their old idolatrous customs. The converted natives however, had become habituated to the wearing of clothing, which the idolaters eschewed, and their houses had an air of neatness and cleanliness which you sought for in vain among

their heathen neighbors. I was much impressed with their reverent obser-
vance on the Sabbath and the assemblage of the natives in their house of
worship. I could not of course understand their language, but was much
affected in listening to one of their hymns, which had been adapted to
one of our familiar Sabbath School tunes. The Rev. Mr. George Turner
was their missionary while we were there, and on the wall of their church
was a tablet to the memory of Rev. Mr. Williams, who as a pioneer at
first brought the gospel to Samoa and to many other of the South Sea
Islands. Sadly, he had but a very short time before meeting a martyr's
death on the island of Erromanga. Here I saw my first banyan, breadfruit,
and coconut trees and enjoyed their delicious fruit. The yams here grow
to an enormous size, and there were many other vegetables and fruits on
which we feasted to our heart's content.

A rainy day, December 11th was a fairly exciting day. We cleaned the
anchor line, then the starboard watch got liberty, with 25 cents each. The
captain discharged Mr. Lockwood today, the 3rd mate, who had become
dissatisfied and desired to leave. He shipped at once on the *Marengo*,
she is full and bound home. Then Jack Frost, Ben Smith, John Smith,
George Spooner, Stanley Craft, L. Wardell, and Tom Burns all ran away
from the ship. The next day, the larboard watch got liberty, but no money.
For crew, the captain shipped four kanakas and four "beachcombers," as
men who have run away from their vessels and have been living ashore
with the natives are called. The beachcombers were Jack Thurston, a 3rd
mate, a boatsteerer, and another. Jack Thurston had left the *Gratitude* to
come on board with us. One of the beachcombers the captain had seen
on the last voyage, one had been on the brig *Margaret*, and another on
the *Warren* of Sydney.

Bill Grosvenor insulted the captain on shore today. When he came
on board he repeated it, and so was put in irons and placed down in the
run. We took in 770 coconuts today and put them in the lower hold and
got a raft of water. Tom Burns was also caught today and brought back.
He too was put in irons in the 2nd mate's cabin. That evening the pilot
came on board and we took up our anchors and kedged the ship out
toward the entrance of the harbor, and then dropped our larboard anchor
for the night. Having secured wood, and water, and laid in a large store

of yams, coconuts, bananas, and hogs, the next day we hoisted our anchor and left the port of Upolu to the joy of the crew. After we got our jib and flying jib and our bow port shrouds all set up, our cable stowed away, and the decks cleared off, the captain had Bill Grosvenor and Tom Burns brought up and tied to the rigging. Bill he flogged, but Tom was let off. Both were then sent forward to their duty. All hands were then called aft and the newly shipped men were divided among the watches.

Later that week, at 7 a.m. one morning, just as the starboard watch was called, Gilbert Marsh raised spouts three points on the lee beam. The sea was very rough and the weather squally, but we lowered away. The 1st mate's and 2nd mate's boats each brought their whale aboard the ship, though the 1st mate struck two others that we lost. By night we had them cut in and stood quarter watches. Then next day we commenced cutting up the horse pieces and the heads. While in the act of tackling one of the heads, it gave a start and slammed into Winnie, but did not injure him too badly. We spent the rest of the day trying out. On Christmas Eve, the captain auctioned off the chests of the men who had run away. We bid goodbye to Upolu, and the Old Man directed our course for the Kingsmill group of islands, or the Gilberts, a famous feeding ground for sperm whales. They lie on either side of the equator, between 165° and 180° east longitude.

At daylight on January 10, 1851, the cry of "Land Ho!" rang from the masthead. Shortly after, we got our first view of a coral island with which we afterword became very familiar, but this was our first acquaintance with Byron Island, one of the most easterly islands of the Kingsmill group. It appeared very strange to see the tops of coconut trees growing right out of the sea, and yet that is just the way it looked until we got within a few miles of the shore. Nowhere did the island rise higher than about eight or ten feet above the level of the ocean. As we got still closer, we noticed from the masthead that the island was shaped something like a huge ring of sand, with an outer circle of white water where the seas broke over a submerged reef, while within the sandy circle lay a lovely lake, or lagoon. Its surface was smooth as glass and glistened like a mirror in the rays of the meridian sun. No grass was to be seen on the island, but there were very many coconut palms, whose fruit furnishes the only food for the islanders except that which they take out of the sea. Shortly after the island was seen from the masthead, the white sails of the natives' canoes began to appear, and by the time we had got within two or three miles of the land we were surrounded by them to the number of sixty or eighty. Each one had an outrigger on one side, which enables them to sail in quite a strong breeze without being capsized. Each canoe carried from six to eight men, with skin brown as a berry, entirely naked but for a narrow waist cloth. Some of them were greatly marked with tattooing, and with their bushy heads, they looked fierce enough to eat one up. From all the stories told of them, they are undoubtedly cannibals.

They kept up a great outcry of which we could distinguish but one word "tobac," for tobacco. On throwing a small piece of that weed into the water they would dive after it, and seldom failed to recover it. After a while we threw our foreyard back, checking the progress of our vessel, and the natives were then permitted to come on board causing considerable terror to some of us. There were hardly less than three hundred of them on our decks, while we numbered less than thirty. We had yet to become accustomed to what we soon learned to call a "kanaka day." However, they had a wholesome fear of firearms and behaved themselves tolerably well. We had been cautioned with regard to their thieving propensity and endeavored to keep out of their sight any little thing they could lay their hands on. Still, after they had gone, various little articles were missed. The natives brought with them green coconuts, and the shells of coconuts filled with a kind of molasses called "lica mi-mi," which they made from the sap of the palm tree. They also brought spears and knives, the cutting edges of which are formed of sharks' teeth, which they tie onto coconut wood sticks with a fine sennet, a fiber made from coconuts. With these things they gladly barter for a little tobac, or a few fish hooks, or pieces of hoop iron.

We were now on good cruising grounds, seeing whales very frequently and having some exciting times in chasing them, sometimes catching them, sometimes having an unsuccessful pursuit. One day, after breakfast we raised whales. We lowered the boats at 8:30 a.m., and soon the 1st mate and 2nd mate each harpooned a whale. The captain fastened too, but his boat lost his whale, then we got two more. All were back aboard at 5 p.m. We spent the next day cutting and trying out the whales. The first two whales turned up 45 bbls. of oil. The day after when we were still trying out, 2nd Mate Caulk assaulted Tom Burns, something he richly deserved. We finally finished trying out that night and then cooled down the fires about 3 a.m. The four whales turned up a total of 98 bbls. of oil. As the sun came up, we washed down the decks and got the ship in good trim. After leaving the Galapagos, as we sailed west along the equator to Samoa and then the Kingsmills, between September 22, 1850, and February 16th, 1851, we took in ten whales amounting to 192 bbls. of oil.

On January 26 we passed Round, or Banaba Island. The next day, a fine day, we raised a fast whale, lowered away and pulled from seven to ten miles to windward. It proved to be a finback, and the boats came aboard after about four hours of time. In the evening we raised whales again, but we did not lower. On February 9, we reached Pleasant Island, or Nauru. That night we saw canoes of the natives out around the island with their lights, as they were out fishing. These islands are fairly large, and Round Island is very symmetrically shaped, rising in the center to the height of about two hundred and fifty feet and sloping regularly in all directions to the sea. In favorable weather it may be seen from the masthead for more than twenty miles. On a subsequent occasion I was part of one of the boat crews to go ashore on Round Island, and I saw much that interested me.

We landed on a small sandy beach at the foot of an old coral reef, now six or eight feet above sea level, indicating that the island was still slowly rising up out of the depths of the ocean. The shore was lined with kanakas, old and young, male and female. The men were entirely naked except for their waist cloth, while the women wear a short "tapa," a girdle of strips of coconut leaves, tied around the waist, and not more than a foot in length. They are fine-looking lot, and some of the women are quite handsome. The young girls, some of them almost women, have not even this scant covering. Most of them wear necklaces of human teeth, and the lobe of their ear is pierced. By constant tension, the hole is stretched until the hole becomes large enough to carry some kind of large green leaf, which is rolled loosely and worn as an article of personal adornment. The natives thronged about us, pushing and crowding each other in the hope of attaining some tobac. Walking over a very rugged path composed of broken coral, we reached the summit of the island, where we found Captain Tobey in the midst of a number of kanaka houses, surrounded by the natives, with whom he was trading. As his interpreter he had a white man, who had been living here for two years, having been put ashore by a Sag Harbor ship in consequence of having a broken leg. He speaks the native language fluently, and being a favorite of the king, he seems satisfied with his condition. We learned from him that the greatest trouble experienced by the natives is on account of the difficulty of obtaining good drinking water. The best water has to be brought from a cave in the center of the island. The women, who are the "workmen" here, have to descend underground nearly half a mile to get it, as the "lords of creation" are too lazy.

On another visit on May 9th, 1851, which was a delightful day, we again landed at Round Island. Shortly after breakfast the natives began to come out to us in their canoes, and during the best part of the day the ship was fairly crowded with them. They brought with them, for the purpose of trading for tobac, fowls, eggs, coconuts, pumpkins, "tica mi mi," poles and paddles of coconut wood, swords of the same armed with shark's teeth, mummy apples, and a kind of nut much resembling peanuts in taste. The ship laid off on the weather side of the island during the best part of the day, while the captain went on shore in the waist boat for the purpose of trading with the natives. We obtained two boatloads of pumpkins, coconuts, and fowls. Later, as we circled the island, two or three canoes came out to us from the lee side. Their canoes are the best I have seen. They display more ingenuity, industry, and perseverance than one would be disposed to give them credit for. They exhibit the greatest desire for tobac, and for small quantities of this weed they will part with most anything they possess.

During the afternoon one of our cruisers, an Oahu kanaka boy called Jim, attempted to escape in one of the canoes. He was, however, discovered, pursued, taken, and brought back; seized up in the mizzen rigging, he received half a dozen lashes with a rope's end. We then took the ship on her way. From May 16th to the 17th, we passed within a few miles of Simpson, Woodle, and Hendersonville Islands, and the vessel was crowded nearly all the time with the natives. These islands are much like Byron Island, very low, and produce scarcely anything besides coconuts and fish. I have mentioned these islands to convey some idea of their nature, as during the six months of this leg on our cruise, we were in sight of one or more of the Kingsmills almost every day. During this time, we very frequently had natives on board, or as often we would meet with other whaleships, gamming with them through the evening and until late at night.

On one occasion while off Simpson Island we were approached by a jolly boat, manned by natives and steered by a white man. He made himself known as the 1st mate of the barque *Belle*, under Captain Handy, of Sydney, employed in trading among these islands for coconut oil, which is made here in large quantities. The natives smear themselves with it daily from head to foot, and while the odor is not very pleasant, it is very useful in these tropical regions where flies and various other insects abound, as none of them will alight on a surface protected by it. The natives of Hendersonville Island seemed gentler, and more modest than those of the other islands, and some of the women wore shirts, which was very noticeable in the midst of the prevailing nudity. They offered in trade quite a number of mats, fowls, eggs, and quantities of rare and beautiful seashells, etc. From Woodle Island we obtained some taro, and breadfruit, with "kolak" or Areca, nuts. Shaped something like a sickle pear, from these nuts the islanders extract the "tica mi-mi," and from which they also make a paste resembling jujube paste.

CHAPTER 8

Islanders and Beachcombers

AFTER TWO OR THREE DAYS RUN TO THE WEST, ON JUNE 12TH AT DAY-light we reached Strong Island, or Kosrae, about forty miles distant. We lowered the anchors from the bow, letting out sixty fathoms, or three hundred and sixty feet, of cable. About 2 p.m. the captain went ashore in the waist boat to obtain a pilot, and three hours later he came off, bringing with him Captain Hussey. Hussey piloted us in through a narrow tortuous channel, with dangerous reefs on every side, and it was nearly dark when we anchored. In the morning we found ourselves in a lovely, landlocked basin, not over one thousand yards in diameter, and with a depth of about forty fathoms. We were lying within a biscuit throw of the shore, and on every side the land rose gently to a height of about two hundred or two hundred and fifty feet.

There were three beachcombers living here, Captain Hussey of whom I have spoken, a Captain Brown and his wife, of Sydney, New South Wales, plus a carpenter from Baltimore, who gave me his name as Kirkland and claimed to know me and be the son of the head of the firm Kirkland, Chase & Co. I always doubted his claims, although he might have been a Baltimorean. From them the captain obtained a tierce and a half a bbl. of tica mi mi, and a number of pigs, fowls, etc., and a couple of puppies. One of the men showed the captain a kind of shipping list of the ships that had visited the island, and he added our ship's name to the list. We also heard of the murder of a young man belonging to the *Morgan* of New Bedford, while she was lying here.

Strong Island is clothed with the most luxuriant tropical vegetation and presents to the mind a picture of restful beauty and quietness that suggested an earthly paradise. We were so close to the shore that we could not help being greatly surprised at hearing many of the natives conversing in fairly good English. We learned later, that several months before our arrival, the barque *Mary Frazier* of New Bedford came in here to replenish her supplies and recruit beachcombers. While coming in was comparatively an easy matter, when they were ready to depart they found themselves unable to go. I have alluded to the crooked and dangerous channel, and it appears that it is necessary to have a westerly slant of wind in order to get out. Although the island lies in the path of the northeast trade winds that blow almost continuously from that direction, and it hardly ever happens that a month passes by without a change of the wind to a favorable direction for a day or two at a time. In the case of the *Mary Frazier* however, the northeast wind blew from that direction for four months straight and prevented them from putting to sea. As the natives here are very kind, it is customary that when ships are anchored here all hands spend the night on shore, leaving only one or two men on board as a watch. Not having any work to occupy them, the crew of the *Mary Frazier* virtually lived on shore, and being brought in constant daily contact with the islanders, they, that is the younger ones, obtained such familiarity with our language that they were enabled to converse in it quite fluently.

Strong is composed of one large island and two or three smaller ones, only separated from each other by a narrow arm of the sea. All are governed by a chief who rejoices in the name of King George, and he has a son named "Cankar." King George possesses arbitrary power, and whenever he, or Cankar, make their appearance, the natives fall, or squat on the ground until they have passed by. With the exception of a favored few, who wear shirts which they obtained from the *Mary Frazier*, the natives wear no clothing except the "tapa." There is no spirituous liquor here either, as the king has "tabooed" it and confiscates to his own use all that is brought here. The natives, however, are greatly addicted to the drinking of "cava," which is prepared by pounding a root of that name, mixing it with water, and straining it through the fibers of the coconut husk. One large coconut shell of this drink will produce stupefaction, but without much if any of the exhilaration caused by alcoholic drinks, therefore it rarely becomes a favorite drink with "Jack." In Samoa, where we first became acquainted with cava, the method of its preparation is rather disgusting, for the young maidens sit around a large earthenware bowl, chew the root, and spit the juice into the bowl. When a sufficient quantity is thus prepared, the coco husk is used as a strainer. Of the two methods, my own preference is for that of Strong Island.

Here on Strong, we found the islanders gentle, but lazy and indolent. Nature, however, produces all they require in the way of food, and that very abundantly, and the hot climate calls for very little in the way of clothing. The women are quite expert in weaving the "tapa" on a rude and singular sort of loom. Their houses are made of long grass, thatched, over a framework of poles. When new, they look very pretty, and when they become infested with vermin the houses are burned, and new ones built. There is a very large house known as the "Sing" House, where four or five hundred natives gather in the evenings and go through their dances, which they accompany with plaintive, and rather doleful vocal music, which the sailors call "hoolah—hoolah." This seems to be a custom everywhere in all the islands of the Pacific of which I have any experience. So far as I could learn, the only deity of which these people have any knowledge is a species of conger eel, which are very numerous here. The one great curiosity of the island is a very high wall, probably forty or fifty feet in height, and extending perhaps a quarter of a mile in length. More than twenty feet above the ground there are huge stones in the wall, which evidence the fact that the builders must have possessed far greater mechanical ability and must have been aided in their task by implements of which the present inhabitants have no knowledge. To all our inquiries, the unvarying reply was given that the wall has always been there.

One day, some of our crew's unhappiness came to a head. Seven of them went aft to the captain to obtain their discharges, which he refused to give. He gave as his reasons that he did not consider their cruise as being completed and that he only came here to obtain wood and water and there was no consul here. Here they found out for the first time that, contrary to their intentions and express wishes made known to him and the consul in Upolu, instead of being shipped for one cruise, some of them were down for two cruises, others for the last port, and one for the voyage. In consequence of this, one man, Jack Thurston, ran away, but was captured and brought back the same day. On June 30, after a little more than two weeks on this lovely island, we had a favorable breeze. So, we fired a gun at daylight for the pilot, Captain Hussey. He soon came aboard, and we weighed anchor and stood out through the passage. All of our boats were let down to aid in towing the ship clear of the coral reefs, which were clearly visible as we passed them by. With the aid of the westerly breeze, we made our way east back to our old cruising ground around the Kingsmill group.

Mid-month, after five days of heavy weather and rain, the seas so rough and so many of us were getting sick, we began standing half watches. Finally, we had a fine day, with just some rain, but then George Ambrose and Tom Burns quarreled, and so were seized in the mizzen rigging and flogged.

In late July, when between Sydenham Island and Drummond Island, a number of beachcombers came out to us in their canoes, bringing a quantity of blocks, irons, lances, chains etc., from the wreck of the barque *Flying Fox*, under Captain Brown, which they offered for sale. We were at that time sailing in company with the *Columbia* of New Bedford and our captains bought the goods for a small sum. The next day, when out of sight of land, we picked up a canoe containing two white men and five kanakas, who had been blown off from Clark Island by a strong breeze four days back. They had no water, or anything to eat, and in a very short time, without our assistance, would have died. We landed them the same evening at Sydenham Island.

A few days later, while off Woodle Island we spoke to the *Ganges* of Nantucket, and by a newspaper obtained from one of her crew, I learned that there had been a large fire in Baltimore. This was my first news from home. Soon thereafter, we spoke to the *Mohawk* of New Bedford. At Ocean Island, they saw one of the men we had landed at Sydenham Island, the natives on Sydenham had stripped him and sent him adrift in his canoe. An English ship had picked him up and landed him on Ocean Island. On August 11th we spoke to the *Ganges* under Captain Coffin of Nantucket. They were twenty-two months out and had 900 bbls. of sperm oil. Then on the 14th we spoke with the *Hector* under Captain Smith of New Bedford, thirty-eight months out and with 2,000 bbls. of sperm oil, and on the 23rd with the barque *Star* under Captain Ewer of Sydney [a different man than the captain of the *Emily Morgan*]. They were only five months out and had 300 bbls. of oil.

One day in early September, we raised whales going to windward at daybreak, but we did not lower for they were all out of sight quickly upwind, on the weather beam. Later I raised a breach to leeward, and when the whales came up, we lowered the captain's boat. We fastened to a cow whale and brought her in. The 1st mate fastened too, but his whale, another cow, carried the line out. He returned to the ship, got another line, and went off and then fastened to a blackfish, but the sharks ate him all up before we got him back aboard. The 2nd mate's boatsteerer darted at a large whale but missed him. The next day we had finished trying out by daybreak and got the decks cleared off before 10 a.m. We then raised whales again going to windward and lowered away at 11:30 a.m. The 1st mate harpooned a large whale, and then the 2nd mate and the captain fastened to him too. We killed him and got him alongside by 2 p.m. and cut in the body and severed the lower jaw before night. After trying out for a few days, we raised whales again on Saturday. We lowered and the 1st mate fastened to a whale and killed him, but the whale sunk and so we lost him. The captain's boatsteerer darted at, but missed two whales, while the 2nd mate got a small whale. We got that one alongside and cut him in.

On September 5th we gammed with the *Ganges*. She was twenty-four months out and had 950 bbls. of sperm oil. After five days of heavy weather and rain, with the seas so rough and many being so sick, we began standing half watches. At last, September 12th was a fine day, with just some rain. On September 23rd, we spoke with the *Macquire* under Captain Comstock of Hobart, and then on the 28th we gammed with the *Mohawk* under Captain Swain of New Bedford. She was sixteen months out and had 420 bbls. of oil.

At the beginning of December, we left the Kingsmill group and steered a southerly course for Vava'u, an island in Tonga. Along the way we stopped at Probies, or Corbett Island, on my 23rd birthday, December 9th, 1851. There, the captain shipped a beachcomber from the island, a carpenter, by the name of John Caron, a Canadian. The next day in sight of Keppel Island we raised whales. At noon we lowered, and the 1st mate's boat harpooned and fastened to a large whale. In succession, the captain's and then the 2nd mate's boats fastened. The whale then stove in and capsized the 2nd mate's boat. All three boats had to cut the line. Then the 1st mate's boat got onto the whale again and fastened to him. The captain's boat stayed by the stoven 2nd mate's boat. The 1st mate finally killed the whale and we got him alongside. We commenced cutting in, and it took two days to try him out. The great whale's fluke measured fifteen feet across, and he turned up 92 bbls. of oil.

Cruising around the Kingsmill group and then south by the Kermadecs, between July 14th, 1851, and December 10th, 1851, we took in eleven whales amounting to 269 bbls. of oil. The last, a large bull, accounted for 92 bbls. by itself. We missed another seven whales, that is our iron pulled out, the rope broke, or they ran the rope out. As I mentioned, we also had one of our whales, a blackfish, consumed by sharks before we could get it in, and on another occasion we pursued a pod of whales until we realized they were killer whales.

A few days later we reached the entrance of harbor of Vava'u in the evening, but the wind being ahead, we could not go in and so came to anchor for the night. The pilot came on board, and at daylight the next morning we pulled up our anchor and tacked in through a very narrow and winding passage. We found it rather exciting and hard work, as we were compelled to tack every few minutes, running our jibboom into the bushes on each side. The water in the channel was very deep, the shore close, and the tide ran like a mill sluice. Our good ship promptly obeyed her helm however, and about noon we anchored in a very safe and capacious harbor. We've found a very marked contrast between the natives and their houses here with those of Strong Island of the Kingsmill group. The influence of the missionaries here is very apparent when we call to mind the fact that not more than twenty-five or thirty years back, these natives were similar to those in their habits and customs. These Tongans are now modestly clad and living in neat houses which they have learned from the missionaries how to build; some of wood, some of stone neatly whitewashed. All with a general air of cleanliness that is perceptible everywhere. None of the houses have floors, the ground both in the houses of the missionaries and the natives being covered with mats, in which the natives exhibit great ingenuity in weaving in different colors and patterns. The houses of the missionaries are distinguished from those of the natives only by their larger size and by their having glazed windows. The natives also have very fine, large canoes in which they make voyages of considerable distances. Their language and music are quite similar to that of Samoans. On Vava'u, King George Tupou, not the same as the Strong Island's king George, is now a devout Christian. Formerly a great warrior, he is now the ruler, not only over this group of islands, but also over all of Tonga, or the Friendly group. He is very tall, athletic, and finely formed, with regular features and an open countenance. He wears a large tapa, in loose folds 'round his waist, and falling to the ground. His chest and arms are bare. He has been very kind to the missionaries but has been very ambitious to rule over the whole group of these islands.

We gammed with the *Huntress* there, under Captain Gibbs of New Bedford. She was seventeen months out, and had 950 bbls. of sperm oil. After two weeks spent laying in considerable stores of wood, water, yams, sweet potatoes, bananas, coconuts, breadfruit, sugarcane, shaddocks, limes, Papua apples, and melons, we put to sea again bound for Tongatapu. On the night of January 3rd, the first watch saw an island with an active volcano erupting. Two days later, we ran down on Tongatapu, and after breakfast, the captain ordered the starboard boat lowered. Selecting a boat crew, of whom I was one, after nearly four hours hard pulling and sailing, we landed on the beach. After being unsuccessful in his endeavors to ship some men, we went aboard again about 3 p.m. Of course in such a brief visit it was impossible to see much of the place. I was very favorably impressed with the beauty of the town, which is laid out with great regularity, the houses possessing a great similarity to those at Vava'u, exhibiting the same neatness and cleanliness, and the people in their general appearance, and deportment evidencing influence which the gospel has brought to bear upon them.

We learned that King George Tupou, whom we had left at Vava'u, had arrived here before us, having been sent for to settle some difficulties which had arisen between his people and some of the missionaries, of whom there are both English Wesleyan and French Catholics. We did not see the Catholic church, but the English have a fine church in the center of town. Instead of a bell to call the people to worship, they use a native drum formed from a large, sonorous, hollow log, shaped something like a pig-trough, and which when struck with a mallet may be heard at a distance of five or six miles.

CHAPTER 9

The Southern Seas

ONE FINE DAY AT SEA I CROSSED THE FORE-TOPGALLANT YARD! A FEW days later on January 12th, just northeast of New Zealand, we caught our first view of Sunday, or Raoul Island, one of the Kermadec group. This group consists of Sunday or Raoul Island, and farther south stretching toward New Zealand, Goats or Macauley Island, Curtis Rock, and French Rock. The islands lie about sixty or seventy miles distant from each other, and around this group we cruised with varied success for about three months. This is a famous feeding ground for sperm whales. Today, Winnie and the cooper made a big bet, for a new thick shirt. Winnie bet that eighteen months from today, the *Smyrna* would still be on this side of Cape Horn. On January 14th, being within a few miles of the island, the ship lay off, while the captain went ashore in one of the boats. I had the good fortune to be one of the boat's crew. The wind was very fresh, and the sea quite rough, the landing was difficult and not without danger, for great breakers, almost masthead high, rolled onto the beach with a tremendous roar. The bay at the head of which we landed was small, its entrance being to the southwest. The habitable part of the island, being confined to a shores, embraced perhaps twenty or thirty acres.

The island has the appearance of having been heaved up from the depths of Old Ocean by some mighty convulsion of nature. From the shore of the bay it rises precipitously, except the small uninhabited beach, to a height of six hundred or seven hundred feet. Presenting the appearance of a perpendicular wall, the regularly stratified rocks have for ages been subjected to the pounding of mighty waves, which have been beaten back and fallen in spray at its feet. We found sixteen persons, men, women, and children, living here, none of them, however, longer than about five years. The men are nearly all white beachcombers, who have been left here at different times by ships that have chanced to touch here. They have wives whom they have obtained from some of the kanaka islands. One of them has two wives, sisters, half breeds, and their children are nearly white. I think I have hardly ever seen more beautiful children.

Here they cultivate sweet, and Irish, potatoes, Indian corn, onions, etc., mostly for the purpose of supplying them to the ships, which occasionally stop here, and send their boats ashore as we did. They have no meat to eat, depending largely for their sustenance upon the fish they catch and the eggs of birds which frequent the island in great numbers for the purpose of breeding. Having shipped a man here, we came back on board the *Smyrna*, and bid goodbye to the island. On February 7th, we spoke with the barque *Australia* under Captain Wilds of Sydney. She was five months out, had 250 bbls. of oil, and was trying out as we paused to gam.

On February 13, 1852, we gammed with the *Montréal* under Captain Fish, which was trying out. She was nineteen months out from New Bedford and bound for the Arctic Ocean. From her I obtained some newspapers, in one of which I saw a notice of the death of Robert W. Armstrong of Baltimore, who died on the ship *Young Phoenix* of New Bedford. Two days later we raised another sail on the lee bow. She was the *Christopher Mitchell* under Captain Sullivan of Nantucket. She was thirty-nine months out and had 2,000 bbls. of sperm oil. This is the ship in which the "female sailor bold" came out from Nantucket. A few days later on the 19th we just exchanged signals with another ship, for she proved to be an Englishman trying out. We passed her; she was the *Earl of Hardwick* of London. Later that afternoon we spoke and gammed with the *Christopher Mitchell* under Captain Sullivan, of Nantucket. A few days later, when we crossed with the *Mitchell* again, I wrote, and sent with them a letter to my uncle.

Being nearly in the latitudes of New Zealand, we experienced a good deal of very rough and stormy weather. However, we were finding whales quite plentiful, and meeting with tolerable success in taking them, and so we continued our cruise until April 20, when we bore away for the Bay of Islands, New Zealand. Sighting Bream Head on the morning of the 26th, and coming to anchor that evening off Kororeka Beach, Russell. Our vessel lay here for about three weeks, during which time we laid in our supplies of wood, water, and fresh provisions. We found the place very dull, as there was very little to be seen on shore. During the greater part of the time, ours was the only vessel lying in here. The town seem to be confined to a row of one- and two-story houses, situated about one hundred yards back from beach. There are one or two stores here, with scanty stocks of goods, and two or three barrooms, where we sailors spent all the liberty money with which the captain supplied us. My confession is a very humiliating one, for although I have been living a very abstemious life for the past two years, I found when we reached a place where my cursed thirst for liquor could be gratified, that time had built up no barrier that could withstand the force of the raging appetite within. My craving was only limited by the extent of my ability to purchase the poison. We thought our captain was very mean when he doled out to us each day what we regarded as a pitiful pittance, as our share of liberty money, when we went ashore. He knew however that with most of us it should have been more truly called "slavery money," for when we were brought back on board at nightfall, many of us showed plainly enough that we were in reality the slaves of King Alcohol.

While we were here a British whaler, the *Lord Nelson*, under Captain Dobson, of London, came in and remained about a week, in which time two of her boatsteerers ran away. She was two years out, with only 200 bbls. of oil. After their vessel had gone to sea, when they made their appearance on the beach, they were arrested and lodged in the calaboose. Meanwhile one of our crew had run away, but he was caught, and after two nights in the calaboose, was brought back on board. Several others of our crew also ran away, including two boatsteerers. So, when we were nearly ready for sea, Captain Tobey paid the fine of the two Englishmen from the *Lord Nelson* and shipped them in place of our runaways. Leaving the bay, we went back to our former cruising grounds around the Kermadec Islands, but the weather proved so stormy that we remained there but a couple of weeks. We then steered a course northeast by east, and we found ourselves on June 11 off Tutuila, one of the Samoan Islands. We kept close to the land for several days, and the captain, picking a crew, in which I was again included, went into Upolu, where we found quite a little fleet of whalers at anchor. We gammed with the *Swift*, under Captain Vincent of New Bedford, thirty-eight months out and with 2,200 bbls. of oil, and with the *William & Henry* under Captain Mayo of Fairhaven. Six months out, and burning candles, and also with the *Commodore Morris* under Captain Lawrence, and the *Lion* under Captain Nichols, and the California schooner *Mr. Allen*. Captain Tobey stayed ashore all night, while the boat crew went back on board. Returning the next day, we found that he had shipped five men, a Spaniard, a kanaka, an Irish man, and two Americans, to take the places of those who had run away on New Zealand. Leaving the Navigator or Samoan Islands, we sailed for our former cruising grounds around the Kingsmill group.

On July 14, 1852, I noted in my log that "we crossed the equator this day for the fiftieth time since leaving New Bedford." Three weeks later, we sighted Howland Island, and when within about five miles of the land, I counted from the masthead seventy-eight canoes in each of which there were at least two kanakas, while many of them carried four or five. We estimated the number coming on board our ship as between three hundred and three hundred and fifty. They have darker skins than some of the other islanders, and being more frequently visited by vessels, they appeared to be more experienced in trade. They brought with them a good many hats, mats, baskets, seashells, and coconuts. In one of the canoes there was a white man, a Portuguese, who had been a shipmate of Tom Burns, of our crew, on a former voyage in the ship *Oliver Crocker* of New Bedford. With his aid, Tom made his escape from us, so in his place Captain Tobey detained one of the natives, a likely looking fellow, but who understood not a word of our language.

We cruised for several months again around the Kingsmill islands, and meeting with considerable success in whaling. On August 19th we gammed with the brig *Inga*, under Captain Barnes of New Bedford, they are fifty-one months out. Then on August 23rd we spoke with the *Omega* under Captain Russell, of Nantucket; thirty-nine months out and with 700 bbls. of sperm oil. On September 22nd we spoke with the

Lord Duncan of the Auckland Company, she was two years out with only 60 bbls. of oil. We then set a course south by west, and all hands are employed in scrubbing the ship. We raised a sail on our starboard bow, so we ran down and spoke to her, the *Oliver Crocker* of New Bedford. She's twenty-eight months out and has 1,000 bbls. of sperm oil. Our captain went on board and got some letters. Shortly after he got back around 10 p.m., the lookout sang out for another ship. We hauled back the sails and ran down to find our old friend the *Omega* again. She had taken two whales since we saw her last.

Of interest, at this time our 3rd mate and two of our boatsteerers had been part of the ship's company of the *Ann Alexander*, which about a year prior to this date was sunk within two hundred miles of our present location, by the attack of a large whale which they had been chasing. The crew had barely time to make their escape in their whaleboats, touching first at those islands and afterwards reaching Callao on the Peruvian coast. We have been tacking for several days to get to the anchorage in the roadstead off Pitt, or Makin, Island, one of the northernmost of the Kingsmill islands. We have been buffeted by the strength of the currents and by the weather which has been quite stormy. This evening however, we finally got in and dropped our anchor in thirty fathoms. There is no harbor here, so we can only remain anchored so long as the wind is favorable. The next day we began to raft off our water and to gather some wood.

On Saturday, October 9, our watch went ashore on liberty, however about 4 p.m. during a heavy squall, our anchor began to drag, and our barque was in danger of going ashore. Without a crew, Captain Tobey had to get a number of beachcombers, who are living on the island, to man a boat and take him on board. With considerable exertion they were able to heave up the anchor and put out to sea, leaving our watch on shore. It was rather a novel experience for us, and I cannot say that I enjoyed it much, for knowing the strength of the currents, and the uncertainty of the weather, there was no telling how long our liberty onshore would last. We concluded however to make the best of it, and the beachcombers were exceedingly hospitable, putting all that they had at our disposal. We split up among them, and I found myself the rather unwilling guest of a big negro whose name I cannot recall. When night came he divided, or rather shared, his bed with me. As it was quite a large one, and looked clean, and moreover was protected by a large mosquito net, and the mosquitoes here might have been the progenitors of our New Jersey pests, I was really not sorry to be so well cared for.

There was not a great deal to see on the island, the natives being similar to those of the other islands, and their food principally of coconuts and fish, and so I concluded I would not care to run away from my ship on Pitt Island. Greatly to our joy, the old *Smyrna* got a favorable slant of wind and hove into sight, returning to her anchorage about noon. Several of our men, kanakas from other islands, succeeded in escaping from us here, while in their places our captain kidnapped two of the natives of this island. One morning at daylight, the 1st mate began to pick a muss with some of the foremast hands, and one of them, a boy, chased him aft, "skearing him 'til he turned the color of chalk." A few days later we left the area for the last leg of our cruise, the captain intending at the end of the six months to go into Auckland, New Zealand, and there refit for Cape Horn and home.

While in the tropics, it being so hot in the forecastle, the men have been accustomed to bringing a mat or blanket on deck at night, and those who are not on duty lie down and sleep almost anywhere. It is also customary to shorten sail at sundown when on the cruising ground and stand boat crew watches, so it is frequently the case that the whole ship's company except the officer of the deck, the man at the wheel, and the man who has the lookout forward are fast asleep. On the night of October 17th, I had the first lookout in the middle watch, from midnight until two. It was a lovely night, scarcely any breeze, the sea quite smooth, the sky full of bright stars, but no moon, yet it was not a dark night. The old barque was slipping through the water at three-knot pace. I was sitting on the end of the windlass, looking out forward, humming an occasional song, and thinking of the folks at home when my attention was aroused by the movement of someone who was moving about restlessly and peering into the faces of the sleeping men all around me. I had just recognized him as the elder of the two men we had kidnapped from Pitt Island. Raising himself up and looking out over the bows, he uttered an unearthly yell that startled the sleepers and brought them to their feet. When he shouted I had jumped up on the end of the windlass, and following the direction of his eyes, I saw hanging from the end of the jibboom, his companion. Rushing out between the knightheads, followed by our boatsteerer, and others, we found the poor fellow, who must have crawled out of there and secreted himself before our watch was called. He had untied the jib gasket, and fastening one end of it around his throat, had deliberately lowered himself to its full length, and then letting go the rope with his hand, suffered himself to strangle.

It was no easy task to haul him up, for we knew the rope was so rotten that a sudden jerk would have caused it to break, but we succeeded in doing so. Cutting the rope about his neck, we then passed his body in between the knightheads. Just then he gave a convulsive sigh, and we began to hope that life was still in him. We carried him back and laid him on the main hatches. We bathed him in hot water and he soon recovered his breath, but his life evidently hung by a slender thread. He was unconscious and continued so all night, suffering terrible convulsions, but began breathing easier toward morning, under the influence of a large dose, five drops, of laudanum. The captain also gave him such restoratives as wine and water peppermint. He had had a very narrow escape, and later in the morning when I saw him again, the flesh of the throat had puffed up so that you could lay your hand in the crease which had been made by the rope. His comrade seemed almost crazy, moaning, wringing his hands, and chanting in a doleful tone, even as he watched his friend gradually rest easier. Neither of them could speak a word of English, and so all our efforts to communicate with them were in vain.

Though the young man gradually grew better, when able to go about the decks he made repeated efforts to throw himself overboard. At last the captain put fetters on his legs and passed between them a heavy fluke chain, which was secured at each end. This enabled the man to walk the full length of the chain but prevented him from throwing himself overboard. It would have been amusing, had it not been so serious a matter, to thereafter watch our men as they prepared to lay down after that for the night. They were terribly afraid of the kanaka, who had been so greatly wronged that he might seek to revenge himself on them while they slept.

One of them would take a belaying pin, another a marlinspike, another a club of wood, and lay it by them when they lay down to sleep. The man who was on lookout was threatened with the direst consequences if he should happen to go to sleep on his watch. The young kanaka had evidently become crazy. One day when we raised whales about three weeks after his attempted suicide, and the boats were being lowered in chase, the shipkeepers, that is the cooper, who had to be at the masthead to watch the boats and the whales, the cook, the steward, and another man whose business was to steer the ship and look after her movements while the boats were away, were so much afraid of these men, that before the last boat left the ship, they had the crew take these two kanakas and nail them up in a bin on the quarterdeck. It was a room which we used to store yams. Here they were kept all day until the boats came aboard again, and the captain determined, as he could get no service of them, that he would put them ashore on the first island he came to, which he shortly afterwards did, giving them some yards of calico and several pounds of tobac.

In early November at Byron, or Nikunau, Island, the two English boatsteerers from the *Lord Nelson*, whom the captain shipped from jail in the Bay of Islands, were today put ashore here, having made themselves quite obnoxious to everyone on board. Two or three nights ago they had a disturbance with Captain Tobey, and showing fight, the captain called up the mates. At the point of the pistol he put them in irons, and in consequence of this, two of our men were promoted to fill their positions. During the first week of December, at Sydenham Island, we heard a "cock and bull" story from the natives who came aboard here that the two whaleboats containing about thirty-five kanakas from Oahu had recently landed there in two whaleboats after having killed the captain of the whaleship to which they belonged. As it was evident that there was something wrong with the story they told, Captain Tobey determined to try and sift it, to see if he could get at the truth of the matter. We stood off the island until midnight, then came about and tacked back to return at dawn.

The next day crowds of canoes came off the island, and among our visitors there was a Portuguese, who had boarded us several times, when we were off Drummond Island. From him we learned that Captain Hussey, whom we met at Strong Island when we lay in there during June and July 1851, had shot one of his crew when he was captain of the *Planter* of New Bedford. On account of that he feared to return to America, and so took refuge at Strong Island. After we left there, the brig *William Penn* from California came in, and in some way Hussey got possession of her, fitted her out for a whaling voyage, and shipped a crew consisting of four white men and a number of kanakas from Oahu, Patience, and Strong Island. One of his boatsteerers was a Tahitian named Harry, a man of large and powerful frame, who became the ringleader of the gang. One night about a month ago, when the brig was near Simpson Island, as the captain came on the deck, he and the cook were killed, and the 1st mate and one of the men were severely wounded. The four white men were sleeping below, and the Fijian kanakas headed by this Tahitian took everything of value they could find, and arming themselves and lowering two boats, steered a course SE which brought them to this island. Since their arrival they have behaved very badly and had killed several of the natives. The Tahitian, Harry, had seized the chest of the Portuguese and had made several attempts to kill him, but was himself slain yesterday by some of his friends. The Portuguese told Captain Tobey the Fijian had in their possession a "hatful of gold and two stockings full of silver." The Portuguese also had with him a percussion-lock musket, which Captain Tobey at once recognized as having been the property of Captain Hussey, and several pairs of the captain's trousers. Captain Hussey had also taken two kanaka women to sea with him, and they are now with these kanakas, as well as two boys. He also stated that the Fijians declared their innocence of any participation in the murder and said that the Tahitian had threatened them with death if they failed to cooperate with him.

The Portuguese earnestly besought our captain to arm a boat's crew and land with him, assuring him of the aid of the natives, who were greatly enraged at the conduct of these men but dreaded their firearms. He also told him that he would be able to secure not only the money they had stolen but also the two whaleboats. As the natives of this island bear the reputation of being the wildest and most treacherous of the Kingsmill group, and this also being the place where it is only a few years since an attempt was made to capture the *Triton* of New Bedford, our captain declined to go ashore. He did supply the Portuguese with powder and gave him orders in the name of the American Counsel, an imaginary person, to shoot down the mutineers at every opportunity.

Three days later, we heard new details when we spoke with the ship *Atlantic*, under Captain Gardiner, of Nantucket. We learned that they had picked up one of the whaleboats with the mutineers one evening, who reported that they had stolen the boat and run away, but they said nothing of the killing, and they were allowed to depart next morning. The next day the *Atlantic* sighted the brig *William Penn*, and seeing her signal of distress, they ran down to her and put a man on board of her. The crew of the *William Penn* stated that Captain Hussey was killed by an Oahu kanaka named Harry, who stabbed him with a lance while he was sleeping in his berth. The cook was also killed, being literally chopped limb from limb and thrown over board, the steward was still living but mortally wounded, and the 1st mate was recovering. After the murder of Captain Hussey, and while the kanakas were all aft, one of the white men, a Scotchman, attempted to blow them up by setting a match to a keg of powder in the wheelhouse. The explosion burned him severely but injured no one else. The crew of the brig stated that the mutineers had then taken thirteen muskets, about one thousand dollars in gold, and had departed.

By December 21st, we were cruising in company with the *Lion* of Providence, Rhode Island under Captain Nichols. At about 3 p.m. when we sighted some whales, the *Lion* being on our weather beam, set her colors at the main and at the mizzen peak to let us know we were mated. In "mating," an agreement is made to share and share alike in all oil that either vessel may take, whether they are together at the time of catching the whales or not, and to render each other every possible assistance. Where vessels are cruising together, which are not mated, and whales are being chased, it sometimes happens that the boats of one ship will do all they can to prevent the other boats from taking any of the whales. We then lowered and pulled to windward chasing the whales. After about seven or eight miles we caught up with her boats but were shut in by a heavy squall. After this passed, we saw the whales and chased them in close to the beach and got on to them. Our mate fastened first, however he was soon stoved in. We came up to give him assistance, while the 4th mate of the *Lion* fastened to, and then lanced, another whale. Our Old Man then also fastened to him and killed him. Meanwhile our 2nd mate fastened to another whale, as also did the 1st mate and 2nd mate of the *Lion*. We took the first whale alongside the *Smyrna* with night coming on, and we let the *Lion* pick up the two others. We spent the next two days cutting in and trying out the whales. In all our share of the three whales was 32 bbls. Later in the day we stowed our oil, filling the hold up to the main hatchway. We now count 871 total bbls.

We have experienced much bad weather in the way of heavy squalls of wind and rain for the past two weeks. The full moon of January 24th, 1853, led to hopes of a change in wind and weather, although there appears to be little prospect of it at present. Someone heaved a coconut shell overboard today, and it had scarcely touched the water before a bird of the petrel kind had lighted on it. There he was, a small sailor in a small frail barque alone on the heaving ocean. Unrest continues, and a month later on February 15th, near Sydenham Island, we gammed with ship *Herald* of New Bedford. She reported that the brig *Inga* had been taken by kanakas at Pleasant Island and all hands were killed.

Shortly after, steering southeast we raised a sail. During the forenoon, the wind dying away, at 11 a.m. we lowered a boat and the captain went aboard the *Milton* under Captain Jones of New Bedford. While we were gamming with her crew, whales were raised. We mated with the *Milton*. We then lowered and after a short chase, each boat secured a whale, our captain in their larboard boat and our 2nd mate in his boat. Then I saw the most wonderful site I had ever beheld. After the first whale had been struck, the whales stopped on the surface, heads and tails together, and for a few minutes they appeared utterly disconcerted, not knowing which way to go. As far as the eye could see, whales lay all around us in every direction, and in numerable multitude, and as close together that it seemed as though I could go for miles, stepping from the back of one whale to another. Their 2nd and 3rd mates' boats got whales likewise. We got our whales alongside and got our chains around their flukes. In the middle watch at night, we broke out the blubber room. The

1st mate's watch got up and set up cutting blocks and tackles. The next day we commenced cutting in. We got one whale cut in before breakfast, and the other cut in and tackles taken down before 10 a.m. The other ship let off her sails and we ran down to her. Our skipper went aboard of her. We commenced trying out before noon, and when the captain came back we tacked around and stood away from them. It took another day to finish trying out, and by late that night we had got 35 bbls. of oil.

After six months of cruising around the Kingsmill group, in early March we left the islands for good and are now steering a southerly course back toward the Kermadecs. Stopping at Rotuma, one of the Fiji Islands, the captain went ashore in a boat, returning about nightfall with a boatload of fine large yams and a dozen watermelons. By April 1st, we were back off Goat Island and Curtis Rock of the Kermadecs. Plenty of whales around, but in the stormy weather we did not succeed in taking any. So, on April 25th we put the ship's head off to southwest for New Zealand. Two days later, at 7 a.m. we raised whales, and at 8:30 a.m. lowered and chased them. In the captain's boat we chased a large 80 or 100 bbl. fellow until the 1st mate fastened on to another, some three or four miles away. Our whale instantly took the alarm and went off to windward, eyes out. We then went down to the other boats and found that the 1st mate had struck him, and the whale was sounding out his line. The 2nd mate "bent on" too, but the whale carried them both off with 2,700 feet of line. We chased the whale until near night, but although we could go faster than he, when we would get up to him he would settle so we never got another chance to fasten. We left him about 5 p.m. and went back on board the ship.

By May 6th we raised Cape Brett of New Zealand on a fine day. The next night we lay off Auckland, but during the night it began to blow a gale and our situation became desperate. At daylight we saw a small schooner and followed her into a cove and dropped anchor. We stayed until noon, then when the schooner pulled up her anchor, we did the same and followed her. As we began to make sail, we saw a large ship come in behind us, and pretty fast. As we came together, it was the pilot, and when he came aboard he told us to follow the other ship, which we did. The weather was moderating, and by 5 p.m. we got to our berth, dropped the anchor in six fathoms, furled the sails, and came to rest in the Waitemata River, off the city of Auckland.

Our barque had now been three and a half years out from New Bedford, and we had taken a little more than 1,000 bbls. of sperm oil. We had just made our last leg of the cruise, and it was definitely known that when the *Smyrna* left Auckland she would be homeward bound. Of all those who left New Bedford in her, there were only about a half dozen remaining in her, and but two of those, a young lad named Edward J. Mosher and myself, who were from before the mast. All the others had run away from the ship at different times during the voyage. Indeed, I do not remember that we ever went into a port that someone did not leave, except in our first port, Santé, Peru. To fill the places of the deserters, new men had been shipped from time to time, some of them joining the ship for a leg of the cruise, or a year, but most of them with the understanding that they were to be discharged in the last port.

As greenhands, we had shipped in New Bedford on a 175th lay, getting 1 bbl. of oil out of every 175 bbls. taken. As we learned on our arrival in Auckland that, at the latest quotation, sperm oil was only worth about thirty dollars a bbl. at home, a very simple calculation showed that on reaching home, after paying for my original recruitment price, and then for the liberty money, tobacco, and clothing I had drawn during the voyage, the sum standing to my credit would be but little more than forty dollars, hardly sufficient to get me a suit of shore clothes. Mosher and I talked the matter over pretty thoroughly. His circumstances were very different from mine, for his family lived in New Bedford, and his father was the captain of a whaleship, somewhere in the Pacific Ocean at this time. As he fully expected to follow whaling as a livelihood, his return home at this time was comparatively a matter of indifference to him, while on my part I felt sure that if I should return home, I would not care to continue a seafaring life, although I greatly enjoyed it. Yet at this time my pride would not suffer me to return to my friends as a pauper after so long an absence, and hope beckoned that I should find more and better chances of improving my condition in New Zealand than I would in America. We had both, therefore, from different standpoints, arrived at the conclusion that it would not pay us to undergo the hardships and perils of a winter's cruise around Cape Horn for the sake of the little pittance that was due us, and had agreed that we should avail ourselves of the first good opportunity to run away from the ship.

CHAPTER 10

Into the Forests

AUCKLAND IN THE LATE SPRING OF 1853, WITH A MAGNIFICENT HAR-
bor, was quite a busy, bustling place. The Waitemata River, on which it
is situated, being in its lower portion rather an arm of the sea, is nearly
two miles wide opposite the city. The water is of sufficient depth for the
largest vessels, and so the anchorage is considered quite good. During the
time we lay here, there were whalers, merchantmen, steamships, and an
English man-of-war lying here. The port was in consequence a very lively
one. Having remained with the ship the whole voyage, I was under the
impression Captain Tobey felt sure that Mosher and I would go home
with him. Consequently, we were allowed unusual privileges in the way
of going on shore and in visiting other vessels in the harbor. We had our
regular liberty days, and as we were more liberally supplied with money
than in former ports, I had indulged in my old propensity to a greater
extent than at any time since I left home. I did not, however, cease to look
out for a chance to desert, but I did not mean to be caught and brought
back to the ship. The police of Auckland were numerous and vigilant, and
several of our crew who had attempted to run away had been arrested
and thrown into the "calaboose" to remain there until our ship was ready
to sail.

As most of our refitting had been completed, we knew there were
not more than three or four days before our departure. Mosher and I
began to be considerably downhearted at the process of an enforced
trip home. One day on the beach, when we were talking over matters,
a good-looking fellow accosted us, wishing to know why we looked so

"blue." Seeing that he was an English sailor, we told him our story. He bid us to cheer up, for he would gladly lend us a hand in carrying out our plans. He was 1st mate of a coasting schooner called the *Antelope*, running between Auckland and Hawke's Bay, on the west coast of New Zealand, and they expected to sail in two days. They would not return to Auckland for three weeks, and by which time, the *Smyrna* would be well on her way to Cape Horn.

His schooner was lying but a short distance from our vessel, and he arranged with us to have his small boat come under the bows of the *Smyrna* on the following night. We were on the lookout for him, with our worldly goods done up in as small a bundle as possible. At a signal, the boat was to come near enough for us to jump in, and he would take care of the rest. Everything turned out as we had planned. The man on the lookout was a friend of ours, and he took care not to see us leave the ship. The 1st mate of the schooner hid us in her hold, and the next morning as the schooner's anchor was raised, we peeked from our hiding place behind the bulwarks as we passed the *Smyrna*. We could see the officers on her quarterdeck and the captain with his spyglass scanning the beach, doubtless looking for us. With a fair wind and a favorable tide, we were soon beyond pursuit and turned with hearty good will to our duties on the schooner. We returned to Auckland in three weeks to find the *Smyrna* gone, and ourselves at liberty to begin the world anew.

In reviewing my life on the *Smyrna*, it is proper for me to say, that when I left her I was a worse man than when I joined her. I was conscious of a great lowering of the moral tone of my life. I had been well taught, yet my conscience continually condemned me. Day by day the Holy Spirit strove with me, convicting me of sin and urging me to turn to Christ and lead a new life. I refused to listen to his persuasive voice and madly continued to resist his appeals and fought against his warnings and reproofs. Happy? How could I be? At the masthead, on my lookout in the silence of the night, during my "trick" at the wheel, in times of peril and danger, on the yardarm in the storm, or in a boat chasing the monsters of the deep; ten thousand times and for thousands and thousands of miles over Old Ocean, God's Holy Spirit never left me, though richly I deserved he should have done so. As I look back on those days, and all the days of the following years, I have felt thanks that, largely to the earnest prayers of my sainted parents, the wonderful forbearance of my God was exercised towards me.

Being entirely without money on my return to Auckland, it became necessary that I should find some employment at once. In May 1853, I was indeed a stranger in a strange land. My companion Mosher shipped at once in another whaler. He was very desirous that I should go with him, but I had had enough whaling for a while. Though I had opportunities to ship on a far better "lay" than that which I had on the old *Smyrna*, or I could also have gotten a berth also on some of the merchant ships if I had desired. Instead, I had made up my mind to a life on shore for a while at least. I succeeded without much difficulty in getting a place in the Customs House Service; to pull an oar in the boat by which the Custom House officer boards every vessel coming into the harbor. Sometimes very dangerous work, especially when vessels come in during a gale, or on account of the velocity of the tide, or during the rough choppy seas in the harbor when the wind and tide are in different directions. However, the pay was good, I had a good deal of time to myself, and a good bed to sleep in at night, and no watch to stand, so I remained in the service for a couple of months, until I had had a chance to look around and decide upon some work of a different character.

Having formed the acquaintance of some "bushwhackers," or loggers, I decided to accept their offer and go with them into the kauri forests and learn to cut timber. All the northern part of the North Island was covered with an immense growth of the kauri. This tree grows to a very large size and furnishes one of the most valuable woods known to commerce. It is highly sought for house- and shipbuilding purposes, and the English navy depends almost entirely upon them for the masts and spars of their men-of-war. Just about this time the discovery of the goldfields in Australia caused a great demand for lumber there, and thus offered work at very good wages for those who would engage in the lumbering business. The country covered by these forests is quite rough and hilly, and as the timber is very heavy, the work is quite laborious. Men go in gangs of four, and having selected a place for their saw pit, usually at the bottom of a ravine. Here the trees, growing on the adjacent hillsides, can be gotten to the pit with the least labor. Usually, not too far distant from another gang, they first put up a rude shanty which will become their home for months. After this, the framework of the pit is constructed of young trees near at hand, the bottom of the pit is leveled, and everything is in readiness for the first log.

With sharp axes some giant tree about six feet in diameter is attacked, usually by two men. With well-directed strokes and considerable wood craft, "scarfs," as they are called, are cut into the butt of the tree so as to throw the tree in the most favorable position for future operations. The kauri is a "hard" pine, and it will usually take two expert axe-men a whole day to cut down a tree of this size. As it begins at last to totter, warning is given to the men. Slowly at first, then with increasing velocity, the mighty monarch of the forest, that had been centuries in attaining its growth, comes to the ground with a thunderous crash, shaking the ground and causing the echoes to vibrate from the neighboring hills. Early the next morning all the men are at work with the butts of their axes, breaking off the bark of the tree, often inch and a half in thickness. Then the length of the trunk is measured, probably sixty to eighty feet to where the branches begin, and once the number and length of the logs into which it is to be divided is decided upon, the cross-cut saw is put to work, and the logs cut to the requisite length. Then comes the hard work, for the timber is very heavy. An eighteen- or twenty-foot log weighs many tons, and it must be lifted over various impediments by means of levers, drawn up out of the hollows with blocks in tackles, guided and directed with caution at every step of the way, until at last it rests on the pit. Supported by heavy transoms or supports, the log is placed into a proper position for sawing and secured there by driving iron "dogs" into the log and the braces. Now for more hard work. Having marked a plumb line down the center of the end of the log, and continued the line on top, the top sawyer takes his position with his eight-foot saw on top of the log, and the pit sawyer wedges his box, or handle, to the tail end of the saw. Now at it they go, until the great log is divided into two nearly equal halves. These in turn must be cut into "flitches" of the width that the boards or planks are to be. These flitches are then laid on their flat side and are marked and cut into boards with a lighter, thinner saw, into one-inch, three-quarter-inch, one-half-inch, or other thicknesses as may be desired.

Now for even more hard work, the pit has been put in a place that is inaccessible to the oxen and wagons which haul the lumber to market. So every day before stopping work, all the boards and planks that have been sawed must be put on the shoulder and carried out over a very rugged road; sometimes crossing a ravine, or chasm, on a narrow bridge, even on the trunk of a tree that has been felled for that purpose, sometimes for a quarter of a mile. As the green timber is very heavy, and the long boards swing with the motion of walking, our shoulders become sore and our limbs ached before each day's tasks are ended.

I will never forget my first day in the pit as a sawyer. Clasping the handles of the box, fastened to the tail of the saw, my work was to raise the box about six inches above my head, laying the saw against the wood, then with a steady sweeping motion as I stooped, the box was brought all the way down to my ankles. My eyes were filled with the sawdust that constantly fell from the log, and this motion had to be repeated regularly, steadily all the day through. I do not know how I ever got through that day, but I've very well remembered how I lay and cried with pain through the whole night, with every bone and nerve and muscle in my body writhing in torture from the unusual and long protracted exercise. It was several days before I got through with my aches and pains and was able to get to work again, but I soon became accustomed to it.

In those sheltered forests where the breezes hardly ever penetrate, such exercise brings out profuse perspiration and causes great thirst. In consequence, we sawyers became great tea drinkers. It was our custom that the first man awake in the morning, and we were very early risers, jumped out of bed, and putting the coals together that had been carefully covered over the previous night, put the kettle on to boil. By the time the rest of us were up and dressed, about 4:30 a.m., he had a quart pot of tea ready for each one of us. We would then go to work 'til about 7 a.m., when one of us would go in and prepare breakfast, usually of broiled bacon, bread and salt butter, and another pot of tea. After breakfast, we worked until 10:30 a.m., then the kettle was boiled on a fire made near the pit, and we had another quart of tea. Dinner, with its pot of tea, came at noon, when we enjoyed some boiled canned pork, or salt beef, Irish potatoes, and beans. We had to have our "4 o'clock," as we called it, of tea, and supper was between six and seven. As there were no neighbors to visit, or books to read, we were in bed by 8 o'clock and slept without rocking until daylight. So the days and weeks and months rolled away for nearly two years. We varied the monotony at times by building a new pit, when we cut out the timber around the old one, or by going to Auckland from time to time for a fresh supply of provisions and then leaving our hard-earned money, or most of it, with the saloon keepers there.

Among my many accomplishments, I learned here to make good bread, though, as I call to mind, the first loaf I baked was thrown at my head. The kauri bark makes an exceedingly hot fire, makes good coals, and retains its heat a long time. First, we started a big fire in our fireplace, which was about ten feet wide and eight feet deep. When the ground beneath the fire was very hot, we shoveled the coals to one side, brushed the hearth clean, and put our dough, when it had raised sufficiently, right on the hot earth. We put an iron pot over it, which we covered with hot coals, heaping them up on every side around it. Sometimes instead of the iron pot, the hot coals were put directly upon the bread, which when thoroughly done was then called a "damper." The crust was very thick, but the bread was very sweet and palatable, and none of us ever suffered from indigestion.

Towards the close of almost two years, near the end of 1854, whenever we went to Auckland, we found the harbor filled with shipping. Everybody we met seemed excited over the wonderful news from the Melbourne goldfields. It has been known for years that the precious metal was to be found, both on the Coromandel coast of New Zealand and also near Melbourne in Australia, but no one seemed to concern themselves greatly about it, until a short time before the period I speak of. Now the air was filled with the rumors of great fortunes to be had for the picking, and every vessel that arrived brought the intelligence of huge nuggets of gold that men stumbled over when they were out walking. We found all of Auckland giddy with excitement, men leaving their businesses and their families to go to the diggings, and every vessel in the port seemed to be bound thither.

We had, prior to this, been living a quiet life in the bush, where no news of great interest ever seemed to penetrate, but when we got back again to our work everything seemed to be changed. We could think of nothing, and talk of nothing, but the wonderful news. It was harder for us to work. The very quietness of our forest life, that we had hitherto enjoyed so much, now became distasteful to us. We could no longer content ourselves in the forest; we had become infected with the "gold fever." It was not that any of us thought of "seeking our fortunes" there, I'm sure it was not on my part, and the result showed that my comrades were similarly minded. However, there was something in the excitement of the multitudes in the city with whom we had been mingling that had communicated itself to us, unfitting us for work, and putting us in a mood to undertake anything that gave promise of adventure or novelty. By common consent we abandoned our pit and returned to the city. We had become very much attached to each other and had agreed that whatever might happen, we would stick to each other. We were all able-bodied Yankee sailors, who had come out from the States in different whalers, but since we had come together, we have become like a band of brothers.

When we reached Auckland, the excitement had increased rather than diminished. Building materials were in great demand, and the vessels in the harbor were being loaded with cargoes of lumber and found no difficulty in additionally obtaining all the passengers for Melbourne they could accommodate. Ships, and brigs, and schooners of all nationalities were daily arriving, making a stop here on their way to the land of gold. Among others, our attention was directed to a Chilean barque, the *Dolores*, that had arrived about a week before with a crew of cholas. She was in a very leaky condition, and on her arrival her crew had left her on account of her un-seaworthiness. She was a beauty as she sat on the water, and a remarkably fast sailor. She had originally been a large Baltimore-built clipper schooner, and had been a slaver, but having been caught by a British man-of-war, had been condemned, and sold at auction. Her purchaser was a Chilean, who had rebuilt her and had changed her rig from a schooner to a barque. She had sailed from Valparaiso, with a Yankee skipper, Captain Throop, who had his wife, a pretty woman, on board. The *Dolores* had sprung a leak on the way over, but they had been unable to locate it, and so had been compelled to keep pumping night and day to keep her afloat.

Since she came in to Auckland, she had been hauled out, and divers, caulkers, and carpenters had sought and found the leak and repaired the damages. Captain Throop found no difficulty in getting a cargo of lumber, and all the passengers, about twenty, that he could accommodate, but how to get a crew for his vessel was a different matter. For as may be supposed, sailors were in great demand, and his former crew had already shipped on other vessels and left the port. A vessel of its size should have had a crew of at least ten or twelve men beside her officers. The captain had retained both his mates but had been able to secure only two men beside. As these things became known to us, we were moved to sympathy, perhaps because Captain Throop was an American, and perhaps because of his wife's presence on board. We made up our minds to ship with him for the passage across to Melbourne, about fifteen hundred miles, and back. I do not remember what wages were agreed on between us, but they were quite high. In those days seamen were so scarce in Melbourne that captains were known to have put one hundred gold guineas on the capstan head as a bounty in order to get a seaman to ship for thirty or forty dollars a month. Our wages were not quite on that scale!

Finding it impossible to secure another seaman, we left Auckland [likely late May, 1855[1]] with but six of us before the mast. Our vessel was filled with all the timber which could be stowed, leaving barely room below decks for the crew and passengers, twenty in number. We were compelled to carry our water on deck, in large casks. These were securely lashed to the bulwarks on either side of the decks, with the smaller casks forward and the larger ones aft, as our vessel sailed fastest when she was "down by the stern." Immediately in front of the wheel was a large cabin skylight, and lashed on either side of it were the largest casks of water, leaving but a narrow passageway between the casks and the skylight.

We had beautiful weather for our start. The wind was a whole topsail breeze right on our quarter, and the old barque soon showed her heels to the New Zealand coast. Early the next morning we were off the North Cape of New Zealand. We then bore away west by south for Melbourne, thus bringing us close-hauled on the wind, and running at the rate of ten knots an hour everything promised a speedy passage. Three other vessels left Auckland at the same time with us, bound for the same port, one of them was the brig *Waterwitch*, while the names of the others I cannot recall. The second night out the wind increased in violence, the seas became very rough, and the captain reported the barometer falling, indicating the approach of a big storm. With great effort, aided by the mates, and a passenger who had been a sailor, we succeeded in reefing our topsails and getting everything ready for a gale. And it came, a regular cyclone, striking us about ten o'clock at night, stern first, and throwing the barque nearly on her beam ends. How the wind did howl and shriek through the rigging. The *Dolores*, pressed down by the force of the blast, drove bodily through the big seas instead of riding over them. The passengers were fastened below, for had they been on deck they would only have been swept overboard by the seas.

The seamen secured themselves with lifelines as best they could, watching for a break in the gale to obey such orders as were necessary. As the ship labored and plunged violently, the fastening of some of the casks became loosened, and they worked with the motion of the ship. The night was quite dark, yet the phosphorescent glow of the waves enabled us to see objects quite plainly. During my trick at the wheel, it was all that I could do to keep the ship's head into the wind, for if I let her fall off into the trough of the sea, we would have finished our voyage there and then. The ship was so heeled over by the force of the gale that the deck was a steep inclined plane. As the vessel plunged forward, and then raised her bows high in the air, a big cask by my side, but from the position of the ship really above me, worked so in its lashings that I momentarily expected it would get loose, and sweep me, wheel and all, over the ship's side. Just then Captain Throop came aft, walking on top of the casks and clinging to the mizzen rigging. I expressed my fears to him. "If that goes," said he, "it is all up with us." He had hardly got the words out of his mouth when our foresail blew out of its bolt ropes, with a noise like thunder, and he started forward calling some of the men to help repair damages. Just then the barque, relieved of the pressure from the sail, righted a little and made a tremendous plunge. The cask broke from its lashings, and following the motion of the ship, slid forward so as to just clear me and the wheel and strike the skylight. It sank into the hole thus left in the deck, lodging in it so tightly that we were unable at the time to remove it. It was a message, and a very narrow escape for me. It ought to have humbled me before my God, but my proud rebellious heart was still fighting against him and would not surrender.

The storm continued in great force, but having less sail on the ship, we were having rather an easier time of it, until one of the officers whispered to the captain that the straining of the vessel had caused her to spring a leak again. With our shorthanded crew nearly exhausted from battling with the storm, which showed no signs of abating, we would have been unable to man the pumps and keep the ship afloat, so the captain gave orders to call the passengers. He told them it must be for them either to pump or sink. In such light, they very cheerfully went to work, and dividing themselves into relays, kept the pumps going night and day, until we reached Melbourne on the seventh day out from New Zealand. The weather did not moderate until we sighted the land of Australia. As we drew near the entrance of Port Phillips bay, on which Melbourne is situated, we found quite a fleet of vessels making for the same port, most of them giving evidence of the violence of the storm through which we had just come. Among the others we saw one of the vessels that had left Auckland with us, almost dismantled, having carried away her topmasts and flying jibboom. As we approached nearer the shore, several wrecks were to be seen on the rocks, one of them the ill-fated brig *Waterwitch*. I never learned whether any of those who sailed in her were saved or not.

We soon entered the smooth waters of the bay, one of the largest and finest in the world, and we were surprised to witness a forest of masts. Between two and three hundred vessels were lying useless at anchor, for it was impossible for them to secure crews of seamen at any price, as their crews had left them and gone up to the mines. In most cases, no one except the captains were on board, and those captains who had their wives with them had turned their ships into laundries. The wives were taking in washing, and the rigging of the vessels was strung with clothing hung out to dry. As soon as possible the lumber was taken out of our vessel and she was run into the dry dock, where the leak was effectually repaired. All hands went on shore. Here we found a great city of tents, there not being anything like houses enough to shelter the multitudes that had come and were continually coming from all parts of the known world. Drawn thither by St. Paul's *auri sacra fames*, the accursed greed for gold.

The sound of the axe, and saw, and hammer were heard on every side, and no one need go without a job who could drive a nail or handle a saw. The lumber, or at least part of it, that was being brought from the ships was turned into houses as fast as possible. Great trains of wagons, drawn by oxen, were being loaded with provisions, building materials, hardware, etc., and with great cracking of whips, hurried to the diggings. Everything was in a bustle, everybody was in a hurry, and every eye was lighted up with hope. Everyone was just on the point of making a fortune. We remained here about three weeks, but not one of us four went to the diggings. We had brought the *Dolores* over and meant to take her back again. Although we were laughed at, and jeered at, and called crazy, we were not moved from our determination. Captain Throop succeeded in getting a couple of crewmen, and with about a dozen passengers, some of whom had made money at the mines, and others who had not, we started on our return voyage. It seemed as though the winds had blown themselves out. The sea was like a millpond, the breeze was fair, but hardly strong enough to lift the leech of the sails. With every sail set, the *Dolores* hardly seemed to move through the water at all. The passage that took us a week to make in the storm, took us fourteen days as we came back in fair weather. We were glad to drop anchor in Auckland Harbor and bid goodbye to Captain Throop and his pretty wife, with many a kind word from them.

CHAPTER 11

Wairoa

I HAD A PRETTY GOOD SUM OF MONEY COMING TO ME FOR MY SIX-WEEK trip, but it was soon gone in the same way in which all my previous earnings had disappeared. Our party of four was then broken up by the determination of two of our number to go to sea again. As the way did not immediately open up for me to go back to my old field of labor, I began to look out for work of any kind. Then a proposition was made to me to join my fortunes with a young Scotchman, with whom I had become acquainted. Accompanying him and his wife to Hawke's Bay, on the southern part of North Island, where he had formerly lived, we would work in the soft pine forests there. As I was desirous of seeing something more of the country, I made up my mind to go, for this would bring me right in the mist of the "Māoris," as the New Zealand natives call themselves. Though having lived on the island for two years, I had seen little of them, for as the English settlements have increased in size and importance, the natives had gradually retreated from the northern part of the island. Taking passage in one of the coasting schooners, after two days sailing in November 1855, we found ourselves at the mouth of the Wairoa River.

We stopped at the settlement of a white trader named William Lockwood, about ten miles up the river, until we could make arrangements for getting to work. Lockwood was known among the natives as "Wiremu Piriwhirri Tawra," the first word being a corruption of his given name and the latter part of it a description of his work, "taura" being Māori for a rope, and the "Piri whirri" referring to the noise of the wheels when put in motion by him to spin the rope. He had been living here for some ten or twelve years with a Māori wife, and a family of their children, and appeared to have made himself very comfortable. He had a good deal of influence with Paul Argeri, who was the high chief of his tribe, which owned the land for many miles on either side of the river, and with whom it was necessary that we should be on the best of terms.

Although not more than thirty-five years old, Paul has been a great warrior, and a man-eater, before the English has succeeded with great difficulty, and the loss of many lives, in breaking the power of the Māoris and reducing them to a sullen submission. Indeed, the year after I left the island, the native chiefs, who had during some years of peace been buying muskets and powder and training their followers in the use of them, broke out again in a rebellion, which was only quelled after great bloodshed and the death of many Māoris. I never learned whether Paul was among the slain or not, but feel sure that he would have been at the front of the fight. Through the earnest labors, for about twenty years, of faithful Wesleyan missionaries, the Māoris in our area had cast away their idols, given up cannibalism, and become nominally Christian. Indeed, I believe that there were quite a number of them who had experienced a change of heart and lead exemplary Christian lives. The Catholics also had their missions among some of the tribes and also exerted considerable influence over them. Yet there were still a great many who in their hearts were vicious and cruel, and who had no love for an Englishman. Paul, I think was one of these, and it was not until he was satisfied that I was a Yankee, and my mate a Scotsman, that we gained his permission to go to work near Wairoa.

I found the country very different here from rugged, hilly, rocky district around Auckland. Here, for miles along the valley of the river, and on either side of it, the ground was as level as a floor. The soil, composed of disintegrated lava, was very rich and almost black, and exceedingly fertile. It was so light in places not covered with vegetation that the strong winds, so common here, would take it up and literally blow it away. The climate here is delightful. Though the islands lie just on the verge of the tropics, yet being narrow, nowhere more than one to two hundred miles wide from east to west and stretching between three and four hundred miles from northwest to southeast, the trade winds blowing directly across them keep the temperature cool and pleasant even in the hottest period of the year. There is no winter, but instead a rainy season takes its place during June, July, and part of August, during which torrents of rain fall, and the rivers and streams are swollen to their utmost capacity. With the ground being so level, it is in many places so overflowed that walking is not pleasant.

High winds, with tremendous storms of lightning and thunder, are of frequent occurrence, especially at the changes of the moon, yet when the wet season is over, vegetation is very luxuriant and abundant and it is not unusual to obtain three crops of Irish potatoes (which grow here in the greatest perfection) and two crops of Indian corn in a season. Earthquakes too are frequent here. In January 1856, while lying in bed one night, I counted more than twelve distinct shocks in succession. Gentle where I was, it is true, yet sometimes they have proved very disastrous. Wellington, the capital of New Zealand, situated on the middle island, has twice already been nearly destroyed by them, and the loss of life and property has been very great.

We found the forest where we were to work, situated about a quarter of a mile from a little stream tributary to the Wairoa, and as my mate and I were experienced woodsman, we were not long in putting up a roomy and comfortable *whare*, or house, on the level land lying between the stream and the "bush," as the forest is called. I was greatly surprised, when I entered the forest for the first time, at the difference between the kauri, or hard pine, with which I have been familiar, and the kahikatea, a soft pine with which I was to become acquainted. The kauri grows to a great size in girth, most of the trees in the kauri forest range from five to nine feet in diameter, and some of them greatly exceeding that. I remember one tree, held by the Māoris in great veneration, and surrounded by them with a fence, which is said to have measured thirty-seven feet in circumference. However, the height of the kauri, from the ground to where the branches begin, is rarely more than fifty or sixty feet. On the other hand, the kahikatea does not often exceed four feet in diameter, while its trunk towers up straight as an arrow for one hundred twenty to one hundred sixty feet before you come to the branches. In the top of the trees there grows a peculiar berry, looking like that of a yew tree with two large berries, a red and a black one, fastened together. The birds are very fond of these, and great flocks of wild pigeons, cockatoos, and birds of rare plumage may be seen feeding on them, perfectly safe from man's attack, unless he be armed with a rifle. My mate had one, and we often enjoyed pigeon pie for dinner.

The wood being much lighter, the logs being smaller than the kauri, and the land so level, two men were sufficient to get the largest logs to our pit. With the wood of the kahikatea being soft, when ripping boards, especially in the sap of the wood, it was not an unusual thing for us to drive the saw three inches at a blow. Consequently, with far less labor two of us could get off as much lumber in a week as four could do with kauri. The wood, however, was not so valuable as the kauri, and being more distant from the market, we received less for our work. Yet as provisions were very abundant and cheap, we were, all things considered, doing quite as well, and having as comfortable a time. After some time, we got tired of our grass, or *raupo*, cottage, and out of the boards we sawed, built a larger and more comfortable home for ourselves, with windows and doors. Being white, the house could be seen over the level land from a considerable distance and attracted the natives near and far who came to see the *Pakeha's whare*, and his *wahine* (the white man's house and his wife). Not long after, while comfortably enjoying our new home, Paul Argeri, who had heard of it, came to see us, and his eyes fairly glistened with delight, as putting his hand out and touching the house he cried "To tika te pakeha nee, a morr taku whare," "First rate the white men, this house is mine." With great kindness, he assured us that he would permit us to occupy the house for a while, but when he wanted it we could make another for ourselves.

We observed Sunday in the bush as a day of rest, though not as a day of worship. Taking a bath in the stream and putting on clean clothes, one or the other of us would jump into our canoe and gliding downstream, would make a call on Lockwood, some five miles below, or crossing the river visit the native "pa." This was a Māori settlement, covering about twenty acres, surrounded by a high palisade. The palisade was made of the trunks of the young trees firmly embedded in the ground, the tops of many of which were decorated with the most intricate carvings, of the most hideous faces and forms. Within the pa, the native houses were arranged in streets, many of them built on platforms six feet above the ground. Not very clean, the houses have peaked roofs, thatched with raupo. The women wear shirts and skirts, except the young girls. The men often have no covering but the waist cloth and a large mat made of the flax thrown over their shoulders which falls to the ground. The faces of the men, and often their bodies, are frightfully disfigured with tattooing. Their bearing is fierce, and though sometimes kind, they are always very sarcastic in their remarks. I never formed any very great attachment to any of them.

Occasionally we would go down to the mouth of the river, which at the close of the dry season would be completely blocked up by the sand that had been brought down the river. A sandbar formed, sometimes one hundred feet in width, stretched completely across the river's mouth, and affording a pathway that was constantly being used by the natives in traveling up and down the coast. Once the river, dwindling daily throughout the dry season, was shut off in its passage to the sea, every succeeding tide of the ocean would add to the size of the bar, while the river inside grew into a little lake hemmed in on every side. Then when the rainy season began this state of affairs was soon changed. Every hour the current of the river increased in volume, and the surface of the lake rose higher and higher, until it soon reached the top of the sandbar. Some native would then, with the point of a stick, make a little gutter in the sand, so the water confined within could begin to flow out, which it did with rapidity and force. Carrying the sand with it, enlarging its channel from moment to moment, the native would have to run rapidly to avoid being carried away. In a couple of hours, the channel would be deep enough and wide enough to permit the entrance of a large man-of-war.

We had been here several years, and 1857 was drawing to a close, when with no cause that we could ascertain, we found our relations with the natives growing more and more unsatisfactory. Paul Argeri's temper became overbearing and threatening, and Lockwood warned us that an outbreak of the natives was imminent. We concluded to discontinue our work and return to Auckland.

CHAPTER 12

Isaac Howland

I HAD BEGUN TO GET VERY TIRED OF MY MANNER OF LIFE AND HAD LONG been terribly homesick. Only my pride, which made me unwilling to return empty-handed, and my wicked and rebellious spirit against God, which refused to yield to the solicitations and stirrings of His Spirit, had kept me so long in exile. I fully recognized the fact that if I ever returned to my home and my friends, it must be with the determination to forsake my old sinful ways and habits and give myself to Christ with the purpose of leading a new life by His gracious help. One day in Auckland, before leaving for Hawke's Bay, I had gone into a bookstore and purchased a Bible. I had been reading it a good deal, though with a constantly increasing sense of self-condemnation and unhappiness. I felt in my very soul that to go back home and lead the old simple life without changing my ways would be but to ensure worse hardships, and a darker ruin in this life than I had yet known. My eternal undoing would be certain and irremediable. With these thoughts and feelings weighing me down, having left Wairoa, I wandered about the streets and up and down the beach in Auckland in a most miserable state of mind. I could have obtained plenty of work at very good wages. There were many vessels in the harbor needing men, and I could have gone in any of them to the uttermost parts of the earth, but I could not get away from myself. At times I tried to pray, but my prayers got no higher than my head, for I felt that I was insincere. I wanted to be rid of my burden, but I was not willing to pay the price. I was not ready to submit to God, and I well enough knew that without that submission I could expect no help from

Him. At length I made a compromise with my conscience and promised myself that I would yield to God, but not yet. I would join some vessel homeward bound, and somewhere in the future, before I reached home, I would give myself to the Lord.

Shortly after I had reached this conclusion, meeting with a young fellow who had come ashore from one of the vessels lying in the harbor, I entered into conversation with him. He spoke in high esteem of the officers and crew of his ship, and I thought I would ship in her if there was a chance to do so. When her captain came ashore next day, I accosted him, and he agreed to take me if I would ship for the remainder of the voyage, which would be a year, before they headed home. This suited me very well, for if she should be successful in taking oil, I would not be altogether penniless when I got back to America. So January 19th, 1858, found me a sailor on the good ship *Isaac Howland* of New Bedford under Captain Reuben R. Hobbs.

Over the course of the next three weeks, we brought on board twelve tierces of beef, a cask of molasses, six casks of water, and a load of potatoes. Also laying in here, we gammed with the *Oliver Crocker*, the *Zone*, the *Amethyst*, and the *Minerva*, all of New Bedford, and the *Sea Ranger* of Nantucket. The last week of the month had us coopering, then painting first the port side, then the stern and lower masts, then the foremasts and jibbooms. Sunday, January 31st, was silent and quiet, with no work expected. I wrote a letter to my uncle Robert, to go home on the barque *Zone*. The next day the *Alfred Gibbs* came in, bound home, and we shipped from them a boatsteerer and a kanaka. Over the next few days we shipped two more men and loaded in nine more tierces of beef and five barrels of pork. On February 5th, the *Zone* and the *Oliver Crocker* went out to sea, while we made final preparations and lashed a couple of casks on deck and brought down all pennants.

At daybreak on Monday, February 8th, we loosed the sails and manned the windlass and hauled up the anchors. After we got out into midstream, we then dropped an anchor under the fort and ate breakfast. By February 10th we were going along the coast up to Mangonui, where we raised some blackfish. We lowered the boats and secured two. We went in to Mangonui the next day and got two men who had run away in Doubtless Bay. We took them out to our ship, then went back in to town again. There we gammed with the sailors from the *William Thompson*, *American* of Edgartown, *James Allen*, *Olympia Kingfisher*, and *Manuel Ortiz*, all right whalers. Later that night we set sails and took her northeast. On February 16th it was blowing fresh, and there was a good deal of sea. We raised whales at 10 a.m. and had a male alongside by noon. We cleaned out the blubber room, got the jaw in, and the next day we, after great labor, cut in the body and got the blubber in. At night we lit the fires and stood our watches. It took us three days of trying, as there was a gale on the second, but the whale turned out 84 bbls. of oil. I regarded this as a favorable token for my return voyage.

[Captain Hobbs's log noted that, on the 16th, they raised a pod of large whales early in the morning. After lowering four boats, one struck a whale. The harpoon then pulled out, so they struck another, but the line parted. They struck again and "saved" that whale. By noon they had the whale alongside and had lowered the topsails to begin "cutting in." That evening, the crew managed to remove the sperm whale's jaw and partly sever the head. Overnight the winds picked up, making operations more difficult, but the next day they were able to finish removing the head and begin the tryworks. On the 18th, the crew finished boiling the "case" and began slicing up and boiling down the blubber. The winds increased to gale level, and the crew double-reefed the sails with the whale's body slamming against the hull in the cresting waves.]

In March, after some very stormy weather, we sighted our old acquaintance, French Rock, of the Kermadec group. After cruising here for two or three weeks in nasty New Zealand weather, we retraced our course, and in April went into the Bay of Islands and came to anchor. While lying here, we took in forty-five tierces of beef and discharged two sick men and a boatsteerer. We also had one man brought back who had previously run away from the ship, and a week later we went out to sea again, going back to the Kermadec group, where we now found quite a number of whalers cruising. [The captain's log noted they had observed up to five sails in the area and gammed with the barque *Awashanks*, under Captain (John) Tobey, and the whaler *Amethyst* under Captain James.]

We spent all day gamming with the *Mohawk* and the *Sophia Thornton*, both of New Bedford. The *Sophia* is commanded by Captain James Nichols, an old friend and crony of our captain, and as they agreed to mate, she was our constant companion during the greater part of our voyage. As we were almost all the time in company with the *Sophia Thornton*, and gamming with her very frequently, our officers and men became very intimately acquainted, and we found them very genial companions indeed. One of the features of gamming, especially with strange ships, is the exchange with them of any books and papers for those which they may have, and the ships thus become something like circulating libraries. Through the first weeks of April, we were off Great Barrier Island, Little Barrier Island, and Mount Many Peaks, then we headed north again to Cape Brett.

Among the books that in this way came aboard our ship was a little one called *Religion and Eternal Life* by J. G. Pike. In my state of mind, it was just the thing that I needed, for I was still fighting against God, and all the more fiercely because of my determination that I would yield to Him before reaching home. Indeed, I became more blasphemous and foul-mouthed than ever, and it was not long before I was the recognized leader of the ship's company in all things sinful. Yet I continued to read the Bible, and this book which seemed to be a sharp probe from the Almighty to search my heart, and they revealed to me my wickedness. It now appeared to me that my heart was fairly honeycombed with corruption, and I wondered that the Holy Spirit did not give me up and leave me alone, yet those prayers of my parents, that long years ago had been poured out for me, were being answered, and I now saw that God's hand "tho then unseen" was leading me back to him.

In early May 1858, after steering a northeast course for the past week, we today sighted land ahead. This proved to be Cantab, or Waya, one of the Fiji Islands, around which we expect to spend most of our time for the remainder of the year. The islands are largely volcanic in their formation, with high hills clothed with verdure rising beautifully from the edge of the sea. The waters around the islands abound in coral reefs, which may be seen rising from the depths beneath, and on which the seas are continually breaking. The next morning, we were close to the shore, and two boats from each ship, *Isaac Howland* and *Sophia Thornton*, went ashore to trade with the natives, returning in about three hours with a load of yams, coconuts, and bananas. Our captain also had in his boat two of the natives, whom he had coaxed on board.

For the past twenty days we have been cruising to the westward of these islands, with the trade winds from the north-northeast, running up to windward and sighting Cikobia, or Thikombia, and then dropping down past Round Island, off Yasawa, to the neighborhood of Cantab, or Waya, Island. We were sometimes in sight of our comrade, the *Sophia Thornton*, and then we would lose sight of her. We saw a good many whales, and both ships took some of them, though they seem very shy. The two Fijians who we kidnapped from Cantab are very unhappy, and although we have other kanakas on board, their language is different, so that we have not been able to converse with them. When they came on board they had great bushy heads of hair, according to their custom. However, we found them so full of vermin that in self-defense we had to cut off their hair, which they did not seem to like. This morning they were both missing, and after thoroughly searching the ship, we were forced to conclude that they had thrown themselves overboard during the night. As we were at least thirty or forty miles from the land, and the current sets here very strongly to the west, it seemed hardly probable that they could succeed in reaching the land, although the natives of these islands are splendid swimmers and are almost like fish in the water. The following day we caught three whales, while the *Sophia Thornton* took two. She had one of her boats stove in by a whale, but luckily none of her men were hurt.

On July 6th, we got our cables ready and our anchors off the bows, and both ships beat through the Round Island passage to anchor in the Bay of Bau, remaining here two weeks. The bay is large enough for one hundred ships. While here, we shifted some of our cargo in order to heel the ship, so that we might get at some of the wormholes that "borers" had made in our sheathing, and which caused our ship to leak a little. After we righted the ship, the natives came on board with coconuts, bananas, breadfruit, citrus fruit, and Papua apples. Karatug is the head chief, and his son's name is Le Macuata. They are very athletic and fierce looking, and very much tattooed as are most of the men. These natives are the most warlike of all the South Sea islanders, and cannibalism is a prevalent custom here, although the missionaries, who are laboring with some success on some islands, have risked their lives in the attempt to prevent it. While ashore here and getting water, we found plenty of lemons, limes, and chili peppers. We also obtained four thousand yams, some of them as large as a man could comfortably carry. A boat from each ship went over to the Macuata coast and returned with a load of lemons. Next we went over to Marley, or Vanua Levu, and dropped anchor. While here, we went ashore and spent a day picking peas of a very delightful flavor, which grow wild here. Four days later we went out to sea again.

A few days later when off Cikobia, three boats went ashore from each ship and brought off loads of coconuts, some sugarcane, and bananas. While here we learned from some beachcombers that our two Cantab islanders, who had jumped overboard, had actually succeeded in swimming to land, but not to their own island, and that in conformity with the custom of these islands, they were killed and eaten.

We continued around the Fijis with varied success for two more months. We were off Round Island on September 19th, it was a fine day with a light breeze, and in the morning, we raised a breach, but then saw no more of that whale. Later that day, just after supper, the following affair transpired. Ned, a Portuguese, was standing barefoot on the forecastle steps. Chambers going up to the masthead happened to step on his foot. Ned struck him and Chambers came down upon his chest and then started off again two or three steps up the ladder. Ned commenced to then give him some saucy speech, and Chambers came back down again and struck him. While in the act of striking him, Antoine, another Portuguese, jumped up and pitched into Chambers and so a regular scuffle ensued. Ned then went up and told the captain, who came down into the forecastle and inquired into the difficulty but could not get an answer until at last Chambers began to tell him. Then he ordered both Antoine and Chambers up on deck, and then sent them aft where the 1st mate seized them up in the mizzen rigging. Chambers was on the weather side, starboard, and Anton on the other. Then calling all hands aft, he asked me to tell him of the circumstances. As I gave him no satisfaction, he called on another, who told him. He then flogged them with a piece of ratline, doubled in his hand, giving Chambers eighteen blows and Antoine two dozen. Then catching Ned by the collar, he gave him a few blows. Then setting them loose, he ordered us all forward.

We continued westward, and on October 24th about six hundred miles southeast of the Solomon Islands, we sighted Erromango Island, one of the Hebrides Islands. This is the island where John Williams the missionary was killed. It is a small island, but very high, and the summit of it is flat tableland, so that it presents appearance of a truncated cone. The day following, we sighted some of the other islands of the group, Anatom, Immor, and Tanna, and we cruised around them for about ten days. Not finding many whales here, and failing to take any that we chased, we then kept away for Lord Howe Island.

In early December, we fell in with our old comrade the *Sophia Thornton*, from whom we had been separated since shortly after leaving the Fijis. She had taken no oil since we parted, but had been in port at the Bay of Islands, New Zealand. On December 9th, 1858, my thirtieth birthday, we sighted Lord Howe Island. Two days later we landed two of the boats and got off a raft of water. On the several following days, we got several boatloads of wood and some water, onions, and hogs. We left here on the 15th, parting at the same time with the *Sophia Thornton*.

Bound for New Plymouth, during the middle of the day on Christmas Eve, we were sailing in company with the *Kingston* of London. She had a great many passengers on board. In the evening she kept off and then ran astern of us. As she steered very wildly, yawing about a great deal, Captain Hobbs thought she wished to speak with us, and also kept off, intending to pass astern of her. When we were about a ship's length from her quarter, her helmsman, who was not attending to his business, brought her by the lee, and finding that she had stern way on, we put our helm hard aport, but too late to prevent a collision. Her stern smashed both our waist and larboard quarter boats, breaking some of our davits, and otherwise injuring our quarter, while we carried away her spanker gaff, doused the British ensign, and smashed some of the fancy gingerbread work on her stern. As we were clearing away the wreckage, her captain hailed us, inquired the extent of our damage, apologizing for the carelessness of his helmsman, and wished us a Merry Christmas. She continued on her voyage.

Today, December 27th, it is nine years since I left New Bedford. We sighted the Three Kings, rocky islands thirty-five miles off the north coast of New Zealand. We then ran along the coast for several days and we saw quite a number of vessels, some of them whalers, others merchant-men, standing in for, or coming out of, Auckland. Five days later, we made our last port, running into the Bay of Islands and anchoring there. Remaining here a little more than a month, during which time we took in fresh supplies, overhauled our rigging, and got everything in trim for our passage round Cape Horn toward home. We also took on board here between 700 and 800 bbls. of oil from other vessels lying in port here. We got underway on February 6th, 1859, and went out to sea. The next day we took a whale that made us 64 bbls. of oil, making in all 342 bbls. since I joined the ship.

CHAPTER 13

Homeward Bound

BEING NOW HOMEWARD BOUND, I HAVE FELT THAT THE TIME HAD COME to redeem the promise I had made to God, to give myself to Him and lead a new life. My old life has been utterly wretched and made me miserable at heart, though before my comrades I have been the same wicked, rollicking daredevil they have always known me to be. Yet as I have continued to read my Bible, the Holy Spirit has shown me the depth of my depravity. I have continued to rebel against God, and while I feel that He should justly cast me off forever, He has not permitted me to despair of His mercy. He has brought to my mind, again and again, the prayers of my parents, the teachings of my childhood, the instructions of my faithful Sunday school teachers, and the exceeding great and precious promises of His word. After a month at sea, I began to pour out my soul to God and asked that he would pardon me and restore to me the joy of his salvation. However, the more I prayed the darker my soul seemed to get, and I continued for several days until one night, March 5th. I remember that night well. I was the lookout in the middle watch during a quite dark night, it was cloudy, blowing a gale, there was a heavy sea running, and we were close-reefed with the main topsail. As I paced the deck my soul was still dark, then when I lifted up my heart in prayer, through our Lord Jesus Christ the brightness of noonday seemed to shine in my soul. The burden that had weighed me down for so long rolled away, and a Divine voice said to me "Thy sins, which were many, are all forgiven thee," and floods of joy and gladness swept my poor heart. Later that night I was enabled to confess my determination before some of my shipmates to become a Christian. May God give me grace to live up to it. And "Oh, may his holy spirit so operate upon their hearts, perhaps through my example and influence, that some of them may be brought to Christ. Oh, may I be ever watchful lest by my conduct I shall bring reproach upon the cross of Christ through my falling away from him. Lord strengthen and uphold me."

I knew it was going to be hard work going forward, and in confessing Christ before my shipmates, but I also knew very well that I could not retain my newfound peace and comfort unless I did so. It cost me many a struggle, and I sought help from God. He gave me the strength to acknowledge what he had done for me and to urge my comrades to forsake sin and seek His favor. A day or two later, in a conversation with my chum William Whitmarsh, he too declared his purpose to seek a pardon from God. This gave me great encouragement. I also had much satisfaction in knowing that there were others on board who were as seriously inclined. I continued to have a pretty hard fight of it however, and Satan hardly ever left me. Indeed, he often gained the advantage over me. When I yielded to his temptations, I would lose my comfort and the sense of His divine favor, and clouds would come in between my soul and God. If I kept on praying however, and reading the Word, after a while the clouds would disappear, and the joy of the Lord would again fill my soul.

One great trouble to me was that there was no place on board where I could find privacy; nowhere that I could retire alone for communion with God. I began to feel the tremendous force of the evil current that I had finally begun to stem. While I was being carried along by it, everything went easily, and I did not realize how rapid and powerful was the tide that was sweeping me to eternal ruin. However, as I fought back, I learned the strength of the evil habits I had formed. They were harder to break than chains of steel. I often became utterly disheartened and discouraged, crying out in the language of Paul, "Oh! Wretched man that I am, who shall deliver me from the body of this death?" I was fully determined however to cling to God, and by prayer and fasting, and by reading my Bible, and through the few religious books I could find on board, to cultivate a closer union with Christ. While He graciously bestowed on me from time to time the assurance of His grace and favor, I became more and more conscious day by day of the presence and power of my fallen, sinful nature that I could neither control or cast out. I saw too, that the God, upon whose service I had entered, was a holy God, and that He expected His people to be a holy people. His word plainly taught us that in the redemption which had been wrought out for us through our Lord Jesus Christ, an abundant provision had been made whereby the vilest sinners might be cleansed from all their sins, so we might live in the enjoyment of Divine favor. So very early in my new Christian life, I began to seek the holiness of heart "without which no man shall see the Lord." As I now look back upon those days, and on my Christian experience for many subsequent years, I realize that my will then was still unsubdued, and that my consecration was so defective that it was not possible for me to obtain any very great degree of victory over sin. Yet, I continued to strive and make hard work of the religious life. Making some little advancement at times, at other times barely holding my own, under the power of temptation and the weakness of my own heart, I would fall back into sin and darkness.

Meanwhile as the days and weeks passed by, our good ship was steering a southeasterly course, sometimes in good weather and with fair winds, at other times beating about against heavy seas and adverse gales. The weather became colder and colder. On April 14th, the clouds which had secured the sun for some days and prevented us from getting an observation cleared away, and we found ourselves on Latitude 56° 54' South, and Longitude 62° 57' West, indicating that in the morning of the previous day, we had passed Cape Horn. After a passage of fifty-six days from New Zealand, we were now in the Atlantic Ocean. With the wind coming from the southwest, we kept the ship away on a north-northeast course. On May 16th, we raised land, which proved to be the island of Ferdinand Noronha, off Cape St. Rogue, on the coast of Brazil. We were now thirty-three days from Cape Horn and eighty-nine days from New Zealand. A week later, after cloudy weather and headwinds, we got the sun today. We found that we had crossed the equator, and we were in 0° 4' North latitude. By the first week of June we were in the Gulf Stream and surrounded by Sargasso weed, indicating that we are drawing near our own beloved land. Not too soon, for we are getting short of firewood and have run out of all sorts of provisions, except salt beef and hard bread. We are daily passing many vessels, either outward or homeward bound.

By our observations on June 12th, we are 477 miles from Bermuda and 1,097 miles from New Bedford. Over the next week, as we continued to approach the coast, the weather became quite foggy and we were obliged to proceed with great caution, making "rope-yarn guns" and firing them from time to time during the night. On June 23rd, 1859, at half-past one in the afternoon, we sounded and found the bottom, with gray sand and shells at twenty fathoms. We then tacked and stood off from shore. We judged by dead reckoning that we were near Barnegat on the New Jersey coast. As the foggy weather continued, and we drew nearer to land, we kept up the firing of the guns from time to time. About eleven in the morning the next day, a schooner passed under our stern, and who, in answer to our hail, informed us that Block Island bore northeast by north at a distance of thirty-five miles. About four in the afternoon the fog lifted a little and from the masthead we discovered breakers quite close to us, which the fog had hitherto prevented our seeing. About 5 p.m., with four ships in company, we were abreast of Montauk Point Lighthouse. Coming out a New London pilot boat took pilots off some other vessels who were heading out. We kept on and continued in. Around 7 p.m. a branch pilot came on board, and on Sunday, June 26th, about 7 a.m. we dropped anchor in the harbor of New Bedford, after a voyage of 130 days from New Zealand.

Before daylight the "land sharks" had already come on board in such numbers that only with the greatest difficulty could we get our sails clewed up and furled. We could hardly get the ship to her anchorage. All earthly things must end though, and by noon we were all on shore, bidding a last goodbye to the old ship that had so long been our home. We were taken by Mr. Henry James to his place of business, on Water near School Street, and after getting a suit of decent shore clothes, Whitmarsh and I went to board at the house of Steven Spooner on Second Street. The next morning, as it would be more than a week before the oil was gotten out of the ship and the men would be paid off, having accepted his invitation, I went with my chum to his home in East Bridgewater. I had the pleasure of witnessing his restoration to his family, from whom I also received the greatest kindness. Saturday, July 2nd, I spent in the company of the Whitmarshes, William, James, Samuel, Kate, and Mary, and we went to the town of West Randolph to see their brother Thomas. It was a very pleasant ride through the country, and I made the acquaintance of some very agreeable people and returned to their home that night gratified and pleased with my visit. Indeed, I was virtually adopted by them as a brother, and nothing they could do for me was left undone.

I found them all, with the exception of the old father, Methodists, like myself. They were the fruits of a recent revival in the Methodist Episcopal Church in this place. I had the pleasure of uniting with them at their family altar, and the flood of recollections that poured in on my soul overwhelmed me. My heart was full of thankfulness to God, and for his wonderful and abounding goodness in protecting me all these years. I remained in this delightful home more than a week, making many acquaintances and greatly enjoying the beauty of the towns and the country around, as well as the hospitality of the people. Then it was time to return to New Bedford to ascertain the results of our voyage, so I bid them all goodbye. Indeed, I had become so wrought up with the consciousness of being so near old Baltimore and the friends at home, from whom I had heard no word in nine and a half years, that I found myself unable any longer to be contented among my dear Massachusetts friends.

I had received my bill from Captain Hobbs before leaving the old *Isaac Howland*, and as it amounted to almost seventy dollars, most of it worse than wasted, and as I had bought a suit of clothes on coming ashore, I had no expectation that there would be much, if anything, coming to me from the owners. Yet I had no money at all. So, I waited to see how my "lay" would pan out. A statement was handed to me showing that there was due to me just twenty-one cents, which they paid me. I could have very readily shipped again, and at a very good "lay" in another whaler, but when the owners found that I had no intention of doing so, and having learned where my home was, they presented me with five dollars to help me on my way. What a munificent return for the investment of nearly ten of the best years of my life! Yet I was very glad indeed to be back again on my native shores. Although I dearly loved a "life in the ocean wave," I determined that the rest of my days should be spent on "terra firma."

Requesting Whitmarsh to forward my chest by Express, I took the night train on July 9th for New York and Philadelphia. I reached the latter early on Saturday, but too late in the day to take either the boat or a second-class train. Not having money to pay a full fare, I had to remain in Philadelphia, waiting for a remittance, for which I had written to my uncle. As none came, at least through the second mail on Tuesday, and with my money being all spent, I bought with my last dime two five-cent loaves of bread, and taking them under my arm, like Ben Franklin did on his first entrance into that city, I started to walk to Baltimore, "a veritable tramp." The weather was intensely hot, and being ignorant of any other road, I followed the railroad track. It was as hot a midsummer walk as one could take. With not a single tree to afford the least shade, and often passing many miles before coming to a stream of water, it is a wonder that I was not sun-struck. When night came, I found a stagnant pool by the side of the track, and covered with a green scum, but not being fastidious, I drew a portion of the scum off and greedily drank the warm water. I finished one of my loaves, and then lay down at a little distance from the track to rest, for I was completely exhausted. The noise and rumble of the trains kept me from doing much sleeping, and so very early next morning I was up. I ate a frugal meal and started in the cool of the dawn on my homeward journey, reaching Havre de Grace in the afternoon, having walked sixty-five miles in two days. Here I found the overnight, or accommodation train, about to start, and telling my story to the conductor, he kindly gave me a passage to Baltimore. So at last, my long journey came to an end.

CHAPTER 14

Redemption

FEW WORDS ARE NEEDED TO RECOUNT THE LATER AND LESS EVENTFUL years that followed. Of course, I found many changes at home. Some of the loved ones I knew had passed to brighter shores, and I found that some whom I had left in middle life had aged greatly in ten years. Most of those, nearer my own age, were now married and had families. Children I had known had grown to man- and womanhood. One of my first acts on returning was to unite myself with my old church, the one I had known and loved in childhood, and to reattach myself to its Sunday school. I soon found that my old evil habits had not been forgotten, and were not likely to be, and that my vices and the consequences they had brought upon me had caused me to be held up "in terrorem" over the children of my friends and relatives. Thus, when I was out in public or at church, I was regarded with a degree of curiosity which, while doubtless very natural on their part, was none the less unpleasant for me. Yet I could not but feel that I richly deserved everything of this nature that I received, and much more. After a week of sightseeing and hand-shaking at the end of July, I became very anxious to find employment, as I had no income. For while my uncles were very kind, I could not but chafe at the thought of my continued dependence upon them. It was quite a long while, however, before I succeeded, and ultimately it was only after a probation of nearly six months, that one of my uncles, Thomas Armstrong, who was at the head of a prosperous business, was finally able to overcome the opposition of his junior partners, one of whom had known me before I left home and had been fully aware of my intemperate habits.

He had but little confidence that I would prove stable for any length of time or that my reformation would stand the test of old associates and temptations.

I feel no sense of condemnation, but a confidence and peace in God through our Lord Jesus Christ. Yet I wrestle with direction and desire. I had tea at my uncle Robert's house today, August 9th, 1859. My friends desire me to return to the dental profession. I feel the importance of the subject and I laid it before the Lord, feelings satisfied if it is to be to His glory, he will carry it through. Awoke with the Lord and enjoyed his presence much during the day. Attended a Eutaw Methodist Church meeting at night, but my mind was much distracted. Many old recollections . . . I find it almost impossible to enter into mixed company and join in conversation without a loss of spirituality and a feeling of condemnation. I find it difficult to engage in devotion with girls in sight. Succeeded to some degree, however, and had a very good meeting. I pray, "Lord assist me to set a guard over my lips and my thoughts as well as my actions that I may think of nothing but thyself and those things that lend to thy glory. That I may say nothing but what I know to be strictly true and in accordance with thy Holy will, and that I may do nothing unbecoming in one who is thy servant and who has been sealed by thy Holy Spirit until the day of thy redemption."

Fifteen years ago, today, August 22nd, my father died. I say, "Oh Savior, help me to follow him as he followed thee." The Savior speaks back to me saying, "We are the salt of the earth, we are the light of the world." With earnest purpose of heart, I strove to serve God, and to do right, but the lessons were painful. "Oh, how the retrospect of my past life makes my heart bleed when I see how I have been outstripped in the race by those who began after me." I remember Alfred Cookman as but a small boy at church before I left. Now he is on the walls of Zion and I am hardly fit to be called a servant of Christ. As regards to myself, I feel a renewed determination to live for Christ. I feel more at peace than I have for some time and am seeking that holiness of heart that I had previously attained. But, "Oh the depths of simpleness remain in me." My other uncle, my aunt, and her aunt returned today from a three-week trip.

I am enjoying great peace and love now, as I am only choosing to do my Lord's will. I have not felt my old enemy in any strength in some days. Lord help me to watch and pray and on thyself rely. I am getting ready to go on retreat to St. James Camp and will board in the Allen's tent. My heart has been much cast down by the state of my temporal concerns. Want of faith in God lies at the bottom of it. "Lord increase my faith," I plea. I enjoy at almost the same time constant peace with God, and an assurance not only of my acceptance by Him, but also that he has deepened his work of grace in my heart, and that he will carry me on to perfection. I am aware that this is a seeming paradox; laboring under an anxious and depressed state of mind, yet in the enjoyment of peace no man can take from me. Although my temporal concerns, that is getting a job, are not so favorable as they might be yet, I still have cause to thank God that they are as comfortable as they are. In reviewing my present position and my past life, I can only say "What hath God wrought?" I do praise him for all that is past and trust him for all that is to come. It is now November 8th, 1859, I have just finished my first month at Dugan's, but I am still seeking better employment.

At last, He came to my aid! He has enabled me to overcome every solicitation to indulge in my old propensity of drink, and He raised up friends for me on the right hand and the left, securing for me congenial employment. On the February 11th, 1860, I finished my fourth month at J. O. Dugan's, but left there, so I could on Monday enter at work for my family's firm: Armstrong, Cator & Co. Here I have left no stone unturned to obtain a thorough knowledge of the business into which I had entered and to conciliate and please my employers. Yet for some months past, I have felt besotted by sin as I have been leading a sad life endeavoring to serve two masters. I have been so mindful and sinful about working that I have not given much to religion. However, through His abounding grace I have been spared and have come once more to the mercy seat and find "his hands for me stand open wide." Through the grace of Christ my Savior and the Father's boundless love and the Holy Spirits favor, I can once more rejoice in the hope of the glory of God. Through more diligent attention to my religious duties, and the Divine blessing, I found myself called by His church to occupy positions of usefulness in both the church and the Sunday school. With such help from God, I was gratified to find that little by little I was painting a more favorable standing of myself in the community and rising in the regard of the firm as was evidenced by the increase of my salary.

A year since my return, today, December 9th, 1860, is my thirty-second birthday. May the Lord help me to keep the resolution I have this day formed to serve him the remainder of my days, be they many or few.

Now this day, January 4th, 1861, has been appointed by the president for fasting, humiliation, and prayer on account of personal and national sins, that God's anger, which now justly threatens our beloved land, may be averted. That the union of these states may be preserved and that we may be saved from the horrors of civil war. I desire to humble myself before the Almighty God in acknowledgment of his numberless mercies to me personally and to us as a people, and also in acknowledgment of my manifold sins and transgressions.

Time rolls onward. Now, November 24th, 1863, and I am still among the living to praise him. I am grateful that I have yet a place and a name among the people of God. Though I have many times wandered from the path of his commandments, and grieved his Holy Spirit, he has not cast me from his presence. Grace abound, how wonderfully my Heavenly Father has led, and preserved, me through these many years. "Oh, how little progress I have made in the Christian life. How rapidly time is bearing me to the grave and judgment." I urge myself, "Awake my soul, bestir thyself, cease to do evil, learn to do well. Break forth into gratitude and praise, the wondrous dying love of thy savior, and let it constrain thee to Him who did for thee, and through whose merits thou hast this day a pardon, peace, and a good helping of eternal life." A month later, as I pause on my thirty-fifth birthday, I recognize that as one who has reached the summit of a high mountain turns to look back from the turnings and windings of his devious journey, so on the occurrence of this day, I look back with wonder at all through which the Lord my God had led me. "Another birthday! Oh, my soul thou has one less to see!" I have this day achieved peace with God.

How time rolls by and what changes it brings with it in its flight. How wonderfully God has dealt with me. Life and health have been given to me with ten thousand blessings of every kind. Now through God's great goodness and mercy I have been brought to this hour. Next Tuesday, November 28th, 1865, I am, God willing, to be united in marriage to Eudocia E. Muller. Through the many vicissitudes of a life not uneventful, it has been, I trust and believe, the providence of God which has led me step by step to this point. I have known her intimately not much more than a year, though slightly acquainted with her for a longer period. But during the past year, I have studied her closely and now think I understand her fully.

I think it is through God that I have come to love her, and she to love me, and in this approaching union I have earnestly prayed that God's glory may be promoted, and our happiness secured. It is the deep desire of my heart that God's blessing may rest upon us in the future, and that united he may bless us both as he has so wonderfully blest me in the past. I pray that he may enable me to make her happy through life, to earn her affection unbroken unto death, and when parted here on earth, we may be reunited above to spend a happy eternity together. I know, just now, that I am stepping as it were upon the threshold of a new life, and with the future all unknown. I am very conscious that new cares and trials and temptations are about to come with this new existence, and that our responsibilities will devolve upon me.

Now nearly thirty years have past, and at age sixty-four, I note that Eudocia Muller has for many years proved to be a helpmate indeed to me. With her I have abundantly realized Solomon's proverb. We at once established a family altar in our house, and He has verified in our home the larger part of Psalm 128. In closing, I wish I could say that my Christian life had always been a consistent one, yet candor requires me to confess that this has not been the case. Sometimes, and for continued periods of time, I have endeavored to walk closely with my God, and in such seasons the "candle of the Lord" has shone upon me, and my soul has been filled with gladness. Yet again, despite the many mercies of my God, my heart has again and again slipped backwards, and gloom and sadness have driven me away from peace and joy. In such times, I have still retained my place in the house of God and attended with greater or less regularity. Yet, sometimes feeling in my heart that my religion was all a sham, and that I was a hypocrite in my soul. Then again, after some lapse of time, the Divine Spirit would come to my heart with His reviving influences. With my soul in penitence, my faith would come back to my Lord's feet, and with a smile that brought the light back to my eye, and the smile to my cheek, He would say "Son, thy sins, which are many, are all forgiven, go in peace, and sin no more." These repeated fallings away, and gracious renewals, have formed the history of my life for over thirty years since I returned and was reunited with the church. I am sure that through the mercy and help of my God, I have made a little advancement in the Divine life. I am grateful that in some faint degree, Christ has, at least in a small measure, made an impression upon my life, but, "o' how far short I have fallen of the glorious standard set up in the gospel for our imitation."

How many the years that have flown, how few those that are left, and how great is the work remaining to be done. I might almost say that I drank in Methodism at my mother's breast, for I was early and faithfully taught the doctrines of Methodism that have been drawn from God's blessed word. I can truly say that all my life long, even when I was furthest from God, I believed and held blessed the truth taught in all the Bible; that there is not only power enough in the blood of Jesus to pardon every sin of the vilest sinner, but also to do for us, what with all our striving we shall never be able to do in ourselves, that is to cleanse our heart from the last and least remains of sin, and make it and to keep it "whiter than snow." For "He is able to save to the uttermost, all those who come unto God by Him." There are not many passages in the Bible with which I was more familiar than with the last one that I have quoted. I have not only heard it, but read it a thousand times, and have frequently quoted it myself. One Monday night in our class meeting when I was sixty-four, a brother who was not a member of our church, in giving his testimony, quoted the passage, and the Divine Spirit brought it with wonderful power to my soul. It was like a new revelation from God, and I cried out "Lord, an uttermost salvation is just what my poor soul needs, none other will do," and "save me to the uttermost." My faith enabled me to lay hold of the promise, and to realize that Jesus did, then and there, come into my heart as never before, and cleanse me from all my sins. I must say that in the past three years since then, my experience has been different from all the years that went before. Personally, I had done nothing but "just to take Him at His word," but since that hour "my life has been all sunshine in the sweetness of the Lord." Since that hour, I have had many, and very sweet, manifestations of my Savior's love and power, and it is to His glory I speak. I have had victory over the enemy of my soul, where I used to only meet defeat. I have consecrated myself with all that I am, and have, to Him. He has come into my poor heart in the power of his Holy Spirit, and he now abides there. In concluding this autobiography, I desire to say that, while I am glad to write for my loved ones this account of my wanderings, my principal purpose in telling the miserable story of my sin and shame is to exalt and honor Him who . . . brought me up "out of a horrible pit, out of the miry clay, and set my feet upon a rock, and established my goings, and he hath put a new song in my mouth, even praise unto our God."

PART III

THE TRYPOT

The Historic Milieu of His Tale

CHAPTER 15

Rob's Youth

LIKE THE BAYEUX TAPESTRY, ROB'S AUTOBIOGRAPHY IS BUT ONE WOVEN recollection of his walk through life. His perspective is but one glimpse of all that was happening around him as he sailed across the South Pacific. Simultaneously, there were an infinite number of additional tales unravelling around his, intersecting, but independent in their own way. Each of these stories is as fascinating in its own right, and each provides its own insights. I pursued a great many of the tales, but ultimately picked just a few to share. I focused on those that clearly intersected with Rob's tale and those that I felt best illuminated the historic landscape of his times.

Rob's version of his journey also falls far short on deep self-reflection, whether about his youthful friends who became pillars in their communities, his stop at the Galapagos with its indubitable horrors, or the mutiny whose aftermath he witnessed. His apparent lack of curiosity later in life served to arouse mine. His story, often after a brief mention, left behind the fate of so many others whose path he crossed; whether those on the *Ann Alexander* or the islanders from Cantab. So hereafter we will sidestep onto the threads of a number of interwoven tales that highlight his journey, and I believe bring greater color and context to his tale and a deeper understanding of America's impact in the South Pacific during his time.

Early in his tale Rob writes that "In my seventeenth year I joined with some ten or twelve young men, all of them older than I was, belonging to the Charles Street Methodist Episcopal Church." This group was largely composed of teenagers attending the Charles Street Methodist Church, who came together under the leadership of Reverend Samuel Kramer, a navy veteran who was their spiritual leader. Rev. Kramer was also well known for having been the son of one of George Washington's body-guards. When he died in 1891, his obituary read "Rev. Samuel Kramer, formerly of Baltimore, died today at his residence at the advanced age of eighty-six years. Mr. Kramer was a native of Baltimore but left there at the breaking out of the [Civil] war to enter the federal army. He rose to be a major and served afterward as a chaplain in the navy. After the war, he established The Navy Yard, and acted as the pastor for a number of years."[1]

Back in the 1840s and before he left Baltimore, Rev. Kramer and the group's first project was to establish the Baltimore City Bethel Church in an old sail loft on Pratt Street. Dedicated to serving constituents of the Inner Harbor, the church focused on providing Christian services to "Sabbath-breaking boatmen and neglected indigent children." A year later, too big for the space, they purchased and reconfigured the hull of an old ship, the *William Penn*. With the church's flag on the masthead and able to accommodate up to six hundred people, it held three services every Sunday and prayer meetings and classes several nights each week. Years after Rob's return, in 1873 the congregation—now called the "Sailors Union Bethel Church"—built a new church on East Cross Street, which stands today. They used the keel from the *William Penn* for the building's foundation, and the ship's railing was incorporated into the prayer rail in front of the altar.[2]

One peer in particular who rose to prominence was Alfred Cookman. His father, George Cookman, was a highly regarded minister based in Virginia and a strident abolitionist. Of Alfred's father, Frederick Douglass wrote:

We slaves loved Mr. Cookman. We believed him to be a good man. We thought him instrumental in getting Mr. Samuel Harrison, a very rich slaveholder, to emancipate his slaves; and by some means got the impression that he was laboring to effect the emancipation of all the slaves. When he was at our house, we were sure to be called in to prayers. When the others were there, we were sometimes called in and sometimes not. Mr. Cookman took more notice of us than either of the other ministers. He could not come among us without betraying his sympathy for us, and, stupid as we were, we had the sagacity to see it.[3]

Sadly, upon returning to England in 1841 to visit relatives, George Cookman's ship, the *President*, went down in a horrific gale and so, when he was just thirteen, young Alfred's family was on its own. It turned out that the partner of Rob's bookselling uncle, John Plaskitt, knew the family well and stepped in and helped them resettle in Baltimore. Soon enough, Rob's uncle himself, Robert G. Armstrong, who was superintendent of the Eutaw Street Sunday School, recognized Alfred's elocutionary abilities and promoted his strengths at school, within the church, and soon the community. By the time Rob ultimately returned to Baltimore, it was said Alfred Cookman had become "one of the most highly regarded preachers in the United States. . . . there was no minister in the Episcopal Church who could draw together a larger crowd of ardent, admiring hearers in the City of Baltimore than Alfred Cookman."[4]

Rob's recollection of his early days seems fairly accurate; independently a biography of Alfred Cookman notes that in Cookman's youth,

A band of young men, most of whom were connected with the Charles Street Church, formed a mission to the seamen and poor children who frequented the upper docks of the harbor in Baltimore. Their hearts were touched with pity as they saw the large number of sailors, most of whom were confined to vessels doing business wholly in the waters of the Chesapeake Bay, and who were back and forth very often, entirely destitute of the means of religious improvement. They first rented a small room at the head of Frederick Street Dock. This proving too limited, they removed to a more commodious and eligibly located one on Pratt Street, at the head of the Upper Basin. It was not the first time that Methodism began a good work in a "Sail Loft." The old Sail Loft, christened "the City Bethel," was the scene of the zealous labors of these devout young men on Sundays and weekday evenings.

. . . In less than a year it was entirely too small to accommodate those who attended the Sabbath-schools and divine worship, and the society purchased and fitted up the old time-honored ship William Penn, capable of accommodating six hundred persons.[5]

Aside from Alfred Cookman's rise to prominence, Rev. T. H. Switzer, the first pastor of the City Bethel, observed that "a number of these young men became able ministers, among whom are Robert Pattison, C. J. Thompson, Adam Wallace, John Landstreet, William Harden, and William Chapman."[6] It was the success of all these men that swirled in the air upon Rob's return to Baltimore. No doubt haunting, if not scalding, him.

While still deeply engaged with these church friends, and still fairly innocent in life, Rob's caretaker, Uncle Thomas, sought to settle Rob into a career. Connected through the church, Uncle Thomas reached out to his acquaintance, Dr. Chapin Harris,[7] who together with his mentor, Dr. Horace Hayden, founded the Baltimore College of Dental Surgery in 1840. Born in upstate New York, Dr. Harris had moved to Ohio to join his two brothers and become a medical doctor, which he did so in 1824. In 1828, the year Rob was born, Dr. Harris moved to Baltimore to learn dentistry under Dr. Hayden, after which he then spent several years as an itinerant dentist in the South. Returning to Baltimore, he teamed up with Dr. Hayden, as they both recognized the need for systematic formal education in the field, and together they established the Baltimore College of Dental Surgery. After Hayden's death in 1844, Dr Harris not only led the school, but also published a series of seminal texts on dentistry and founded the first society for dentists. Today he is considered the father of American dentistry, and coincidently he is buried near Rob in Mt. Olivet Cemetery in Baltimore.

Upon graduating as a dentist, Rob set off across the Appalachians in what then was still a rather dangerous journey. How can one not be fascinated that, the night before, the stagecoach driver froze to death on the same trip? He joined his classmate, John Adair,[8] in Paris, Kentucky. John Adair's father, Richard, had been raised in the backwaters of Maryland and was a skilled tanner. He had moved to Nichols, Kentucky, in 1815 and married Mary Tarr, with whom he had twelve children. Uniquely, for the day and perhaps even now, three of their sons became dentists, of which John Jackson Adair was the oldest. Born in November 1822, John was six years older than Rob and had already established a dental practice in Paris before he went to Baltimore for more training. Shortly after Rob's drinking "deteriorated" and he departed, John married Sarah Ewalt, with whom he had nine children. They stayed in Paris, and he became a very well respected and "popular" dentist. At some point the family moved to Bourbon Farm, roughly where today Route 27 intersects with Peacock Road. Consisting of 175 acres, the farm had a nice house, a stock barn, and a tobacco barn. Near the end of his life, he seems to have had a stroke, for he died precipitously by falling down his basement stairs at the age of fifty-eight in 1880, and it was noted that "Dr. Adair has suffered some time with paralysis."[9]

Mortified by his own conduct, Rob came back from Kentucky to "a very different moral atmosphere in my uncle's house." In shame, for some months he managed to keep "quite sober" as his friends tried to help him out. The dental college faculty rallied to his support and recommended Rob for another position. Thus in the spring of 1849, Rob was admitted to a partnership with Dr. Kemp Strother Dargan, age forty-two, of Winnsboro, South Carolina. He not only already had a lucrative dentistry practice in the area, but Kemp and his wife, Margaret, had four children at the time, ranging in age from seven to one, with another on the way. Kemp was described as "descended from an old Virginia family and noted for his extremely elegant manners and unrivalled conversational powers," while Margaret was "a native Charlestonian of French Huguenot blood, a remarkably handsome and graceful lady." They were well off, having a large house, and in 1860 owned three female and two male slaves according to federal records. Eleven years after Rob's departure, one of his sons made the newspapers in 1858 when he nearly killed his father, hitting the dentist in the right temple with a load of buckshot. Kemp recovered, though he passed away just a few years later. The rest of the family was soon decimated by the Civil War, for it "scatter[ed] the once happy and united family; [and] with the fall of the Confederacy their wealth vanished." Their loss, however, appeared to have inspired, or perhaps propelled, the eldest daughter, Clara, to arise from Sherman's ashes to become a gifted and noted author. She wrote several novels, including *Riverlands* and later *Light or Love*, and along the way married Judge Joseph A Maclean, with whom she had a child.[10]

CHAPTER 16

Smyrna Southbound

FOLLOWING HIS DISGRACEFUL EXIT FROM SOUTH CAROLINA, AND AFTER he had drunk himself into oblivion on the cobblestoned streets of New York, Rob sold himself to a whaling agent and found himself "on the barque *Smyrna*, under Captain Rodolphus H. Tobey." Born February 22, 1813, in Sandwich, Massachusetts, Rodolphus Howland Tobey was the youngest of five children in a seafaring family.[1] His father, Lewis Tobey, was a ship's captain, and his wife, Rebecca Ingraham, was raised in New Bedford. Lewis died at sea on the other side of the Atlantic when Rodolphus was just twelve, thus propelling his son to sea rather early, just to earn a living. We know Rodolphus was already a captain of a whaling vessel at age twenty-six when the 290-ton *William Rotch*, thirty months out, arrived at Pitcairn Island in January 1842. She was heading home with a full load of just more than 1,200 barrels of sperm whale oil on board.[2]

On his return to New Bedford, he married twenty-two-year-old Emeline Macy in Poughkeepsie, New York. Along with the Starbucks and Coffins, the Macys were one of the preeminent whaling families of Nantucket;[3] but as we all know they also had a hand in commerce. After whaling for almost two decades, just a few years after serving as Rob's captain, Rodolphus left his life at sea. By then, he and Emeline had three children, and using Emeline's family connections, they settled in New York City. In 1856, he is listed in Trow's City Directory as a manager and part owner, along with several other Macys, of a grocery store at 808 Sixth Avenue, between 27th and 28th Streets, in Manhattan. At the same time, he and Emeline are living at 60 West 21st Street. Intriguingly, the

Tobey-Macy store was but fifteen blocks north of Emeline's ultimately far more famous cousin's store, R. H. Macy. He opened his first store in New York City at Sixth Avenue and 14th Street just two years later in 1858.

For Rob, signing himself over to Captain Tobey was a desperate act driven by a young man's desire to turn himself around. How he came to choose a sailor's life remains a mystery to me, but most likely it was due to his childhood affinity to Baltimore Harbor and the many sailors he encountered there with his work in Sailor's City Bethel Church. Indeed, Michael Dyer, the Maritime Curator of the New Bedford Whaling Museun, after reading Rob's logs thought that Rob was the quintessential everyman, a vaguely lost soul who came to whaling like many Americans "from all walks of life," particularly as "any strong lad could find a place on ship board, as pay was nominal and hard muscles were the only pre-requisite."[4] But Dyer also commented that while in "the crew list he is described as a greenhand, . . . his journal entries are as fluent in marine terminology as any old salt."

As a greenhand, Rob began to immediately learn the ropes, the terms, and the customs of the ship; later the details of whaling itself. On whaling ships, the "watches" marked the time when various crew members were responsible for the ship's sails and any tasks that needed doing.[5] The crew was divided into two watches: the starboard watch and the larboard, or port, watch. The starboard watch was also known as the captain's or second mate's watch, while the larboard watch was the first mate's watch. One day the starboard watch was on deck for the "first watch" or night watch, from 8 p.m. until midnight. The larboard watch was then on until 4 a.m., and so on in shifts. Each watch was four hours, except for the two late afternoon watches, known as the "dog watches." Each of these was divided into two-hour shifts to facilitate serving dinner among the crew and to encourage them to spend time together. The dog watches were the one time where those off duty usually remained up on deck, and together the crew mended their clothes, sang, played cards, smoked, and whittled ivory. As the watches were offset, the two watches reversed the order the next day, and so on. Of course, when whales were spotted or a storm threatened, the watches dissolved and it was all hands on deck.

The captain was like a god, coming and going as he pleased. He roamed the ship throughout the watches and was in or out of his cabin as circumstances warranted. He certainly was on deck during storms and whaling operations or when landing or leaving a port. While on deck, the captain always walked on the weatherside, upwind. His second-in-command, the first mate, stayed on the downwind side because it was difficult to see around the sails when underway, and throughout the voyage, he was responsible for that side of the ship. The second and third mates, cooper, cook, and boatsteerers gathered midship, usually jawboning while sitting on the hatches. The crew had the forward part of the ship, above and below, to themselves, which was why a crew's life was colloquially called "before the mast." Whenever anyone needed to move about the ship, they did so on the lee side so as not to impede the captain's sight or hamper sailing operations. When at sea during daylight, and especially when underway and hunting for whales, a boatsteerer was assigned to the crosstrees up the mainmast. Often another was on the foremast, and sometimes a third up the mizzen, or sternmost, mast. The mates would spell them. The galley was the cook's castle, and no one else was ever allowed in there. But let there be no doubt, unless they were in harbor or a tropical port, the food was terrible. As one whaler commented "after six hours of hard work, our supper consisted of beef, which means *nothing*, for no one can eat the stuff, and the man who put it into the ship 'ought to be kicked' to death by a Jack Horse, and I would like to be 'the fellow to do it.'"[6]

The logbook was critical, mainly detailing the track of the voyage and its success, and as a written artifact of the voyage it was embedded in the contract with the ship's owners and insurers. Custom and discipline on a ship called for every sailor to be always busy. Each morning the crew washed the decks, hatches, and rails, while the boatsteerers made sure the whaleboats were ready. Other crew members were given specific tasks: sharpening the harpoons and lances, loosening up the chains which grew rusty between use, stowing the anchor, painting, coiling lines, and filling water casks. They also helped the boatsteerers ensure that each whaleboat had sufficient lanterns, candles, matches, and bread in case they were caught out at sea overnight.[7]

Gamming was the great social event on every whaler and happened when ships came together at sea so their captains and crew could intermingle. Often after a day's hunt, and signaling their intent, the ships would cruise close, furl their sails, and drift. Then some mix of captains, mates, and crew would lower their boats to gather on one ship or the other to while away the hours. Captains and crews would exchange letters, especially if one ship was headed home, and swap newspapers and books. Sadly, as we know many of those letters never made it to their destination. Most importantly, there was lots of smoking, talking, and tale spinning.

From the start, Rob displays a great predilection for the sea, and he often mixes in his religious fervor. This is particularly true with his repeated use of "old ocean," a phrase almost certainly derived from William Cullen Bryant's poem "Thanatopsis," wherein "Old Ocean's gray and melancholy waste, are but the solemn decorations all of the great tomb of man." Bryant was a major newspaper editor, a romantic poet, and closely aligned with the era's religious fervor. He was highly regarded by Walt Whitman, who said "Bryant saw God in the sublime manifestation of Nature."[8] From a more distant perspective, I too have always appreciated Bryant's inclination for nature and his social success, for he was a major political force behind the creation of Central Park in New York City.

On February 8, 1850, Rob crossed the equator for the first time. It has been a tradition since the seventeenth century for the line-crossing to be celebrated with an induction ceremony overseen by "King Neptune." Among different traditions, the ceremony can range from being mild hazing to one brutal in nature, from simply beating the greenhands with seaweed and wet ropes to throwing new sailors over the bow and dragging them under the keel to be pulled out at the stern. Charles Darwin described crossing the line in 1832 and being "shaved." "This most disagreeable operation consists of having your face rubbed with paint and tar," he wrote to his father, "which forms a lather for a saw, which represents the razor, and then being half drowned in a sail filled with salt water."[9]

Rob didn't report on his trial in detail, but it's clear he didn't enjoy whatever his particular ceremony entailed. "As is tradition, 'Old Neptune' came on board," he wrote. "His antics afforded an occasion of great jollity to the officers and the old salts, but we greenhands, called 'pollywogs' for the occasion, did not find quite so much enjoyment in his visit, and we were rather glad when the Sea King went back over the ship's side that night."

CHAPTER 17

The Crimson Sea

FARTHER SOUTH, ON MARCH 7TH, 1850, ROB AND THE CREW HOOKED up to their first sperm whale on Brazil's Abrolhos Banks. It was a large bull, and after striking it, the unfazed beast took them on a "Nantucket sleighride" for a good part of the afternoon. Toward sunset, and with roiling thunderheads on the horizon, it sounded and threatened to take out all their line. They cut it off then, attaching a large board called a "drag" to the end, hoping to simply slow the beast's flight. The crew rowed after it for a while longer, then eventually gave up as the line squall closed in.

Killing a whale was a maritime bullfight: a long-drawn-out and barbaric affair, quite similar in many ways to one of the classic Spanish pageants. As in the ring, there was a series of prescribed acts, an array of weapons, and the final *estocada*, or plunging of the sword. Often a terrifying encounter, killing a great whale required superb skill, considerable strength, and good luck.[1] After the whale was spotted, usually by a boatsteerer in the crow's nest who in tradition decried "thar she blows" upon seeing the white vaporous cloud of a spout, the captain ordered the crew to lower the whaleboats for the chase. Mostly rowed, whaleboats also had a small mast with a gaff-rigged sail that could be used to sneak up on a whale quietly, or after a long, unsuccessful chase just to get the tired men home.

Each boat carried six men. Four of them rowed, while a bowman rowed a bit and then took up the harpoon. The sixth crew member—who might be the first, second, or third mate, or even the captain—held the great steering oar and took charge of the action. Each whaleboat had a large wooden tub in the middle, in which a long rope was coiled and attached to the end of the harpoon. There were also one or more lances on board, great wide blades attached to long poles. These were used once the whale was close enough to touch, and they were plunged into its side to help speed the whale's bleeding. Most boats also carried a flense, a huge long-handled knife, like a machete on a broomstick. Near the end, the crew would try to use the flense to cut the tendons of the whale's tail, hobbling it to prevent any further runs or a dramatic escape.

Each species of whale has slightly different patterns of spouting and diving, but generally most take one long dive to feed and then make several shallow surface dives to clear their lungs and reoxygenate their bodies. As the crew rowed toward a whale, if they were lucky they might get to it before a deep dive. If not, they might have to wait up to an hour for it to resurface. In any event, their success depended on rowing as quietly as possible, approaching the whale when it was under, guessing where it would surface, and being almost atop it when it rose. At that point, when close enough to throw the harpoon with penetrating strength, the mate would holler "Let it fly!" and the "darter" would throw or plunge the "whale iron" into the beast. Sometimes the whaleboat was nearly on the whale's back when it surfaced, but often twenty or so feet away. Much beyond that, and the iron would likely not penetrate deep enough to set.

If the darter was good or lucky, the harpoon reached the heart or lungs and would kill the whale quickly. More typically, once the harpoon was set, the whale, reeling from the pain, swam straight away or sounded, heading to the deep. Rarely did they turn to fight, though gray whales were known to do that, and sperm whales, too, on occasion. If the whale "ran" straight away, the crew got a Nantucket sleighride and the line hissed out of the tub, smoking hot, stripping away from around a post amidships. If the whale sounded, the line would equally uncoil, but simply feed straight down into the deep. The men in the whaleboat were left bobbing in fear, since they didn't know where the whale was or when it would reappear. Sometimes the whale "ran the line out," or the line broke, or the dead whale simply sank before the crew could get the carcass back to the ship. Crews lost about 10 percent of the whales they harpooned.

After the whale ran for a while, which sometimes took hours, the crew would slowly haul in the line until they were close enough to use the lance. When the whale was fully exhausted, the harpooner would then use the lance to reach the lungs or heart. One trick was to shove the lance into the thrashing mammal and twist it, in a move known as "churning," ideally deep enough to wreak havoc on the lungs. At last, blowing blood to form a crimson sea, its eyes would widen and then fade into an opalescence of death. Its great tail fluke would pound the sea in a final flurry, then calm as the endmost spasms coursed through, and the great whale would finally turn over, dorsal fin down.

After a short break, the crew would then tow the carcass back to their ship, where a large hawser would be placed around the tail and tied off near the bow. This way the head was facing the stern, lying closer to the cutting and boiling areas aboard the ship. The whale was almost always tied to the upwind, or weather, side of the ship so the carcass would ride against the hull and not slam into it in strong winds. A large "cutting stage," in essence a catwalk, was lowered over the side and rigged to ride twelve feet or so out from, and parallel to, the ship's deck. From the cutting stage, crew members used flensing knives to slice the whale into pieces. Those on the stage generally wore lines around their waists, linked through a block or pulley in the shrouds above and held by a sailor on deck who kept the line taut. Sharks, large oceanic ones, often came to feed on the whale, and if a crew member slipped from the stage and fell into the water near the carcass, the results would be gruesome.

The head was the most valuable part of a sperm whale, with high-quality oil held inside the special "case" or melon behind the forehead. A huge spongy area below was called the "junk." Unlike the oil derived from boiling the blubber, the case and junk oil were much purer. The head oil is synthesized by toothed whales to create specialized fat bodies, which play a key role in sound transmission and reception. The melon focuses a sperm whale's high-frequency echolocation clicks, effectively making it a sonic amplifier critical to a creature hunting fast squid in the dark of the deep.[2]

With other men manning the great windlass on deck, its lines straining through pulleys clamped to the mainmast, huge chunks of the head would be raised to the deck. After oil from the case and junk had been removed and placed in specially marked barrels on deck, the crew turned to the body still lashed alongside. The rest of the whale's outer layer of blubber, often more than a foot thick, was then slowly cut off in a great spiral and hoisted aboard in strips. Usually about four feet wide and ten feet long, sometimes weighing a ton, these strips were called "blanket" pieces. On deck, other crew members would start portioning them into smaller "horse pieces" that could fit into the "try-pots."

At the same time, other crew members were getting the "tryworks" going. The tryworks was essentially a large stove built on the deck, eight feet deep and ten feet long. It was built of brick and mortar and had two large iron pots above the firebox beneath. Two thick, black, iron doors guarded the firebox, below which a second layer of bricks held a reservoir for water, which the crew kept constantly filled when the fires were stoked. This water-cooled firewall protected the wooden ship. The tryworks were probably the most dangerous element in whaling. A few whaleships simply disappeared at sea when the fires of their tryworks escaped and reached their hulls, and in an era before radios, there was no way to call for help; the vessel just disappeared. News at the time would occasionally carry a report of a glimmer in the night sky where the previous day a ship had been seen. The crew tossed the minced horse pieces of blubber into the boiling tryworks pots, stirring until eventually the blubber was reduced to oil. The resulting dark black cloud of thick smoke permeated the deck and ship, and soon enough the crew all looked like colliers.[3] Decent-sized sperm whales might take from sunrise until noon to render, producing thirty to forty barrels of oil. A great bull sperm whale could net upward of one hundred barrels and took days to try out. Once all the blubber was gone, the carcass, now headless, was cut loose. Without the buoyancy of blubber, it simply sank, becoming fodder for sharks and crabs.

The whole process, from sighting a whale to cleaning the ship's decks, often took two or three days, and on occasions when several whales were secured at the same time, a ship might give over almost a week to processing. Eventually the ship's cooper would finish the job of barreling all the oil and the crew would stow it below. After a break, the crew was then tasked with cleaning the decks, which began with backbreaking scraping to remove the "gurry," the congealed blood, guts, and oil. The next step was a thorough scrubbing with lye made from the whale's ashes, and finished with a polish using special stones, often pumice acquired during a visit to the Galapagos or another volcanic isle.

A review of five hunts from the log of the *Isaac Howland* in 1858[4] shows that whales were typically spotted first thing in the morning. The boats were lowered immediately, and the whales were darted fairly quickly. In two cases, though, whales had to be chased all day before being harpooned. "Cutting in" took about a day for each whale. Inevitably, at least half the first day was given over to cutting the head off and getting junk and jaw in. In one case, it took five days to cut up two whales, but that was because there was a storm raging the entire time. In sum, Rob's first ship, the *Smyrna*, came home with 870 barrels of sperm whale oil, roughly that from thirty-five to forty whales, while his second ship, the *Isaac Howland*, brought back 1,383 barrels of sperm oil from about sixty whales. So even though Rob was only aboard for the last leg of *Isaac Howland*'s voyage, my best guess is that he still had a hand in slaughtering between fifty and seventy-five great whales in his time at sea.

CHAPTER 18

The Carapaces in Darwin's Wake

FOUR DAYS AFTER LEAVING THE COAST OF PERU, AND ONE HUNDRED twenty out, on July 14th, 1850, the *Smyrna* was among the Galapagos Islands. Rob's ship intersected and gammed with many other whaling vessels, "and saw many whales as well as great multitudes of seafowls, boobies, gannets, and pelicans, all of which reside there for breeding purposes," he reported. As an ornithologist, I have long been particularly fascinated by the unique wildlife of the Galapagos, especially given their role in Darwin's epiphany regarding evolution. While supposedly the lights actually went off in Darwin's head on the transformative nature of speciation from watching the islands' mockingbirds, the renown finches and tortoises certainly also shaped his thinking. In fact, when writing about his visit to the Galapagos in 1832, he recalled

> *that from the form of the body, shape of scales and general size, [a person] can at once pronounce from which island any tortoise may have been brought. When I see these islands in sight of each other, and possessed of but a scanty stock of animals . . . , but slightly differing in structure and filling the same place in nature, I must suspect they are only varieties. . . . If there is the slightest foundation for these remarks the zoology of the archipelagoes will be well worth examining; for such facts would undermine the stability of species.[1]*

With such an observation, Darwin opened the world to the twin notions that God's species were neither immutable nor "stable," nor perhaps

155

even due to God's proximate guidance. Thus, it was with great interest that I read Rob's short piece about his visit to the archipelago, only to be immediately struck that, curiously, he remained silent about most of his time there. The *Smyrna* spent two weeks in the archipelago, and as I explored the world of whaling, I shuddered when I later realized how they assuredly spent their time. The crew of the *Smyrna* likely joined thousands of other whalers of the era in their own descent into barbarity as they captured and savagely slaughtered the archipelago's most renown inhabitants.

Prior to the whalers, the great lumbering tortoises dominated the islands. Even as late as the 1860s, an old whaler recollected that

> *the older skippers of his day often said there were thousands of them even on the smaller islands in the [eighteen] thirties and forties. Some of them were of enormous size. He had heard of two or three up in the mountains of Albemarle Island too big to be moved, but instead had dates cut on their shells as far back as sixty or seventy years. The whalers who had seen them thought they might weigh seven or eight hundred pounds.*[2]

It was with horror that I came to understand the role whalers played in Darwin's crucible of evolution. Ships like the *Smyrna* and *Isaac Howland* did cruise the islands for whales in the mid-nineteenth century, but they primarily visited the Galapagos to gather information from others and *re-victual*, that is, to collect fresh water and meat before sailing west "along the line," the equator. Nearly every whaler visiting the islands partook in the rapacious behavior of "tortoising."

As early as the 1680s, William Dampier, the early English adventurer and buccaneer, wrote: "There is no place in the world, so much stored with iguanas and land-tortoises as these Isles. The first are fat, and of an extraordinary size, and exceedingly tame; and the land-tortoises so numerous that some hundred men may subsist on them for a considerable time, being very fat, and as pleasant food as a pullet; and of such bigness, that one of them weighs 150–200 pounds, and are from two feet to two feet six inches over the belly."[3] Another visitor, Amasa Delano, said "Their flesh, without exception, is of a sweet and pleasant a flavour as any that I ever ate."[4]

To really understand what Rob must have engaged in, we turn to the tale of another young sailor; one who will also reappear later in this tale.[5] Late in his life, this same sailor posed for a photograph. In the daguerreotype he sports a great horseshoe-shaped mustache that blends into thick muttonchops and wears a buttoned-up peacoat over a starched white shirt with a neat bow tie as he gazes into the distance. His chin tilted up, William Paddack is looking toward some distant object, miles offshore. Ultimately, William spent his final thirty years at sea as a successful captain on various merchant ships. But in the beginning, in a book covering his very first voyage, William wrote of his victualing visit to the Galapagos in 1848, one year before Rob's voyage.

Paddack described the vile act in fair detail. "The captain and second mate took their boats and went on shore after terrapin," he wrote. "We succeeded beyond our most sanguine expectations, having captured ten large ones in the space of two hours. Some were of immense size, weighing from one to three hundred pounds. The boats came on board about seven o'clock, when we had one of the terrapin killed and cooked for supper, the crew telling (of) their experience on shore, which was very interesting to those who remained on board." The slaughter continued the next day, of which William wrote, "We found considerable difficulty in capturing the terrapin, not only on account of their size, but from their color, which bore exactly the same appearance as the ground—a dark brown. At four p.m. the boats returned, bringing on board fifteen large terrapin, and the quarters of two others they had killed on shore." The third day, he went on, "the boats returned with eight very large terrapin. We came across one immense terrapin. The captain thought he would weigh some 600 pounds. He had more than fifty ships' names and dates marked all over his back."[6]

Ecologically the Galapagos tortoises are what is known as a keystone species, one intrinsically important to the archipelago's biology. While they may look like innocuous and lost wanderers on the parched islands, over millions of years they have become an essential link in the islands' food webs. The tortoises' selective herbivory helps maintain a mosaic of vegetation, and their castings during their slow and arbitrary wanderings are critical to broad seed dispersal on the islands. Regardless, without remorse whalers lashed thousands of tortoises to oars and carried them from the hills, completely unappreciative of their role in Darwin's epiphany on evolution or in the islands' ecology. Every day they were flipped onto their backs and with ropes dragged to different ships to be confined, starved, kept as an object of amusement, and ultimately killed. Indeed even Darwin's ship the *Beagle* took aboard thirty tortoises from Chatham Island for their consumption. Others took more. Capt. Benjamin Morrell, a sealer visiting the islands in 1825, wrote: "I have known whale-ships to take from six to nine hundred of the smallest size of these tortoises on board when leaving the islands for their cruising grounds; thus providing themselves with provisions for six or eight months, and securing the men against the scurvy. I have had these animals on board my own vessels from five to six months without their once taking food or water."[7] In the 1920s, a scientist from the New York Zoological Society, Charles Townsend, studied whalers' records and found of "seventy-nine vessels that had visited the Galapagos at various times between 1831 and 1868 and [they] had carried off thirteen thousand tortoises."[8] Extrapolating from such numbers, and multiplying by the fleet size, divided by the probability of stopping in once every four or five years, a reasonable guess is that between five hundred thousand and a million tortoises were hauled off for food and oil between the 1820s and 1959, when the Galapagos were finally declared a national park.

Nearly every island in the Galapagos had its own species of tortoise. Naturally, the smaller islands lost their tortoises first.[9] Thankfully, with the waning of whaling in the Pacific and the nascent rise of conservation, the tortoises rebounded a bit in the twentieth century. Still, today five of the fifteen known species of Galapagos tortoises are now extinct.[10] The death of Lonesome George from Pinta Island in 2012 was the most recent extinction, and hopefully the last at human hands. Five of the remaining ten species are distributed among many islands, and the other five are all found on different volcanoes on the largest island, Isabel. Fortunately conservation programs were initiated shortly after the Galapagos were declared a national park, and they continue today. Most recently, on some islands where tortoises are extinct, sterilized individuals from other islands have been released to ecologically restore the island's natural vegetative diversity. In the meantime, biologists and political leaders ponder the ethics and genetics of reintroducing viable sibling species to empty islands—something I think we should encourage.

CHAPTER 19

Jackson's Belligerence

NOWHERE IN HIS VOYAGE DID ROB SPEND MORE TIME THAN AROUND the Kingsmill islands, now known as the Gilberts in the nation of Kiribati. They formed the crux of his ships' wanderings during the years they searched for sperm whales, and the Kingsmills also serve as a microcosm of what was happening all across the South Pacific at this time. The *Smyrna* in particular made repeated landfalls among the islands to resupply and give the crew an opportunity to stretch their legs. While then the islands looked substantially as they do today, it was superficial. In fact, during Rob's visit they were on the cusp of their cultural asphyxiation. The islanders' dress, customs, and technology were still their own,[1] yet shortly to be doomed by the unremitting invasion of whalers, missionaries, beachcombers, and others with foreign customs and conventions.

A collection of sixteen groups of islands, the Kingsmill archipelago sprawls on a southeast to northwest axis along four hundred miles, from two degrees below to three degrees above the equator. For whalers sailing west along the line, they lie at the intersection where a ship either headed north "off the line" to cruise these islands and adjacent archipelagoes, or continued westward "sailing to Japan." The Kingsmills' attraction was that they lie atop a large undersea shelf which drops off precipitously into the Pacific deep. This bathymetric feature consistently attracted sperm whales to its waters. However, unlike many other famous South Pacific island archipelagoes, such as the Fijis or Samoas with their tall verdant mountains, lush foliage, and ample fresh water, the Kingsmills are dry and monotonously covered with coconut palms. Neither Henri Rousseau nor Marlon Brando ever wished to live on these arid and ecologically depauperate islands. The Kingsmills did, however, manage to have their own unique role in history as they repeatedly illuminated the brazen edges and sharp clashes reflective of American and British expansionism. The islands featured epic social collisions as Westerners faced off against some rather resolute indigenous people.[2]

The Kingsmills came to Europe's attention less than ninety years before Rob's time, but in reality probably only had regular Western visitors in just the last decade or two before his arrival. It is believed that Captain Bishop, when he visited on the *Nautilus* in 1799, bestowed the name "Kingsmills" on the islands, for they first appeared so labeled on an English map in 1803 just after his return. The nomenclature of the islands is quite confusing, for since Rob's time, not only have the borders defining the archipelago shifted, but individual islands that were initially given English names by the first European visitors were then renamed in recent years to reflect their indigenous heritage. For example, of the islands that Rob visited most, Pitt Island is now known as Makin, Woodle is Kuria, Hendersonville is Aranuka, Sydenham is Nonuti, Drummond is Tabiteuea, and Byron is Nikunau.

Of the sixteen islands, all but two are actually sets of low coral islets surrounding a beautiful turquoise lagoon. An English explorer, C. M. Woodford, wrote after visiting them that "the islands are clothed from end to end with a dense growth of coconut palms and other vegetation, and present a beautiful appearance when approaching them from the sea. The reefs and lagoons teem with fish."[3] Young William Paddack, the same sailor who tortoised the Galapagos, recorded his observations of the Kingsmillians. "The inhabitants . . . are in general above the middle size, and some are very large," he wrote. "They are well made, walk gracefully, run nimbly, and are capable of enduring great fatigue. They have fine open countenances; and the women, in particular, have good eyes and teeth, are sensible looking, and possess manners of engaging sweetness . . . The king, chiefs, and married women wear a small mat around them, while the slaves and children go naked. Tattooing the body is largely practiced, but the women are far less decorated than the men."[4] A sketch of a family from one of the islands, drawn in 1851, shows a naked child with earrings and a man with shoulder-length straight black hair and a loincloth. Next to them a woman wears a short palm frond skirt and matching shell bracelets on both arms. In addition, she has a headband and a necklace of shells, the latter with a great one in the middle. The islands' warriors were more famous though for their martial garb, described as "a defensive armor, consisting of a cuirass, made from the fibers of the coconut, woven into a compact mass, a helmet of the skin of the porcupine fish, and coverings for the thigh and arm of netted sennet. Their weapons are numerous, but the three-forked spear, barbed with rows of shark's teeth, is the most formidable."[5]

Like other South Pacific islanders, the Kingsmillians lived in houses with low thatched roofs, thatch-plaited mats serving as walls, and dirt floors. Most villages had a community meetinghouse as well. On Woodle Island, Paddack recounted "the village contained about fifty huts, and was surrounded by coconut-trees, and before each door was a brood of chickens and cats. The houses were thatched to keep out the wet, and looked neat and comfortable. They have no floors to their houses, but the earth is beaten smooth with constant use. They have no furniture, but, as a substitute, grass mats are spread in various parts of the room." Perhaps one of the most difficult things for us to imagine today is the very limited diet the islanders survived on. Other than fish, Woodford wrote that the coconut was everything. Its milk was their primary drink, and the inner kernel, or "meat," their staple food.

Rob arrived in a time of profound change; thousands of years of a simple lifestyle were being overturned in a cultural heartbeat. In the 1820s early whalers and sailors introduced coconut oil lamps and mosquito netting. Tobacco came too, but it was not consumed to any significant extent until the 1840s, when it suddenly became the primary intercultural currency. The use of clam shell adzes, coral rasps, and wood digging sticks was fading, while steel, calico cloth, fish hooks, pots and pans and similar trade goods began to appear in substantive numbers.[6]

Having left the Galapagos in July 1850 to sail along the line, the *Smyrna* is among the Kingsmills', Ocean Island, and Nauru in May 1851. Their first break from ship was apparently on Ocean Island, now Banapa. Rob writes that they were helped by a "white man, who have been living

here for two years, having been put ashore by a Sag Harbor ship in consequence of having a broken leg. He speaks the native language fluently,
and [was] a favorite of the King," a classic beachcomber. Indeed, Ocean
Island was famous for its beachcombers at this time. As early as 1845,
there were at least seventeen noted, "several of whom were runaway convicts from New South Wales, or Norfolk Island."[7]

A month later, in June 1851, the *Smyrna* then stops in at Strong
Island, eight hundred miles northwest of the Kingsmills. Later known
as Kusaie and now Kosrae, the forty-two-square-mile volcanic island,
surrounded by beautiful coral reefs, is a lush island with plenty of fresh
fruit, fresh water, and three good harbors; thus was a regular stop for
whalers.[8] Of this visit to Strong Island in June 1851, he notes meeting
three beachcombers. The first was Captain Isaac Hussey, who reemerges a
year and a half later in the tale when his fatal flaws unravel into a Greek
tragedy. The second was Captain Brown of the *Flying Fox*, who we will
also revisit in greater detail,[9] and the third was David Kirkland. There was
indeed a Kirkland who was a native of Baltimore who came to Strong
Island in 1850 to establish a trading post. He is known to have served as
a harbor pilot for several years, compiling a list of visiting ships before
dying in March 1858.[10] Whether he was actually related to the principles
of Kirkland, Chase & Co. is unknown, but the firm was well known as a
highly reputable trading firm based in Baltimore at the time. Kirkland,
Chase & Co specialized in the sugar and coffee trade in the Atlantic,
though the firm dissolved in 1872.[11]

Typical beachcombers, about which H. E. Maude observed in his
seminal treatise, "probably we would all know . . . if we were to see one,
yet he is hard to define as a type."[12] They were essentially Westerners
who had deserted their ships, been shipwrecked, or had paused in their
South Pacific travels to stay on an island and lose themselves among the
indigenous residents. Even Herman Melville was considered a beachcomber for a while after he deserted his whaling ship, the *Acushnet*. The
few who were unlucky victims of wrecks were also known as castaways.
To earn a place among the indigenous population on an island, sometimes they would serve as a translator to visiting crews, or just act as an
intermediary in the bartering for locally raised crops or livestock. Others

maneuvered in their sphere of influence to earn a living as a trader of one of the region's commercially sought items, such as salt pork, sandalwood, pearls, bêche-de-mer, or tortoiseshell, while others simply perished. Inevitably there were some callous beachcombers who were escaped convicts, pirates, or thieves, and these often sought to dominate the indigenous population to their peril.

Over the next two and half years Rob and the *Smyrna* spent cruising among the South Pacific's islands, it was particularly around the Kingsmills they heard of, or witnessed, several violent incidents that loomed as a dreadful fate for whaling crews. Three types of mayhem were regularly noted. Foremost were the crews that were "cut-off" on one island or another; implying they were massacred by the islanders. Secondly, there were mutinies, including the one Rob stumbled upon involving Captain Hussey, and thirdly, there were wrecks. In an era with crude means of navigation, errant maps, uncharted reefs, and nighttime sailing, wrecks were relatively frequent. In chronological order during Rob's time in the area, there was the wreck of the *Columbia*, an attack on the *Triton*, the wreck of the *Flying Fox*, a mutiny on the *William Penn*, attacks on the *Charles W. Morgan*, *Inga*, and *Rudolph*, and the wreck of the *Ontario*.

Most stories about these incidents and others, shared while gamming, certainly added a morbid luster to the yarns the crews spun to each other, but in reality mystery will forever shroud a number of the tales, especially for those incidents where there were no survivors. In the period, most narratives simply ascribed the act to barbaric islanders, but in fact history shows the crews were generally attacked in retribution for straightforward felonious acts of kidnapping, theft, and rape that had been served on the islanders. The strongest reactions by islanders were of course elicited by the slavers, who in the same time period began to "recruit" the natives. H. E. Maude wrote about one visiting the Kingsmills in 1847:

> As the *Ellen Elizabeth* stood off and on to the lee of each atoll the islanders sailed out in their canoes and were easily persuaded to come on board to trade, in the hope of pilferage, or out of mere curiosity, as

they had been accustomed to do on their visits to passing whaling ships since the 1820s.

Once on deck many of them were willing to sign on as recruits, misled by what Newbury terms the "fallacious promises" of the captain, for the pressure on food resources in the well populated, but arid islands of the Southern Gilberts made them ideal recruiting country. When persuasion failed Captain Muller used more forcible means, towing the canoes out to sea and scuttling them when too far from the land for anyone to swim ashore; which Newbury describes as "the usual way of capturing natives."[13]

Even those ships that were not unscrupulous slavers or those whose captains impressed islanders for their own staffing needs, still occasionally evoked strong reactions. Puritanical New Englanders, Native Americans, free African Americans, and various distant islanders were regularly tossed together with the indigenous residents as the foreign fleets penetrated the Pacific and routinely sought to trade for fresh water, food, and supplies. Yet each culture retained vastly different views on ownership and sharing. Tumultuous events often began during trading encounters, where the islanders' desire for metal goods and tools, plus the obvious affluency of the Westerners in a comparative light, led to attempts to surreptitiously "share" goods. Sometimes, intercultural differences respecting ethics spun out of control. Pilfering was a normal game undertaken by most indigenous islanders during trading interactions. While annoying to whalers, it was not unexpected, and given the great discrepancy between the amount of material goods the different societies possessed, it was to be fairly anticipated. These intercultural encounters were vastly more complicated in certain archipelagoes, where trading often included sex. Some indigenous cultures "shared" or bargained women for goods. Such actions often led to inter- and intracultural competition and considerably heightened friction, and it's easy to see how interactions that began with felonious behaviors such as stealing and prostitution might easily escalate into the capital crimes of kidnapping, rape, and murder.

In a faded portrait taken on her honeymoon, an attractive woman stares ahead. She has a very pinched waist, a triple-bouffant hairdo, a pearl necklace, and a black scoop-neck Victorian dress topped by white ruffles and huge puffy shoulders. Mary Davis Wallis was one of a few female Westerners who visited the islands in Rob's time. Her husband, Benjamin, had previously been the first mate and an officer on a South Seas trading ship, but he then acquired his own ship to focus on the bêche-de-mer trade around Fiji. Meaning "worm of the sea," bêche-de-mer was a hot trading item. This group of animals, also known as sea slugs, were boiled, dried, and smoked to make a delicious soup highly desired in Asia. To procure them, traders built a network among islanders who would locally gather the animals from the reefs and then sell them to traders.

Mary often sailed with her husband during his rounds and wrote about her experiences.[14] We will reencounter her later in the Fijis, but during one of their cruises among the islands in 1844 they passed the Kingsmills to land nearby on Pleasant Island, now Nauru. Dropping anchor just offshore, she described the wild behavior of the islanders:

Our decks were completely filled with native men and young girls, who stole everything they could lay their hands upon. I saw them handing shirts, trousers, sailors' knives, and various other articles over the sides of the vessel. . . . All they brought was sold for tobacco, and I was almost stunned by the vociferous cry of the girls [to me] of "Captain's Woman, give me chaw tobacco." They placed no value on cloth, which was offered them, although they wore nothing but a leku, made of grass. The whole conduct of this people was boisterous, rude, and immodest in the extreme. The girls came on board for the vilest of purposes, but stated their purposes were not accomplished, as the sailors were afraid of [her,] the "Captain's Woman."

Surprisingly, Mary balanced her moral judgment of the islanders by redirecting her ire at the whalers, continuing, "When [they] visit foreign climes, their conduct shows that they have left their souls at home."

There were indeed tens of thousands of such trading interactions each year as roughly six hundred whalers plied the waters, with each ship making multiple stops at different islands. Most of these encounters were peaceful and productive. However, the stakes sometimes rose, especially when the whalers stayed longer and women were in play. No doubt without a missionary, a captain's wife, or some other foil on board, such trading "interactions" were stretched out over time, often well into the night, and indubitably some turned ugly.

One rather perceptive mariner, John Mahlmann, wrote with respect to the Kingsmill islanders, "judging from only one of the many horrible stories . . . of the barbarous treatment these islanders had received in former years, it is surprising that thereafter they did not murder every white man who landed on their shores."[15] Indeed, it might well be said though that all of the incidents Rob heard about, or somewhat witnessed, were simply the result of retaliation to acts that had been fanned by the flames of American expansionism. Elected the year Rob was born, the nation's seventh president, Andrew Jackson, was a populist, whose outlook and expansionist ideology coupled with cultural narcissism triggered a sad cavalcade of cultural hegemony in the Pacific.

While only a short portion of the story that follows took place in the Kingsmills, the extended tale is helpful to understand the American behavior that unleashed decades of mistrust and recriminations across the South Pacific. It began in 1838 with the martial whip of America's expansionist agenda, the Wilkes Exploring Expedition.[16] Sent out by Jackson's protégé, President Martin Van Buren, to establish America's dominance in the region, the Secretary of the Navy James Palding charged the expedition with attempting to secure America's rights to the Antarctic and to protect and ensure "the important interests of our commerce in the great Southern Ocean."[17]

Setting off from Norfolk, Virginia, six ships and four hundred naval seamen represented a heavily armed naval projection of American strength. The squadron included the *Vincennes*, *Peacock*, *Flying-Fish*, the brig *Porpoise*, the supply ship *Relief*, and the small schooner *Sea-Gull*. Ostensibly the expedition sought to accomplish America's aims through surveying, cartography, and scientific collection, but it was no secret that it was sent with military heft. Before their departure, they had been admonished to "respect the intercourse with the natives of the South Sea islands as their experience would inculcate." However, military egos of those times could not conceive the cultural empathy necessary for first-contact diplomatic interactions. Confronted with aboriginal dress and manners, most officers and sailors couldn't comprehend the islanders might be equally intelligent and ought to be treated as they themselves might wish to be treated.

Taking advantage of the prevailing winds and currents, the squadron first crossed the Atlantic to Madeira, then sailed southwest back to Rio de Janeiro. Rounding Cape Horn, they spent the heart of the southern hemisphere's summer on the Beagle Channel and attempted to reach Antarctica in March 1839. Halted by pack ice, the fleet turned north and sailed up the coast of Chile, surveying and visiting various ports, before heading west "along the line" in the Pacific. Soon, a thinly veiled corollary to their mission began to emerge; the exertion of "justice" for American interests. Back at home port, in the smoke-filled and burnished naval offices, this had been officially explained to Commander Wilkes as the need to "diminish the hazards of the ocean." In fact, the goal was to intimidate the indigenous islanders across the South Pacific.

On Tonga, in the first such action, the expedition set about capturing a chief, Vendovi, who had been previously accused of murdering nine or ten sailors from the American brig *Charles Dagget* when she had been there four years before. As events unfolded, it became clear that Commodore Wilkes himself was not the iron fist of the expedition; that role had been reserved for Captain Hudson of the *Peacock*. Hearing rumors of the hunt for him, Chief Vendovi hid in the mountains, so Captain Hudson enticed Vendovi's brother, his wife, family, and seventy villagers onto the *Peacock* by offering a feast and gifts. Once aboard, Captain Hudson took them hostage at gunpoint until they agreed to orchestrate the capture and surrender of Vendovi. By any standards, Captain Hudson's subsequent treatment of the prisoner was incalculably harsh. Vendovi was kept chained in the wet hold with only darkness and rats for company, and he remained so imprisoned for the next several years until the remnants of the expedition ultimately reached New York City. There he was transferred to a prison in lower Manhattan where he soon died, without a fair trial or any real justice.

After Tonga, the expedition headed to the Fijis. There, on the island of Malolo in late July 1840, Lieutenant Underwood of the *Peacock* led several crew members ashore by the village of Sualib to trade. Scared by an unusually large number of villagers surrounding the crew on the beach, they took the son of a chief hostage, their new modus operandi. Putting him in one of the tenders, several of the crew then rowed it offshore so they could hover at a safe distance with their hostage. The chief's son did not appreciate his predicament and jumped overboard to swim ashore. A sailor then fired his musket at, or near, the hostage, and on the beach the hostage's father cried out that his son had been killed. The islanders then surged in anger around the crew. In the ensuing melee, spears, sabers, and pistols were all employed, and when the smoke cleared, it revealed islanders running frantically up the beach toward their village and two crew members lying in the surf. Lieutenant Underwood's and a midshipman's blood gave a scarlet luster to the breaking waves, for they had been speared and clubbed in the scramble. The *Peacock*'s crew, now split apart, felt vulnerable and panicked. Those still on the beach hoisted their two comrades up on their shoulders and ran for the tenders. They rowed to the ship, raised anchor, and rejoined the squadron some miles off. It was a mortifying incident, made worse by the fact that the dead lieutenant was the commodore's nephew. Kidnapping begat murder, and soon enough murder begot horrendous retribution. The squadron regrouped, and after pausing to bury the two sailors on nearby Tavua Island, it furiously returned to the lagoon. The fleet's tenders were set as a cordon around the island while the sun slowly dropped against a dreadful pink sky.

The next morning, more than seventy-five sailors and all the officers rowed ashore. The sailors formed a line along the beach, now the site of the Rendevous Eco Lodge, and fired fusillade after fusillade into the flimsy homes. The walls, made of plaited fronds, shook as if being battered by hail in a typhoon. During pauses, officers simply walked up to the windows of the thatched homes, leaned in, and used their pistols to dispatch anything in sight: man, woman, child, or dog. Next, the village was torched. Other than a few cowering women and children, nearly everyone perished; fifty-seven islanders died. It was a numbing display of retribution for an event that was in fact instigated by Americans who succumbed to their fears and kidnapped the first hostage.

Leaving the Fijis, the squadron sailed northeast to Oahu for repairs and resupply, and then south to Samoa, again on a mission of discipline. On the island of Upola, another native who was alleged to have murdered an American seaman was targeted for apprehension. Again, Captain Hudson acted as the hatchet man, directing the *Peacock* to send in several tenders to the village of Salufato to find the alleged killer. When they failed, Hudson demanded that the islanders turn him over. When that didn't happen on the first day, Hudson reverted to his now favorite response, a barbaric one that has repeatedly arisen in human history from the Peloponnesian Wars to Lieutenant Calley in Vietnam; again he resolved to torch the entire village in punishment.

While his subordinates were up early in the pale yellow wash of dawn, putting in fresh flints and loading their weapons, Captain Hudson took his time, enjoying a leisurely breakfast. It was not until late in the morning the onslaught began. By then, according to accounts, not a breath of wind stirred the lagoon; not a palm tree waved. The water was reported to be as flat as a turquoise mirror when he shattered the peace with a thunderous opening salvo from the *Peacock*'s deck guns. Like a gigantic shotgun blast, grapeshot was used as an antipersonnel weapon. Thousands of small lead balls slammed into the guileless villagers watching from the beach. Several more rounds followed, reverberating off the water. The dead lay sprawled on the sands or floating in the surf. Maimed islanders crawled across the beach as others clung to trees, bleeding out.

Upon landing, Captain Hudson shouted evermore bellicose commands amid the lingering pall of the cannons' smoke as he briskly strode across the now sanguine scene. A handful of surviving islanders fled inland as the crew burned the village to the ground. One village wasn't enough, so he ordered his crew to row across the lagoon to torch two more. Hundreds of houses were burned in such a great conflagration that the frenzied fire rose to three times the height of the coconut groves and sent a pall of smoke roiling over the island. The fugitive was never found, but even three decades later the event was well remembered across the

South Pacific, and America's Wilkes Expedition was dubbed "the burning fleet."[18]

The fleet then split up for various errands and missions as it made its way home. Separately, the *Flying-Fish* and the *Peacock* under Captain Hudson sailed east back "along the line." So, in April 1841, just a decade before Rob's arrival, Captain Hudson came to the Kingsmills, and the *Peacock* and the *Flying-Fish* approached Drummond Island. Most of the crew went ashore, and all seemed to have had a fine time of it, including several who bedded female islanders. However, at sundown, when the crew returned to their tenders on the beach, one man was missing: Seaman John Anderson. Whether his absence was because the islanders seized him for his valuables as the crew believed, or because Anderson had "misbehaved," will never be known, but he was never found. However, given that Captain Hudson was known to allow his "officers and men to seek amusement after their own fashion and free from any hindrance that his presence might create," a good guess is that Anderson tried to take unwanted liberties with an islander. In any event, the stage was set for the crew's next descent into their moral vacuity as they assumed the worst.

With Anderson unaccounted for, two tenders returned to the village in the looming dusk to search for him but were driven from the beach by islanders. Wreathed in fear reflective of their ethnocentric perspectives and their anger stoked overnight by their insecurities, at dawn Captain Hudson sent a heavily armed party of nearly eighty sailors back to the island. As before, the tenders pivoted into a line parallel to the breakers and, without a pause, fired a volley at the islanders gathered on the beach—a sailor's broadside. No guilt established, all innocence aside, no discussion had, American justice was delivered. Scores died and others lay wounded, sprawled in their blood. The sailors then landed as the survivors ran into the undergrowth and blithely burned their homes to the ground. Then after a round of self-congratulations, the sailors returned to the *Peacock* and raising their sails for home left behind another great pall of smoke ascending into the blue sky, an event long remembered in the Kingsmills.

The first ship to feel the heat left behind was the *Columbia*. In January 1844, three and a half years after *Peacock*'s departure, the *Columbia*, under Captain Kelley of New London, slammed into the reef off Sydenham Island in the Kingsmills.[19] She, obviously, was a different ship than the *Columbia* that Rob gammed with seven years later in 1851. While the crew survived and were picked up by another ship three days later, they reported having been roughly treated by the islanders and feared for their lives. Gamming spread this tale widely, and lingering salvage from the wreck opened the doors to the next sequence.

The next ship was the *Triton*. She sailed from New Bedford in 1846 under Captain Thomas Spencer, and then arrived in the Kingsmills in January 1848, just three years before Rob and exactly four years after the *Columbia* went aground.[20] Anchoring off Sydenham Island, the captain and crew were soon surrounded by canoes. The teeming islanders traded the normal fare of coconuts and fresh meat for trinkets, as well as offering some articles that came from the *Columbia*. In one of the canoes was a surly Portuguese beachcomber named Manuel, a recent deserter from the whaleship *Nantucket*. He enticed Captain Spencer ashore with the promise of some "first rate fluke chain." After landing on the beach and visiting the village to examine the items, the captain bought the *Columbia's* chain, plus two great wooden booms, a topgallant mast, and a whaleboat. However, when the deal was concluded and it was time to return to the boat, he found that the islanders had hidden his oars. Visibly annoyed, but not yet alarmed, Captain Spencer and his two crewman, William Peet and John Grue, tracked down a noisy group who had hung the oars up in a tree. Unfortunately, by the time they retrieved the oars, the tide had fallen so low they could not cross the lagoon to reach their ship. Forced to return to the village, they reluctantly spent the night at Manuel's house.

In the dark just before dawn, the sailors heard a commotion and looked out. By the faint starlight they could see some of the islanders again purloining their oars. They dressed and grabbed their belongings and weapons as the islanders vanished in the dark. On the beach, the captain discovered their boat was missing, too. The three men split up to search the island. Shortly, Captain Spencer found the whaleboat being dragged away by some islanders about a quarter mile down the beach. He ran to catch up with them and was immediately surrounded. Manuel and more than a hundred villagers closed in from all sides, many armed with pistols, rusty cutlasses, whaling lances, and knives. At first Manuel lied and mumbled some incoherent story about protecting the whaleboat from the islanders, but when Captain Spencer pushed for the truth, Manuel said brusquely, "We are going to take the *Triton*." Before the captain could come up with a response, the crowd suddenly grabbed him and tied him up. Desperately he asked Manuel why he and the islanders would do this. Manuel told him they had been cheated three weeks previously. The *James Stewart* of St. John, New Brunswick, had stopped at the island, and after intense bargaining had also agreed to purchase several items from the *Columbia* for three hundred dollars. However, after all the items were safely aboard the *James Stewart*, the captain, Joseph G. Kenney, drew his sword, drove Manuel and the islanders overboard, and then sailed off without paying. Perhaps it was the same *James Stewart* that the *Smyrna* had gammed with when outbound from New Bedford in February 1850.

In any event, Captain Spencer begged Manuel to allow him to make good and pay the *James Stewart*'s debt. Manuel cruelly replied, "I have the bird in my hands, and I will pluck him at my leisure." Soon the captain and his sailors were dragged back to Manuel's hut, where they were placed under guard to await sunrise and their fate. While the *Triton* had remained well offshore overnight to clear the reefs, in the morning's light she sailed slowly back toward shore. Manuel and his crew of eight islanders then rowed out in the captain's whaleboat across the now glassy sea to meet the *Triton*. After a long dialogue, the captain's heart plunged as he saw Manuel and other islanders climb aboard his ship, which then sailed away from the island. As the day slid toward evening, there was still no sign of either the success or failure of Manuel's plot. Darkness soon cloaked the ship, and in anguish and unable to sleep, the captain and his crew members awaited dawn's light.

With sunrise, the great and empty blue ocean shared no secrets. The captain and his crew pushed their way out of the hut and down to the beach through the hostile throng of islanders. Finally, they spied the *Triton*. She was far out at sea, just a white wisp on the horizon, and appeared to be drifting listlessly with her sails at an odd angle. Trembling with the sure knowledge that his crew must have been slaughtered, the captain pushed his way back through the massed islanders into the hut and prepared to die. Nothing happened. Hours passed. Then late in the afternoon, the captain and his two sailors heard a tremendous commotion down on the beach. Peering out from the hut, they saw three whaleboats and an equal number of canoes heading toward the beach. A great cry went up among the islanders as the boats landed, and the throng immediately turned to storm the hut. Several islanders entered and grabbed Captain Spencer, telling him in broken English that the ship had been taken and his crew killed. But it also seemed that Manuel and most of his pirates had perished in the effort, so revenge was in the air. The terrified captain was dragged from the hut and pulled along a path deep among the coconut trees.

At last, the seething horde came to a shallow bay, with a small island in its midst, upon which sat a single hut. The islanders began to chant and dance, waving their spears, whaling lances, and clubs as they tossed the captain inside. One islander jumped into the hut with a huge spear, one used to kill wild boars, and advanced with the clear intent of skewering the captain. At that moment, an old and bent woman hobbled in and wrapped her arms around the captain, shielding him and mumbling incantations. After a sizzling exchange with the brute, for no reason apparent to the captain, the standoff dissolved. The furious killer and the old woman left the hut to join a group of elders gathered outside. After a long conference with much gesticulating and harsh words, the captain was dragged back to what had been Manuel's hut and thrown inside. The sun set soon after, and the captain and his mates, hungry and exhausted from fear and sleep deprivation, dozed in their corners. Late that night there was a gentle tap from outside, and a young Hawaiian kanaka named William called out. William had been a crew member on the *Triton*. Wet, weary, and with sand still clinging to his clothes, he told the captain he'd just swum to the island. He then went on to relate what had transpired aboard the *Triton*.

After Manuel had rowed out to the ship, he had shouted up to First Mate Wells, who was on deck managing her in the captain's absence. Falsely reporting that the captain's boat had flipped in the surf and he was injured, Manuel told them that the captain had sent him to ask the crew to send ten barrels ashore to be filled with fresh water. Wells and crew remained skeptical, but reluctantly allowed the marauders to board the ship, but without weapons. Wells brought Manuel into the main cabin to keep watch over him with two pistols. However, near ten o'clock that night, Wells eventually nodded off, giving Manuel the opportunity to grab the pistols and arm his accomplices on deck with whaling spades and lances.

The clattering of steel awoke the second mate, who ran to find Wells. However, before the second mate and other crew members could get on deck with their weapons, Manuel shot the seaman at the helm and badly wounded the suspicious cooper. A fight erupted, and Manuel used his sword to force the second mate to dive overboard. When First Mate Wells lost his sword dueling, he was terribly cut by Manuel and almost run through before he could retreat below. The cooper, Andrew Folger of Nantucket, just twenty-three years old, was badly sliced himself but still came to aid Wells and managed to kill two islanders. However, he was then quickly surrounded on deck and cut to shreds in a horrible death witnessed by all. The third mate fought his way up onto the deck, grabbed a whaling lance, and ran eight inches of steel through Manuel, pinning him to the deck, where he bled out.

The courageous third mate turned and killed another islander, but then he, too, was quickly surrounded, backed into a corner, and badly cut. With no recourse, he too dove overboard. The two mates, now in the water and trailing copious amounts of blood, swam over to join five other crew members who had earlier escaped in a whaleboat. Holding together their grave wounds, the men in the whaleboat pulled away from the ship to safety. At this point, there were three natives left alive. Two were badly wounded, but together they still held possession of the deck. During this melee the *Triton* had drifted out to sea, and day had turned to night.

In the morning about twenty-five islanders paddled out in their canoes for plunder. In searching the ship, they managed to flush out one of the last crew members, William Paisler, just fifteen years old, from his hiding place in the hold. He was mercilessly hacked to pieces. The only other crew member left was the Hawaiian kanaka, William, who had climbed aloft for safety. Way up at the masthead, as the sun rose higher and the plundering ebbed, he pondered his predicament. At last, employing sharp wits, he cried out "Sail Ho!" The islanders thought another whaler or a navy ship was approaching, and so panicked and abandoned ship. They leapt into the sea with their plunder, scrambled into their canoes, and paddled back to the beach. As soon as they had cleared the ship, the savvy kanaka climbed down to join the badly wounded First Mate Wells, who emerged from his hiding place. The two managed to sail the ship to the whaleboat where the second and third mates and remaining crew members were cowering. As the natives who had swarmed out that morning had told the kanaka that they had killed the captain and the two seamen still ashore, once the crew was aboard, the *Triton* simply sailed away from the dreaded Kingsmills, though William decided to stay and swam for shore.

Meanwhile back on the island, the islanders now feared an impending naval warship would soon arrive and kill them all, and so they reversed course and sought Captain Spencer's favor. He demanded his freedom and a canoe. The captain and his two crew then attempted to sail after the *Triton*, but she was long gone. Over the next several days, they made repeated attempts to sail offshore toward various ships they saw at great distance, but none spotted them in return. Finally, on the third day, two ships were silhouetted far offshore at the break of day. The three men rowed hard for six hours until at last they caught up with the *Alabama*, commanded by Captain Coggeshall. Greeting them effusively and taking them aboard, Captain Coggeshall immediately raised his ship's flags, signaling the other ship, which tacked and sailed over to join them. She was the *United States* under Captain Calvin Worth. The three captains and two ships returned to the island, and with three large squads of armed sailors, they secured a few remaining artifacts from the *Triton* before sailing away. Captain Spencer and the two sailors went aboard the *United States*, which sailed toward Guam. Several days later they intercepted the *Japan* bound for Hawaii, who had met with the outbound *Triton*, and so told them of her passing. Without a ship and destitute, upon landing in Hawaii, Captain Spencer decided to remain there. He was soon joined by his brother, and together they started what became a highly successful ship's chandlery. By 1855 the papers reported he "had more money than anyone else in town."

The third incident involved the *Flying Fox* and Captain Brown, who Rob first met on Round Island with Captain Hussey, and was the second of the three wrecks. In September 1850 when Rob was sailing west down the line, the *Flying Fox*, skippered by Captain Brown, went aground off Sydenham. Slamming into a reef with all sails flying, it was a terrible wreck.[21] The speed and mass of the ship and the unyielding nature of reef led to the immediate destruction of the ship and the deaths of many of the crew. The captain and his wife made it to the nearby island where they were fortuitously soon rescued by Captain Hussey, which is why these three were together when they first met Rob a year later.

The other survivors didn't stay at Sydenham either, but instead set off north for Simpson Island, now Abemama, fifty-eight miles away. Under the command of First Mate Walker, the cooper and nine crew members made the trip safely and soon settled in as beachcombers. Their fortune in surviving soon shifted, for their greed and offensive behavior overcame their gratitude to the islanders who welcomed them. Seven of the *Flying Fox*'s crew decided to engage in the lucrative, but competitive, coconut oil trade and joined with another beachcomber, Walter Holliwell, who had come off the Australian whaler *Genii* in June 1848. Together this group was fronted "a considerable quantity of tobacco, with which to purchase cocoanut-oil" and several hundred casks. Soon though the group "made such a nuisance of themselves" that shortly after "they had all been killed on the order of the island's High Chief Baiteke, who kept the entire trade . . . in his own hands."[22] Thereafter, in whalers' gams, a muddled tale of the *Flying Fox* often commingled the two threads of the story, and the crew were considered "cut-off."

As these stories spread, legends about the ferocity of the Kingsmill islanders continued to grow, unrestrained by the truth about the root cause. Later in 1851, and directly overlapping with Rob's time in the archipelago, the famed whaler *Charles W. Morgan* also visited Sydenham Island.[23] After being at sea for a lengthy period, she was eager to resupply with fresh water, fruit, and meat. As she approached the now notorious island, the winds died, and the ship and crew found themselves becalmed

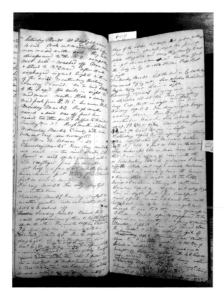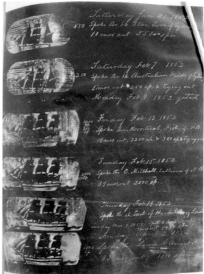

Rob Armstrong's original log found at NBWM (Item #1267). Photograph by author, log courtesy of the New Bedford Whaling Museum, and photostatic copy from his second logbook; author's copy.

Photostatic copy of R. W. Armstrong's map and handwritten autobiographical manuscript. Photograph by author.

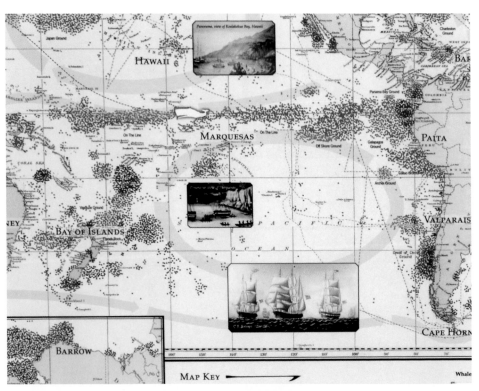

Where whales were taken in the Pacific, especially "along the line"; sperm whales in red, baleen whales in blue. From "New Bedford: The City That Lit the World," one of the museum's graphic panels, courtesy of the New Bedford Whaling Museum.

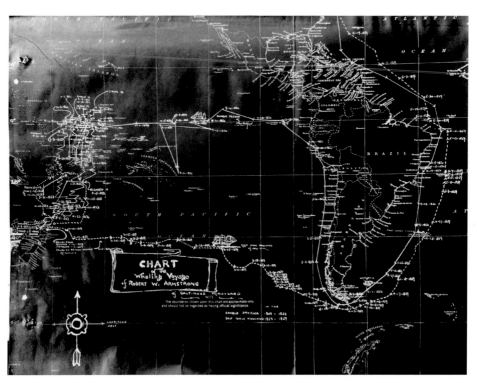

A close-up of R. W. Armstrong's full map (circa 1885), detailing the routes of the *Smyrna* and *Isaac Howland*.

Nantucket Sleigh Ride by Robert Sticker. Image from J. Russell Jinishian Gallery; permission from artist's daughter.

A crimson sea; the whale's lungs have been lanced. *Whales off Twofold Bay NSW* by Oswald Walters Brierly (1867). Art Gallery of NSW, Sydney, Australia

Several ships "mating," or partnering, to savage a pod of sperm whales. *Offshore Whaling with the* Aladdin *and Jane* by William Duke (1849). Tasmanian Museum & Art Gallery.

Rob wrote "as far as the eye could see, whales lay all around us in every direction . . . " *South Sea Whale Fishery* by Thomas Sutherland (1825). Library of Congress.

A decent-sized sperm whale brought alongside. *Removing the Hook* by Clifford W. Ashley (1904). Image courtesy of the New Bedford Whaling Museum.

Cutting in a Whale by Marian Smith (1903). Image courtesy of the New Bedford Whaling Museum.

Boarding the Case of a Small Sperm Whale by Clifford W. Ashley (1904). Image courtesy of the New Bedford Whaling Museum.

Cutting up the blubber as laundry dries in the background. *Stowing Blubber* by Clifford W. Ashley (1904). Image courtesy of the New Bedford Whaling Museum.

Bailing the Case by Clifford W. Ashley (1904). Image courtesy of the New Bedford Whaling Museum.

Tending the "try works"; rendering the blubber into oil. *Trying Out Blubber* by Herbert Lincoln Aldrich (1887).

Trying Out a Whale in the Arctic on the Helen Mar, artist unknown (1887). Image courtesy of the New Bedford Whaling Museum.

One ship's return, roughly 1,000 bbl. of oil on Rotch's North Wharf in New Bedford. By Joseph G. Tirrell (1876). Image courtesy of the New Bedford Whaling Museum.

Gilbert Island warriors; "a defensive armor, . . . a helmet of the skin of the porcupine fish . . . three-forked spear, barbed with rows of shark's teeth." (1890s). Alamy Photo Stock.

A Maori family in their whare. *Family at Mangaakuta, Homebush* by James Bragge (1865). Alexander Turnbull Library, Wellington, New Zealand.

Team to Cross-cut the Giant Kauri. Artist unknown, undated. The Kauri Museum, Matakohe, New Zealand.

The author, A. R. Brash, with a kahikatea near Wairoa, NZ, in 2022. Self-portrait.

Bushman sawing a great kauri. *Big Log Omahuta* by artist unknown (1910). The Kauri Museum, Matakohe, New Zealand.

"A Fruitful Vine"—the whaler's family and in-laws—circa 1892: Back row: William A., Ada A., C. Muller, H. Muller, Louis A., Minnie A. Ludington, Eudocia Muller, John Ludington, Jane Ludington; Front row: Eudocia M. Armstrong, Rob A. (whaler), Gelston A., Harry A., and Jenny Armstrong. Photographer unknown, at Mountain Lakes, Maryland.

Armstrongs and Ludingtons—circa 1896: John Ludington, Minnie A. Ludington, Jane Ludington, G. Franklin Ludington (on lap), George F. Ludington, Eudocia M. Armstrong, and Robert Armstrong (whaler). Photographer unknown, at Mountain Lakes, Maryland.

Family of the whaler's grandson: Nicholas, G. Franklin, Marian, and Nancy Ludington. By Dana Wallace (late 1940s), Fire Island, New York.

Current generations: Emily, Jane Q., Alex, Diana (sister) Brash, Nancy Ludington Brash, Leland Ludington (Nicholas's son), and Ian Brash. Photograph by author (2020), Riverside, Connecticut.

The inspiring "Ship Followers" diorama in the American Museum of Natural History, New York. Photographs by Branan Edgens, Genetic Films.

Pelagic bird-watching with Steve Howell off Cape Horn. Photograph by author (2020).

Wilson's storm-petrels dancing on the ocean's surface like St. Peter. Photograph by Brian L. Sullivan (2005), Macaulay Library, Cornell University.

The ethereal light-mantled sooty albatross. Photograph by author (2022), off Auckland Islands, New Zealand.

Beautiful in the cobalt sea; a sperm whale. Alamy Photo Stock.

Chinese fishing vessel mass-harvesting squid; a tragedy of the commons. By Isaac Haslam (2021). Courtesy of Sea Shepherd Conservation Society.

in its great lagoon. Suddenly, sixty or more canoes were launched from shore, filled with islanders shouting, waving, and shaking objects at the crew. Greatly surprised, they panicked. The captain, J. D. Samson, urged the crew to grab their weapons and man the ship's small cannons. The canoes surged forward and spread out, apparently to encircle the ship. We will never know their true intentions, because without waiting to find out, Captain Samson unloaded the *Charles W. Morgan's* small cannons on the canoes. Sending grapeshot rippling across the still lagoon, she shredded the canoes, killing and maiming numerous islanders. As the smoke cleared, capsized canoes and writhing bodies peppered reddening waters. The remaining islanders immediately turned their canoes about and fled toward shore. Today in Connecticut's Historic Mystic Seaport, the seemingly innocent *Charles W. Morgan* is safely docked and visited by thousands, yet unknown to most, she is haunted by the specter of her deeds.

By December 1851, just after Rob and the *Smyrna* had left the Kingsmills and were south in the Kermadecs, another incident took place, one he never mentions and may not have even known about. The cargo ship *Rudolph* under Captain Charles D. Perry was cut off.[24] Having left San Francisco in October 1850, she stopped in at Sydney in January 1851 and then dropped a load of coal in Callao, Peru, before heading to the Kingsmills in July for coconut oil. The demise of the *Rudolph* was ultimately reported by the first mate, but without any firsthand knowledge for he had left the ship in Callao. However, he told the newspapers that in December 1851 the crew was massacred and the ship burnt in the Kingsmills. Rallying to the defense of his captain, he noted that the man was of "good character" and there was not a Westerner in the crew.

The third wreck and last incident in Rob's time in the Kingsmills occurred shortly after Rob and the *Smyrna* were in the area. The whaler *Ontario*, under Captain Slocum of New Bedford, was homeward bound by way of Hawaii with 1,000 barrels of whale oil when she struck a reef off the northeast corner of Pitt, now Makin, Island, just before 4 a.m. on January 24th, 1852, a moonless night.[25] The captain had been using an older, erroneous chart that placed Makin some miles away from its true position. Within a few hours the seas broke her back and ripped her hull open so her cargo spilled out. Lost in the ocean on a black night, the crew could only cling to the wreck. At last with the first tinges of light to guide them, they struggled to shore on nearby Butaritari. Some swam, while others rowed the surviving whaleboats. They were lucky, for they landed on the island that a local and beloved trader, Richard Randell, had made his home and he protected them. With Randell's help, not only were the islanders "restrained" from exercising their traditional rights of pillage, but using Randell's small trading ship, over the next few days the crew managed to salvage hundreds of barrels of the *Ontario*'s oil.[26] Shortly after, the British schooner *Supply* swung by and took some of the crew on her way to Sydney in return for 500 bbls. of oil. Then the whaler *Phocion* stopped by a few days after that, and her captain purchased the remaining oil and took Captain Slocum and the rest of the crew aboard. As *Phocion* left the island, she paused near the wreck site to fish another 200 bbls. from the seas, making it home to New Bedford nine months later.[27]

A year later, while near Sydenham in the Kingsmills, Rob hears a final tale, one that perhaps cut a bit closer to the bone. It was about the brig *Inga* being cut off at Pleasant Island, now Nauru, just north in the Carolines in February 1853. She was a ship the *Smyrna* had gammed with just seven months previously. The facts surrounding the incident are again unclear, for the newspapers reported contradictory stories, but the *Inga* is known to have left New Bedford on May 9th, 1848, and been at sea nearly four and a half years.[28] The first version the newspapers covered began with a crewman who reported that while the *Inga*, sailing under Captain Barnes, was at Pleasant Island a great swarm of islanders came aboard under the pretense of trading. Instead they attacked the captain and the crew, killing all the Westerners, with the exception of the crewman himself. The islanders then plundered the ship and attempted to sink her. Being unable to accomplish that, they sought to burn her instead. However, the fire went out, and before they could ground her, a strong current swept the *Inga*'s smoldering hull out to sea.

Soon a second whaler, the *Bartholomew Gosnel*, stopped at the island, and a slightly different story unfolded. The crew of the second whaler were struck that the islanders offered money instead of produce to buy tobacco, and then were even more surprised when one of the two beachcombers on the island brought out the *Inga*'s chronometer and offered to trade it. This elicited a few questions. It turned out that one of the beachcombers had previously been part of the *Inga*'s crew, and he now offered a fuller version of his tale. His name was George Mayhew, and he claimed to have come to Pleasant Island in January 1852 aboard the *Inga*. At his own request, he says, he was discharged on the island. Then after he had been on the island for nearly ten months, on November 28th of that year, the *Inga* returned. Once she set anchor off the beach, Mayhew went out to his old ship along with a great number of islanders in their canoes. Mayhew stated that after a brief conversation with Captain Barnes, the captain told him he was ready to get under way and was going to cut the islanders' canoes free. When he went to do so, he was killed, and Mayhew was thrown overboard by the islanders.[29] In another newspaper, Mayhew reported that after talking to the captain he went below to trade and talk to his ex-mates and then heard a great commotion overhead. He came up the ladder to find the captain shouting at the islanders to leave the ship, but as the islanders did not appear to be leaving the ship quickly enough, the captain then ordered the crew to begin cutting their canoes loose. Likely thinking they were all about to be kidnapped by a slaver, they aggressively responded. At that moment, Mayhew claims he was seized by the islanders and bodily thrown off the ship, and once he was in the water he swam to his own canoe. He was "held" there while the natives still on board killed the crew and plundered the *Inga*. Mayhew then said, fearing for his life, he crept out of the village and climbed up into the island's interior, where he hid in the forest. After two months, a whaler visited the island, and at that point Mayhew snuck down out of the hills and managed to get aboard her to escape.

What exactly transpired on the deck of the *Inga*, and what sins were committed, will never be known, but certainly Captain Barnes and likely Mayhew were a lot less innocent than supposed. The moral pillar in the region, Reverend Gulick, observed the killing of Captain Barnes and the crew was *to the surprise of every one acquainted with peaceable character of the natives [of Pleasant Island]. It is surmised that it must have been in revenge for a Pleasant Island native who died at his hands in th[at] very harbor . . . Captain B. has for the last four years been practicing high-handed outrage on the inhabitants of these seas.[30]*

CHAPTER 20

A Mutiny, a Wrathful Whale, and a Blackbirder

PAUSING IN FEBRUARY 1852 NEAR THE KERMEDECS, THE *SMYRNA* gammed with the *Christopher Mitchell*, a ship famous even then for having had the "female sailor bold" on board four years previously. A jilted young woman, Ann Johnson, had left Massachusetts in pursuit of her lover, a whaler, and sailed surreptitiously after him under the name George Johnson. She lasted aboard for seven months by tucking her shirt in tight and playing coy. She successfully made it south down the Atlantic and 'round the Horn undiscovered, until she got quite sick in the Pacific. Off the west coast of Peru, when she was ministered to for her fever, her sex was discovered. Whereupon she was immediately dropped off at the American Consul in Peru to the great chagrin of the captain.[1]

Next, the *Smyrna* stops in at Sunday Island, whose sorrowful tale we will return to in a bit. She then visits New Zealand for a brief respite in April 1852, where Rob again succumbs to his "cursed thirst," and in June they sail north and east to Samoa. Along the way, Rob crossed the equater for "the fiftieth time since leaving New Bedford" on July 14th, 1852. Returning to the Kingsmills the *Smyrna* stumbles into the aftermath of a blown-out mutiny. In early December, Rob reported a "cock and bull" story from the islanders who came aboard. "As it was evident that there was something wrong with the story they told, Captain Tobey determined to try and sift it, to see if he could get at the truth of the matter," Rob wrote.

Mutinies have played out in ships at sea over time immemorial: on Henry Hudson's *Discovery* in 1611, the HMS *Bounty* in 1789, and the whalers *Globe* in 1824 and *Sharon* in 1842, as well as many others, often unreported. In the Kingsmills such a savage drama replays as a hard captain, a long voyage, and a disgruntled crew simmer, until just a little something ignites a boil. While Rob witnessed the final scene, the stage had been set for this play by the Husseys years before and far away. For on the heels of the Macys, the Husseys were one of the earliest families to settle in Nantucket. They, too, quickly excelled in fishing and then the subsequent expansion into whaling. However, a life carved from the sea is never easy. As difficult as it was to navigate the oceans, it was no easier to raise the capital necessary to outfit a whaler. Captains like the Macys or Husseys tended to be tightfisted, puritanical New Englanders. Even after garnering the funds for a voyage, they then had to be tough enough to recruit a crew along the world's waterfronts amid the saloons and back alleys. Their resolve was tested again as soon as they were underway, for they had to meld a fractious crew to sail to distant waters in a quest of elusive beasts. Along the way they ran a gauntlet of hurricanes, typhoons, pirates, and other terrors. Thus, the Husseys were not faint of heart, nor did they lack grit, and through the years, they became a stern and unforgiving clan.

This drama might be said to have begun in 1847, and the first parting of the curtains took place in the hazy hot days of that summer on Nantucket.[2] At that time, Hussey's sixteen-year-old nephew, William Paddack, whom we have previously heard from, had just finished his schooling and was looking for a career. After visiting his uncle's ship, the *Planter*, placidly at anchor in the harbor, William begged his mother to let him go to sea. She acquiesced, whereupon he returned to his uncle's house and asked to be recruited. The captain said, "William, you have chosen a life full of toil and hazard, and as this voyage will perhaps be one of great peril, it would be well for you to reflect maturely upon the measure you are about to adopt." Soon after, with his sea chest packed with clothing, books, and other sundries, William was pulled aside by his aunt, the captain's wife. With her calico dress flapping in the breeze as she crossed the porch of her house, she sat him down and counseled:

"You are now about to enter upon the world, and will soon be far beyond the control and friendly advice of your mother and friends; you will be thrown upon your own resources, and it will depend much upon yourself what your future condition in life may be." How true.

The *Planter* sailed on July 4 of that year, crossed to the Azores, then cruised back southwest to 'round Cape Horn by late October, just as the southern spring was sliding into summer. The ship lost a man near the Horn in a turbulent storm and then stopped briefly to resupply in Chile. They continued northwest, whaling along the way, and arrived in the Galapagos in December 1847. After collecting fresh water, tortoises, seals, and other supplies, the *Planter* sailed straight for the Kingsmill islands, reaching them a month later. For the next two years they sailed around the islands. In addition to collecting a few hundred barrels of whale oil, Captain Hussey set up trading posts on several islands, leaving a few crew members ashore to trade trinkets for palm oil. Then things soured on the ship. As recalled by William; May 4, 1850, was a notably beautiful day, azure skies melding with the blue waters. The *Planter* was miles out at sea questing for whales, but without success. As dinnertime approached, the cook directed the crew to haul up a barrel of beef. Upon opening it, a rancid odor poured out. Captain Hussey descended from his deck to have a look. He told the cook to boil the beef a bit more to compensate, then "go ahead" and serve it for dinner. Here the stories diverge, with one told by young Paddack, the captain's nephew, and the other later reported by the crew. According to Paddack, the beef served that night and again the next day seemed to go down well. In the newspapers later, the crew recollected it was rancid and poisonous. Either way, the beef somehow fell overboard that night. When the mate reported this at daybreak, the furious captain ordered the entire crew on deck and had them sent aft to meet with him. He demanded to know who was responsible. William innocently observed that "it seemed to be one of those things no one knew anything about." The captain reiterated his demand, adding that, until the perpetrator was found or came forth, there would be no more meat for the crew; then haughtily dismissed the men. The air was fraught with tension, but the ship slowly settled back into its routines. After several days the ship then returned to the Kingsmills and Captain Hussey went ashore, his back ramrod straight. Several of the crew worked up their nerve and told one of the mates "they would not do any more duty on board that ship until they had their meat." The mate immediately sent a note to the captain, who quickly returned, and with a more sensitive nose this time, smelled mutiny. He ordered the crew aft again and asked to hear their gripe. Shuffling, with eyes downcast, the crew repeated their demand, but Captain Hussey insisted there would be no meat until the beef-tossing culprit was exposed and then archly dismissed them. However, when the captain sought to return to shore, the crew stoically refused to man the davits and lower his boat. Incensed, he advanced angrily to midship and directed the crew again to come aft so he could talk to them. They balked. Now enraged, he commanded them to go below to their bunks. They refused this, too, rightfully worried that the captain might lock the hatches and imprison them.

The rancid meat now blazed into infamy as a rebellious mutiny. The captain told the mates to bring up the ship's firearms, and, in response, the crew began arming themselves with hand spikes, the cook's axe, and flensing knives. Again versions of the tale diverge, no doubt reflecting familial affiliations.[3] According to his nephew, Captain Hussey lost his temper, cocked his gun, and fired indiscriminately toward the crew crowded near the bow. William maintained that his uncle's shot just happened to strike a certain James Henry Clark in the head, killing him instantly. As the captain reloaded, the crew stampeded in terror to the forecastle and jumped below. With his gun reloaded, and the mates all carrying theirs, the captain ordered them to lock down hatches. The crew was now trapped, as they had feared. After a bit, the captain's temper cooled, and with weapons trained, he and his mates stood by one hatchway, opened it, and ordered the crew to come back up on deck, one by one. Those who didn't, he snarled, would be "shot like dogs." As each crew member arose, they were manacled and laid out in lines on the deck.

A slightly different version of the story, reflecting the crew's perspective, was that Captain Hussey shouted at the mutineers, "I am the captain, and will remain so on this ship." Facing the crew, the captain then gave the troublemakers half an hour to reconsider their stance. After a dramatic pause, he told the mutineers the first person who refused the next order would be shot. Knowing the group's leaders, he then called out to one, James Clark, and commanded him to come aft. When he did not, Captain Hussey fired, shooting him cleanly in the head. Clark was dead before his body fell to the deck. With that, Captain Hussey then called upon the rest of the crew to resume their duties, which they sullenly did.

When the *Planter* sailed into Sydney to be refit six months later, rumors of the event had arrived well before her. Captain Hussey's actions had already been discussed all along the waterfront, and British authorities in charge of the port stirred. Days later, a British officer rowed out in a tender to find him, with an arrest warrant in his hand, probably really just a letter summonsing him to a hearing. In response, Captain Hussey pulled his pistols from his belt, leveled them at the officer, and warned he'd shoot if he came any closer. Clearly unprepared for such a response, the officer retreated. However, recognizing that such actions would provoke a stronger official reaction, the captain quickly packed his belongings and sailed with a friendly captain just departing for Lord Howe Island.

Weeks later and with repairs complete, the *Planter* was at last ready to sail. She went directly to Lord Howe Island, where Captain Hussey rejoined her. Back under Hussey's command, the *Planter* returned to the Kingsmills and resumed whaling and collecting palm oil, until ten months later when she was ready to head home. At that point, she first sailed northwest to Strong Island, for the mountainous island had fresh fruits and the clean water needed for the long trip home. There, the ship swapped out some of the crew and brought supplies on board. However, at the last minute, a trusted friend of Captain Hussey's, Captain Prince Ewer of the *Emily Morgan*, advised him to let his ship go on without him and avoid the trial that was sure to occur. So with his nephew aboard to watch after his interests, the *Planter* sailed for home, arriving at Nantucket on July 12, 1851.

Captain Hussey, as well as Captain Brown and his wife, remained behind as guests of Strong Island's chief for the next year and a half, where Rob and the *Smyrna* first intersected with them. Hussey was well-liked by the chief and credited with building "several attractive houses and making other improvements that drew admiring comments from visitors and made him a favorite." Then, he somehow came to command the *William Penn.*[4] This ship's origins are rather murky, but evidence suggests she was a 159-ton "fast sailor" that had been sold at auction in San Francisco in 1850[5] and then refitted for trading in the Pacific. Somehow Captain Hussey came into her possession among the islands, and before returning with her to Strong Island, he stopped at the island of Ebon. There he managed to aquire a lot of cash, roughly $1,000 in coins, a fatal mistake. The islanders, not appreciating their value, had allegedly gotten them from six sailors who in turn "took them" from the *William Neilson,* a ship that had disappeared near Ebon four years previously on a return voyage from China.[6] Money and ship in hand, Captain Hussey returned to Strong Island and refitted the *William Penn* for whaling, and then he set off to hunt around the Kngsmills before he was ultimately supposed to return the ship to San Francisco by December.

Thus, on July 6th, 1852, while Rob was on the *Smyrna* between Samoa and the Kingsmills, Captain Hussey set sail with the small crew he had rounded up. Far from a decent port, there were slim pickings available, and so his crew was comprised of just two experienced mates, five beachcombers, and fifteen kanakas, altogether a rather rough bunch.[7] As a result, when the *William Penn* left for the Kingsmills, apparently some of the crew had their eyes a bit more focused on the captain's purse than on the horizon.

After whaling in the area for three months, in early November the *William Penn* found herself just off Drummond Island, perhaps a hundred miles due west of the *Smyrna*'s position. One morning, with no inkling or warning, First Mate Christian Nelson was jolted awake by the groans of someone injured and in pain up on deck. He jumped out of his bunk in aid, and as he emerged from below, he was knocked to the deck by one of the kanakas armed with a cutlass. Nelson struggled to his feet, but before he could do much more, he was surrounded by the rest of the crew, each armed with a whaling lance or spade. They warned him to freeze and remain silent. The sailor who had hit him was their ringleader, a Hawaiian known as Henry or Harry. Either because Nelson had been unusually good to the crew, or because they thought they might need him, they didn't seem intent on killing him. However, they still stabbed him in the eye and badly beat him before he fled down a hatchway.

The noise awoke the rest of the mates and the watch below. The mutineers then broke into the aft cabin and attempted to get at the ship's muskets. Luckily, they were wet and useless. Next, the mutineers climbed onto the captain's cabin on the aft deck and, employing the same trick they'd used to fool Nelson, lured Captain Hussey, George Reed, the cook, and Amoy, a Chinese sailor, out on deck. As these men rushed out to respond to the groans and noise, the mutinous crew sliced Captain Hussey's head right off with a flensing knife, speared the cook with a whale lance, and badly wounded Amoy. The remaining mates and crew, terrified they would be carved up next, and believing the mutineers were above them as they huddled in the aft cabin, tried to blow up a keg of powder underneath them. Instead, the keg fizzled and flashed into flames, badly burning two of the remaining crew gathered in the cabin. Now in a standoff, with the rest of the crew trapped in the lower hold and the kanaka mutineers led by Harry above, the two sides parlayed. Finally, Harry concluded the stalemate.

> *"I have killed all I want to," he said, "and if you will give me fifteen muskets and a keg of powder, and let me take what provisions I want, I will leave the brig."*

After a quick discussion, the surviving crew members agreed to the terms, and within an hour the mutineers left the *William Penn* on two of her whaleboats. At this point the remaining crew regrouped, treated the wounded, and set sail for San Francisco.

Five days later, the whaler *Atlantic* under Captain Gardiner spotted the kanaka mutineers in their whaleboats far offshore of the Kingsmills. Approaching them, he saw they were in an exhausted state and almost out of food and water. The mutineers spoke well and lied even better. After hearing their tall tale, Captain Gardiner innocently took them aboard. They remained on the *Atlantic* for several days, until she anchored in the lagoon at Sydenham Island. Here, when Captain Gardiner went ashore one evening and the mutineers got the mate drunk, they took back *William Penn*'s two whaleboats and went ashore themselves.[8] It was at this point in the tale that the *Smyrna* arrived. The conclusion, as we learned from Rob, was that Harry was killed ashore, while the remaining mutinous kanakas cried out their innocence. In the end, the ultimate fate of the kanakas remains unknown, while the survivors on the *William Penn* disappeared over the horizon.

The second story of this trilogy starts with one of the greatest *non sequiturs*, and perhaps most restrained comments, ever made. Restrained that is, for what might have been. Rob pauses amidst his tale to share . . .

> *of interest, at this time our 3rd mate, and two of our boatsteerers had been part of the ship's company of the Ann Alexander, which about a year prior to this date was sunk within two hundred miles of our present location, by the attack of a large whale which they had been chasing. The crew had barely time to make their escape in their whale-boats, touching first at those islands and afterwards reaching Callao on the Peruvian coast.*

First, it should be noted that I moved this paragraph in his autobiography. He actually placed it after he visited the Galapagos, but that was in July 1850. In fact, the the heart of this tale took place in August 1851, and Rob refers to it being "a year prior to this date," so I shifted it to a more appropriate position in 1852. Second, in hindsight one recognizes that Rob brings up the *Ann Alexander* more as a "there but for the grace of God go I" story, and I have honored that. And last, in fact, not three but four crew members of the *Smyrna* were veterans of the *Ann Alexander*'s previous voyage.[9]

In 1845, when the *Ann Alexander* left New Bedford on her previous trip, Charles Lockwood had been a boatsteerer, Jack Frost and Payne Winnie had been "gringoes" or greenhands, and Isaac Ford had been the cook. When she returned to New Bedford in November 1849, these four mariners had just four weeks ashore before they signed up with one of the next outbound ships, which happened to be the *Smyrna*. Ultimately, they were quite lucky, for while they were sailing with Rob, the new crew on their previous ship, the *Ann Alexander*, had a very different sort of adventure.[10]

No small footnote in whaling history, the *Ann Alexander* experienced two memorable incidents that elevated her in the annals of maritime history. The first incident she handled admirably to her credit; the second incident was her downfall. Launched as a merchant ship in 1805, she was a simple barque, nothing ostentatious about her. But, on nearly her first Atlantic crossing, as a merchantman loaded with flour, tobacco, salt, cod, and lumber, she emerged from the fogbanks off Spain on October 21, 1805, and found herself amid the British fleet two days after the battle of Trafalgar. Lord Nelson had perished the day before, his spine shattered by shot. Amid the bloodied and tattered British fleet, scrambling to effect repairs and take care of the wounded, the *Ann Alexander* appeared, her billowing sails a luminous guardian spirit. An officer on Lord Nelson's flagship, HMS *Victory*, signaled her, and upon seeing her cargo, immediately requisitioned most of the food and naturally all the lumber. *Ann Alexander's* captain agreed; as if he had a choice. It was said though, he was especially happy to be recompensed on the spot with English gold. Now lighter, the *Ann Alexander* turned north toward England to complete her crossing.

Her second great moment in history began forty-five years later. Now outfitted as a whaler, the *Ann Alexander* under Captain John S. Deblois set sail from New Bedford on June 1st, 1850, five months behind the *Smyrna*. On a similar track, she headed to the South Pacific. Tragedy first struck as she rounded Cape Horn in March, for she lost one young sailor, Jackson Walker. During a great squall, with huge rolling breakers and shrieking high winds, the captain realized the ship might be lost if the main topsail didn't come down. Walker was called up from below to help, and while at the rail holding a line, as the captain wrote, the *Ann Alexander* "shipped a sea, and over he went, with no hope of saving him."

In mid-August, the *Ann Alexander* split tacks from most whalers and instead of sailing "down the line," she headed due west to what is known as the "offshore ground." In this vast empty area just eight hundred miles WSW of the Galapagos, just before sunset on August 19th, 1851, the *Ann Alexander* spied another whaler, the *Rebecca Sims* under Captain

Jernegan. The two ships signaled each other, and the crews happily gammed under the stars. As the captains shared Madeira and talked in their cabin, the crews swapped newspapers and books and talked all evening on the deck. Late the next day, near sunset, the *Ann Alexander* saw a large bull sperm whale heading away, west-northwest. Captain Deblois set the *Ann Alexander*'s course at sunset, simply seeking to stay with the hundred-barrel beast through the night. Incredibly, the next morning on August 21st, as the stars faded from the sky, the great sperm whale was seen just two miles downwind of them. They had not only stayed with it, but during the night advanced into a more advantageous position.

Two boats were immediately launched, one commanded by Captain Deblois and the other one by the first mate, Joseph Green. When the whale dove, the two crews rowed like the blazes to a point where they guessed he might arise thirty or forty minutes hence. Amazingly, they guessed well, for the whale broke the surface just by the mate's boat, misting the air with his breath. The mate struck fast, but now angered, the big bull wasted no time and immediately turned and charged the mate's boat. The mate gave sharp orders, and the crew deftly spun the boat from his jaws. The captain's boat, rushing in to help and add more iron to tame the beast, ended up sliding up onto the back of the now-vengeful leviathan. Shocked and terrified by their unanticipated collision, and before they could slam another lance into him, the whale flexed its great back and surged ahead toward the mate's boat. This time the whale crushed the boat in its jaws and, swirling among the wreckage, purposefully crunched all the larger remnants. Some of the crew were thrown more than twenty feet into the air, but incredibly all survived. The whale swam off a hundred yards, the harpoon sticking from its back, and paused tauntingly to rest on the surface. The captain then directed his boat to approach the scattered wreckage and they picked up the mate and his crew.

Seeing all this from the deck of the *Ann Alexander*, the second mate, Charles Wills, lowered another whaleboat from the ship to help rescue the swimming crew. The two boats now had nine men apiece, but instead of returning to safety, the captain, his ardor undiminished, had his crew pick up the line still attached to the leviathan. Having barely done this, instead of the expected Nantucket sleighride, the whale dove, turned, and surfaced under the second mate's boat, smashing it to bits in a new round of fury. At this point, with nine men back in the water, and his boat already overloaded, the captain cut the rope and carefully picked up the swimming men. With eighteen men in a boat, and the seas getting rougher, there was nothing to do now but row for the ship.

Clearly still furious, no doubt maddened by multiple harpoon and lance wounds, the whale turned the tables. It rose from the depths of the Pacific and charged them. Making a colossal ripping noise underwater, which the captain called "a noise as of coach whips," the bull missed them by just a few feet. As the whale passed below them, its great mass visible in the clear waters, his angry eye glared at them. Safely back on the *Ann Alexander*, the captain directed the ship back toward the scene where the smashed whaleboat's oars and other reasonably valuable items lay floating. Hot tempered, and perhaps as mad as Ahab, the captain then turned in pursuit of the whale itself. Still in sight, with his rope trailing behind, the great bull was swimming rather slowly and clearly wounded. From the bow of the ship itself, the captain lanced the whale. The bull turned and, with a contortionist's twist, struck the ship's bow, knocking the captain and crew off their feet. Again, the enraged bull charged, and the mate spun the wheel with all his might to turn the ship into the wind, thus avoiding the whale's charge. The whale dove deep then, leaving nothing but dark swirls and an empty sea in its wake. At this the captain gave up on the whale and ordered the crew to brace up the topsails and come to the wind for the evening.

Then just at twilight, with barely a glimpse before he struck, the furious whale rose from the inky depths and slammed into the bow just four feet above the keel. The ship shivered as its forward progress ceased, and the cracking sounds from its great planks were unmistakable. Captain Deblois and the crew knew in an instant. Even as he ordered the anchors and ballast thrown overboard to lighten the ship, the water rose about the captain's waist in his cabin. He grabbed extra navigation gear, knowing it would be a long way to anywhere in the two remaining small whaleboats. In pulling away from the hulk of the mortally wounded *Ann Alexander*, barely visible amid the deepening gloom, the crew took a moment to count their supplies. They realized they had only been able to save twelve quarts of water and no food of any kind.

The crew spent their entire first night bailing the two leaking and overburdened whaleboats. At dawn they were surprised to see the wreck still clinging to the surface of the sea. Demoralized and dismayed by their prospects, and rightfully angry at the captain's ego, at first the crew was understandably unreasonable. Initially, they wanted to set off toward the closest land; the Marquesas Islands, some twenty-two hundred miles distant. Luckily, after just a short distance, the captain asserted himself and reminded them that they had no food and insufficient water for such a journey. The two boats returned to the floating wreck and hovered near it while at first the captain alone dove into the water to see what more could be salvaged. With great reluctance, several additional men tied ropes around their waists and jumped in to help. Try as they might, they could not reach any of the fresh water deep in the hold. A cask of bread was found, but it had leaked. Several barrels did arise from the wreck, but they held only vinegar. After giving them a pep talk, the captain asked if they wanted him to lead them. They reluctantly concurred, and so he proposed they sail across the wind to California, twenty-four hundred miles away. While a greater distance, they were more likely to intersect rain, and thus get fresh water along this route. As they left the wreck, they paused to carve "Save us; we poor souls have gone in two boats north on the wind" on the stern.

With a minimum of two weeks of open ocean ahead, and with so little fresh water in hand, the deeply anxious crews set off with slim hopes. Not having had a real meal aboard their ship during the two days they had pursued the great bull whale, the captain and crew were already parched and hungry as the first day wore on. Shortly, there was nothing in sight but great rolling cobalt-blue waves merging into the endless blue skies of the Pacific, and the mercilessly beating sun. Unbelievably, just one half-hour before sunset, the captain spied a distant sail. Trying to cry out his observation, his cracked lips and parched throat betrayed him, and so he simply weakly waved at his crew. Worried that it might be a merchant ship, and thus without a watch at the masthead, there was a heightened sense of fear in the whaleboats. As the other whaleboat was about six miles ahead, and closer to the ship, the men all watched in great trepidation. Suddenly she tacked and looked to be going away, and the fear in the boat ran like rain in a gutter. Panicked by the implications, the men went silent with dread. Then slowly the ship swung all the way about and headed straight to the other whaleboat. After picking up the crew on the distant whaleboat, the ship turned to the captain's whaleboat. So in exultation and with great relief they were saved by the *Nantucket* under Captain Gibbs.

"About five months" after this disaster, the newspapers reported the pugnacious bull was taken by Captain Jernegan of the *Rebecca Sims* of New Bedford,[11] the ship the *Ann Alexander* had last gammed with before she pursued the whale. Two of the *Ann Alexander*'s harpoons were found still deep in him, "AA" carved in their shafts, and the leviathan's head had sustained serious injuries with pieces of the *Ann Alexander*'s timbers still embedded. Captain Jernegan noted that the injuries had robbed the whale of his "wildness and ferocity," yet gratefully noted he still yielded seventy to eighty barrels of good oil.

The third tale of this chapter requires a small chronological step back in Rob's story and to the beginning of this chapter, when on January 12, 1852, Rob caught his first view of Sunday Island, now known as Raoul Island. Six hundred miles northeast of New Zealand, part of the Kermadecs and undiscovered until 1793, Sunday Island is one of the archipelago's islands that are arrayed along one of the Pacific Ocean's most isolated geologic spines. Two of the island groups consist of only a handful of towering rocks rising from the sea. The largest island, Sunday Island, is roughly fourteen miles in circumference and rises to seventeen hundred feet. The island has fertile soil and a shallow harbor called Denham Bay. Above the bay is a flat plateau of several hundred acres, the site chosen for homesteading by the island's few colonists. Geologically active, the island has numerous fumaroles. Steam rises from the sides of Blue Lake, curls out of crevices on Campbell Hill, and seeps from the sands on the beach. The thermal activity has long terrorized its residents and visitors. Otherwise though, the green hillsides are covered with a shrubby forest reminiscent of northern New Zealand, tranquilly complete with palms and tree ferns.

First settled in 1837 by two families, the Bakers and Reeds, the residents abandoned the island after seismic scares in 1848. Two years later, it was recolonized by an American named Halstead. A year later he was joined by a New Zealander, Henry Cook, with his Māori wife and two additional Māori families. Historians believe the men were whalers who deserted to become beachcombers, arriving at Sunday Island after first stopping in New Zealand to acquire wives.[12]

In his 1852 visit to the island, Rob noted:

We found sixteen persons, men, women, and children, living here, none of them, however, longer than about five years. The men are nearly all white beachcombers, who have been left here at different times by ships that have chanced to touch here. They have wives whom they have obtained from some of the kanaka islands. One of them has two wives, sisters, half breeds, and their children are nearly white. I think I have hardly ever seen more beautiful children.

Sadly, this pictaresque tableau was to be soon heartlessly destroyed by one of the most abhorrent creatures on earth, a "blackbirder."

Many ships plied the turquoise waters of the South Pacific besides whalers, but none was more dreaded and deadly than the *Rosa y Carmen*. Reportedly a sleek barque with a three-masted clipper's rig, fast as any ship, she was also heavily armed, as she needed to be for her mission.[13] The *Rosa y Carmen* was a notorious Peruvian blackbirder, a slaver. Not only did she enslave thousands, but she brought death to Sunday Island in 1862, wiping out the peaceful colony Rob had visited a decade earlier.

Gaining its independence in 1824, Peru was still economically reliant on agriculture and the coastal guano deposits the country sold as fertilizer. To be profitable, both industries required a large subservient and unpaid labor force. The African enslavement that had fed the labor force in Peru for centuries was being curtailed, and it was theoretically abolished in 1854. However, new forms soon took its place. "Immigration" laws were passed, and "contractual" labor encouraged. A law was passed allowing for immigration of "colonists" from the South Pacific, and soon the *Rosa y Carmen* became one of the ships dedicated to "importing" colonists. Her captain, known as Marutani, was ugly in all senses of the word. He snarled at everyone and had a pockmarked face with an empty eye socket covered by a patch. He reputedly carried a musket, a pair of pistols, and a big bowie knife at all times. With previous experience in the African slave trade, he made no real attempt to recruit islanders, but rather sought to pack his hold with kidnapped victims stowed " 'tween decks fettered in irons."

The *Rosa y Carmen*'s first port of call on her maiden blackbird mission was Easter Island in December 1861. There she joined with seven smaller ships, and the crews worked in concert under Captain Marutani to secure their first load of "colonists." Landing on the beach early in the morning, the crew initially pretended to set up a display of goods and trinkets for trade. When about five hundred islanders had gathered, the crews fired their weapons in the air, terrifying them, and proceeded to grab and manacle nearly two hundred. The rest fled inland.

After Easter Island, the *Rosa y Carmen* sailed westward. Midway between the Cook Islands and Samoa, and by then packed below decks with nearly three hundred "recruits," typhoid broke out on the ship. Arriving at Pago Pago, she intended to fill her casks with fresh water, which was desperately needed for the dysentery-damned captives and crew. However, when the Samoans discovered she was a blackbirder, the islanders surrounded the crew members on shore and confiscated the ship's boats and water casks. After a long night of negotiations, the crew on board traded six Samoans on the ship for their compatriots ashore, and the *Rosa y Carmen* sailed on.

Now sixty-five hundred miles from Peru, typhoid's deadly dysentery set in and those on board began to die. Determined to get his precious human cargo home, Captain Marutani set his sights on a small isolated island, Sunday Island. When the *Rosa y Carmen* arrived at Sunday Island, just nine years after Rob's visit, the group of sixteen people Rob had met had grown to twenty-two. Instead of providing whalers with limited produce and sea turtles for meat, the families had expanded their holdings and now offered visitors cattle, pigs, chickens, and a broad array of produce. Wholly indifferent to the small community's welfare, Captain Marutani anchored in the bay and immediately ordered the evacuation of his ship. He sent everyone ashore, including the dead and dying, as he attempted to clear the ship of pestilence. The first tender that came in through the surf was carrying fifty-three men. When it slammed onto Sunday Island's pebble beach, only three men could stand up. All the rest, and most of those in the launches that followed, were simply thrown out of the boats by those who could. A number drowned and many died over the next day or two, never having moved from where they lay on the beach. Eighty died the first day, smaller numbers in subsequent days, and within the week, a passing whaler noted in her logs that more than 130 of the ship's contingent had died. The rest huddled on Sunday Island, barely alive, while with weapons drawn, Captain Marutani absconded with the community's crops and livestock.

After a few weeks and a thorough cleaning of the ship, the captain recaptured what Polynesian "immigrants" he could, 128 in total, and set sail for Peru. The remaining Sunday Islanders were left with no animals, no crops, no seeds to restart, and worse—typhoid. Eight of the twenty-two residents perished, and the survivors—with hearts broken and fields emptied—soon left Sunday Island forever. So, a decade after Rob's departure, this wild, desolate island with its beautiful children was despoiled and emptied by one of the world's cruelest animals, a Peruvian blackbird.

CHAPTER 21

A Bushman in New Zealand

IN AUCKLAND, ROB RELATED HIS REASONS FOR DESERTING THE *SMYRNA*: "at this time my pride would not suffer me to return to my friends as a pauper after so long an absence, and hope beckoned that I should find more and better chances of improving my condition in New Zealand than I would in America." Yet, in a note made by his daughter Jenny years later, she recounts that her father told her that on the *Smyrna*, "the men suffered so terribly of a very cruel mate, that another sailor and he deserted ship in a port in New Zealand." It is an interesting revelation from an otherwise quite taciturn man on a personal subject. Regardless, three and a quarter years out and not ready to go home, Rob and his companion Edward Mosher deserted the *Smyrna* in Auckland and snuck away on the *Antelope* for three weeks.[1] The thirty-five-ton coastal schooner was considered a "pretty schooner" and had been built in Wahapu, Bay of Islands, in 1850. She sailed under command of a Captain Burgess and traded between Auckland and Hawke's Bay for a number of years, and this no doubt whetted Rob's appetite for his later return to Hawke's Bay. Regardless though of their friendship, as soon as they returned to Auckland, Mosher "shipped at once in another whaler" on April 6th, 1853.[2]

Young Edward apparently made it home safely, for it is most likely that Edward Mosher was the same as the child born in 1834 to Edward P. Mosher and Julia Ann Pierce of New Bedford, Massachusetts. He had two younger sisters and a brother, and his father, Edward P. Mosher, was indeed a whaling captain at the time, having skippered the *Fenelon* in

1847 and the *Edward* in 1851. Coincidentally, the *Edward* was reported to have put into Auckland, New Zealand, in late January 1853, where "the captain had disposed of his cargo as the ship was abandoned by her crew."[3] It is also probable that eight years after leaving New Zealand, young Edward was the one who enlisted with the C Company of Massachusetts' 11th Infantry in 1861. Thankfully, he survived the Civil War, though he was discharged with a disability in 1862; Boston newspapers show that as late as 1895 he still proudly attended the regiment's reunions.[4]

Now being "entirely without money," Rob pondered his next steps in Auckland. He needed to find work fast. The problem? "I was indeed a stranger in a strange land," he wrote. Meanwhile, though Rob had opportunities to serve on other ships, he'd made up his mind to stay on shore and luckily succeeded in finding a place in the Customs House Service, "to pull an oar in the boat by which the Custom House officer boards every vessel coming into the harbor." However, after a couple of months, and curious about seeing New Zealand, Rob joins with some "bushwhackers" and heads into the forest.

Rob's first target was New Zealand's great kauri trees, which are both sacred and now quite endangered. A huge coniferous tree, sized like a sequoia, the kauri have evolved a unique symbiotic relationship with the ecosystem they grow in. The naturally dropping organic debris of the kauri, their leaves and branches, are highly acidic, which serve to not only deter other species from growing around them, but also leaches the soils. In a process known as podsolization, this releases additional nutrients for the kauri's roots to absorb. The indigenous Māori believe them to be sacred for "when Sky Father and Mother Earth were locked in a passionate embrace, it was the kauri tree that separated them, creating space for light, allowing life."[5]

Having myself earned good money climbing as a tree surgeon in college as well as having a graduate degree in forest science, I was particularly interested in this portion of Rob's journey and in a second endeavor to follow in his wake, soon after the island reopened from its COVID-19 lockdown, I flew to New Zealand in November 2022. I landed at 5:00 a.m. one morning in Auckland. After retrieving my luggage from the carousel and getting coffee from an Airstream camper on the sidewalk that had been remade as a cafe, with little delay I drove a rental car north into the heart of historic kauri country. Now rare, once kauri trees covered North Island above a rough east to west line near Hamilton, a town seventy miles south of Auckland. In his manuscript, Rob made clear he was not on the Coromandel Peninsa, but north of Auckland, and far enough north that he and his crew visited the town only occasionally. I thus surmised he was based somewhere in the hills near Warkworth, a town thirty miles north of Auckland and in the heart of kauri country. As I navigated the narrow winding lanes amid soaring conifers that morning, the landscape reminded me of the reforested wilds of British Columbia. With little sleep on my long flight, the two-hour drive was hair-raising. I was grappling with sleep deprivation, the novelty of driving on the left, and twisting roads designed for speeds half of what the Kiwis blast by at. Thankfully, just before noon I arrived at my first stop, the quaint Kauri Museum atop the Arapaoa River in the small town of Matakohe. There, after a query at the front desk, a kindly and rather bowlegged curator, with a lovely Kiwi burr, emerged from a back room. Peter Panhuis took me in stride, and after listening to a quick version of Rob's tale and ignoring my awful pronunciations of New Zealand geography, Peter told me about life as a Kauri Bushman. We then walked back to their archives where he shared books and photos from the museum's collection, which he augmented with some tales. After that, I walked the museum's halls and admired beautiful samples of kauri wood. Fashioned into exquisite wall panels and furniture, the wood was lovelier and richer in color than the finest California Redwood I have ever seen.

As the old books and photos highlighted, in Rob's time most of the kauri logged were still great trees. Coupling their size with the wood's density, which made them extraordinarily heavy, cutting and getting the timber to the market was a herculean task, one likely harder and regularly more dangerous than life as a whaler. The great kauri were deep in a near endless forest pierced by neither roads and nor many navigable streams, so getting them out to market was as hard as cutting them down. Oxen teams were the mechanism of choice. After chopping down a massive tree, and Rob noted most of his were about thirty-five feet in circumference, the bushmen then cross-sectioned the trunk into shorter lengths, and these in turn were cut into "flitches," or thick boards. Each stage was dangerous. On steep slopes, or with leaning trees, great trunks sometimes fell the wrong way, cross-sections rolled too quickly, sharp axes slipped. Many bushmen were seriously maimed and even killed in the effort. Peter apprised me of one who was crushed by a rolling log. Barely still breathing, his felling crew sounded their horn to the hills and summoned others to help carry him out. Sadly, the bushman's heart gave out sometime during the thirty-seven-hour travail on a litter to the nearest town. Not only dangerous, a bushman's life was crude and nasty. In the 1850s they lived in squalor. Peter pulled out pictures of crude "raupo," or thatched, shanties, for it wasn't until decades later that bushman had canvas tents. In general they lived and logged in a region beset by endless dreary rainy days. Bushmen drank scummy water from muddy streams, pissed in by those on the slope above. After a hard day's work, they ate sparse coarse fare, mostly just bread and bacon, and if lucky, slept on crude grass mattresses and had a kerosene lantern to read by.

I then asked Peter about seeing some great kauri, for such trees are extremely rare now in New Zealand, a land fairly cut and cleared. He directed me down the road to two sites. So after leaving the museum late in the afternoon, my first stop was the nearby Kauri Bushman Memorial Park, a place dedicated to Rob and all his fellow loggers. A special gated entrance, for biosecurity, forces you to brush your boots and then rinse their soles with a disinfectant before entering the park, for a root rot is now ravaging the remaining kauri today. But here at last I found a living forest, and along the park's boardwalk I gazed up at great spectacled trunks, whose bark reminded me of poplars at home. I wandered there among a beautiful stand of mature, but not ancient, kauri trees. Intense clusters of epiphytes covered nearly every branch, and the soaring trees resonated with beckoning calls of endemic tuis, bellbirds, and the "coos" of New Zealand pigeon. The tui and bellbird are native passerines, the first the size and color of a grackle with a distinctive white tuft on its throat and mellifluous trill of descending whistles. The second is a greenish-yellow species, smaller in size, with a lovely liquid call. The pigeon is a gorgeous large purplish irridescent dove with a starkly contrasting white abdomen. Altogether, with the forest and the birds, I was plunged into a rare slice of native New Zealand.

Spellbound, I was also struck by the distance then, pausing to contemplate how incredibly far Rob had been from home. He had been here, fourteen thousand miles by sea from Baltimore, in an era with no communication, or expectation of any, with all those he knew left so far behind. When cutting kauri in the area, he had bonded with strangers unknown, far beyond any civilization, and with no clear vision of his future. Seemingly lost, he undertook unbelievably backbreaking and hazardous work, endeavors he as likely might not have survived. In such light, I wondered if even unbeknownst to him this may have been the apex of his arc, the point where he ultimately began his homeward journey.

Too exhausted to drive much farther that afternoon, ten miles down the road I checked in at the historic, but very seedy, Maungaturoto Hotel. With threadbare rugs, stained walls, tiny rooms, and a shared bathroom, I was sure I would awake blessed with fleas or bedbugs. Worse was to come. After a dinner of fish and chips, only saved by ample amber Red Lion beer, I headed early to bed. Lying on my thin lumpy mattress, the fading sun still bathing the room, a crowd of local chain-smoking Māoris began a pool tournament in the bar downstairs. With clacking balls and shouted jests, the scene degraded as they shortly began singing the choruses, awfully but gleefully, in karaoke style to every lousy 1980s rock song. It lasted until 2:00 a.m. If I could have left I would have; if my car had been larger, I would have slept in it.

The next morning, I fled at first light, heading south to see the second stand of kauri, this one allegedly with a few remaining giants. Not only were these along my route to Rob's next stop, but they were near Warkworth, the town I estimated Rob most likely logged near. There, on the south side of town, I found Parry Kauri Park, and in an empty parking lot at 7:30 a.m., to my amazement I was met by two grizzled seniors, members of the Kauri Bushman's Association. They seem to manage the park or, like retirees elsewhere, embellish their later years under that supposition. They appreciated my small donation into a box and happily pointed me into the park, which indeed features a pair of huge kauris. Massive giants, fifty or more feet in circumference, the two are named for the site's first owner, a Rev. McKinney, and the subsequent one, Simpson. Each comparable to a giant drive-thru California sequoia, the trees are surrounded by a twenty-one-acre grove of smaller, but still mature, kauri. The rising sun lifted steam from the dew-glittered pastures around, and again tui and bellbirds sang in the forest. I reveled in being there. These kauri were true behemoths in situ, and their immensity shed light on the grueling nature of Rob's endeavors as a bushman. After two hours in the resplendent grove, with much still to do and places to go, I left the kauri to continue my quest that day, but with a feeling of great appreciation for the trees, their sacred nature, and some real insight into Rob's work as a kauri bushman.

After Rob had been logging the kauri about a year and a half, he began noticing that, whenever they made a trip into Auckland, the harbor was "filled with shipping" and everyone he met seemed excited about the "wonderful news" from the Melbourne goldfields. So Rob and his "band of brothers" returned to Auckland in late 1855, just as gold rush fever was building to its height.

He then took a quick run on the *Dolores* between Auckland and Sydney to earn some money, barely surviving a typhoon. However, the demons again ensnared him when he returned to New Zealand, and most of his money was "soon gone in the same way in which all my previous earnings had disappeared." It was during this time in Auckland that Rob purchased a small polyglot Bible.[6] Found in the same black leather trunk as the other papers, the book is six inches tall and three-and-a-half inches wide, with beautifully drawn maps of the ancient Mideast inside. The print is tiny, and when I try to read it and decipher Rob's scrawls in the margins, I must use a magnifying glass. How Rob could have read it in the light of a logging camp or later in the forward hold of the *Isaac Howland* while bouncing around at sea is beyond my comprehension. On the forest-green frontispiece, bold black cursive announces that it is Robert W. Armstrong's Bible, purchased on October 7, 1855, in Auckland, which he notes in his tale was "before leaving for Hawke's Bay." Bible in hand, somewhere in Auckland that October, he met "a young Scotchman" who suggested that Rob accompany him and his wife to Hawke's Bay on North Island. Having visited the area previously on the *Antelope*, and given that the Scotsman assured Rob he'd find work in the soft pine forests there, Rob concurred. With that, he headed south into what then was the deep dark verdant dominion of the Māoris. In 2022, I followed.

With "faces carved with deep blue and black scrolls and curved lines,"[7] the fiercely tattooed Māori were, to Rob, seemingly the scariest natives he had encountered. Reverend W. Yate, a missionary in the 1840s, said of the Māori that "some of them had their beards plastered with red ochre and oil; others, with blue clay and a deep mark of red ochre over each eye, which, together with the tattooing, gives them the most ferocious aspect."[8] In fact, Rob and his mates were quite fortunate to have settled where and when they did. He arrived after the brutal Musket Wars of the 1820s and 1830s and before the Māori uprising in the 1860s.[9] Luckily, Rob was more explicit about his second sojourn in logging. In Hawke's Bay they ventured to the lovely region around the town of Wairoa (pronounced "y-oh-rraa"). The town derived its name from the river, which the Māori called *Te Wairoa Hopupu Honengenenge Matangi Rau*, meaning "long frothy swirling river." Here, Rob and his unnamed Scottish mate cut timber under the guidance of a then-established trader, William Lockwood. He, in turn, worked closely with a local Māori chief who was one of the friendliest toward the pakehas, as Westerners are known.

Perhaps scary to behold, but arguably the most culturally advanced of the many Polynesians Rob encountered, the Māori were a young civilization. At the end of a million years of human dispersal, New Zealand was the last large landmass to be colonized. Evidence indicates Polynesians arrived in great seafaring canoes around AD 1200, just as Angkor Wat was being built, Europe was gathering for the Crusades, and the Magna Carta was about to be cantankerously signed by King John at Runnymede. The Māori then had just five hundred years of cultural evolution between their arrival in New Zealand and the first visits by Europeans. In that period, they developed a unique society similar to sustainable cultures of indigenous people we know on other continents. To Western eyes, they lived more like the Iroquois or Lakota in North America than the Tongans or Samoans they had left behind, and their homes and storehouses were decorated with carved faces as beautiful and ornate as those made by the Haida or Tlingit.

For most of their time before the European invasion, the Māori were at peace. There were plenty of fish and giant moas to eat, the valleys were fertile, and the forests full of timber. The island was large enough for all. There was a far greater need to be mutually helpful than to be competitive. Families grew into clans, and clans merged through marriage to become tribes.

With an infusion of domesticated farm animals and crop cultivars provided by Captain Cook's visit in 1769, the Māori's agricultural prowess flowered. Though sadly the infusion of these species also initiated a massive degradation and destruction of the island's native ecosystems. In any event, the Māori populace shifted from a shoreline existence and marine dependency to increasingly living along interior river valleys where it was easier to grow crops and raise livestock. With more time and food at hand, Māori culture flourished, but it also became competitive. Then just as the pakehas arrived, the increasing human density, concurrent with the first brush with limited resources, led to heightened friction. Intertribal competition exploded and a rather bellicose society evolved. Why this happened continues to be a major subject of academic debate. It's likely the savage fights for territory were simply competitive, but apparently they were often triggered as retribution for social slights. To initially address the growing number of intertribal attacks, more and larger forts, or *pas*, were added around each village. Simultaneously, the great beauty and economic values of New Zealand began to attract larger numbers of pakeha traders, whalers, and sealers. These intrepid vistors came to visit, but then began to stay, and they brought guns.

Years of intertribal warfare suddenly accelerated with new technology, and the era became known as the Musket Wars. One tribe would gather a few muskets earned in trade from the pakehas and then attack another tribe to take their land, possessions, and even human assets. In the Hawke's Bay region where Wairoa lies and Rob went, a northern tribe, the Tuhoe, "visited [the area] during their devastating southern raids between 1818 and 1824, [and] they took back prisoners to the Bay of Islands. Many of the captives were slain and eaten; the others were distributed as slaves among the northern chiefs."[10] The Hawke's Bay region was devastated and nearly depopulated. Across North Island, constant warfare almost overwhelmed society. Māori clans, or *iwis*, shifted from a relatively peaceful and sustainable coexistence to one devoted to acquiring arms and aggressively engaging their neighbors. Used to make rope, flax was the most prized trading item, and it garnered more muskets from the Europeans. Conquered clans were then enslaved and put to work in the flax fields.

In a truly twisted facet of these wars, the Māori began to cash in on their enemies' heads. Historically, in victory Māori had occasionally preserved and displayed heads of their enemies' leaders as a testament to their success and a mark of derision for the losers. However, when they found that some pakehas would trade guns or goods for these shrunken and tanned trophy heads, the market drastically shifted. Not only were heads now more widely taken as trophies in battle, but some captured warriors were then tattooed with patterns chosen to please the purchaser. Like choosing a live lobster in a restaurant for dinner, the captured and now-tattooed Māori were subsequently killed and their shrunken heads sold to the buyer.

Eventually, a number of Māori realized that these wars were not only a grossly injudicious practice among themselves, but had also caused them to foolishly play into the pakehas' hand. Fortunately, missionaries, who began arriving in considerable numbers during the 1830s, forged a unique coevolutionary bond among their two cultures. As more missionaries established themselves, an increasing number of Māori sought their help in finding a more peaceful path forward. In just a few years, with more and more Māori converting to Christianity, the missionaries began to intervene among the Māori factions and brought the Musket Wars to a close. In addition, with their conversion, the missionaries also began standing up for the Māori and protecting them from the onslaught of land-theft by the pakehas. The missionaries forced their own countrymen, and ultimately the British government, to reckon more fairly with the Māori in trade and land deals.

Nonetheless, the pakeha invasion, largely English, continued from afar, and the British government could no longer restrain their own citizens fleeing the Industrial Revolution and attracted to the promises of New Zealand's spectacular landscape, bountiful waters, and lush valleys. Soon they overwhelmed the missionaries, and by the end of the 1830s, the British government became truly concerned.

To address the invasion and the asymmetric cultural relationship, the Treaty of Waitangi was signed in 1840 between some 540 Māori chiefs and the "Crown." In the treaty, the Māori ceded the sovereignty of their land to the Crown and gave the Crown an exclusive right to buy lands they wished to sell. In return, the Crown promised to guarantee Māori ownership of the lands, forests, fisheries, and other possessions they held at the time, and uniquely among its colonies, the indigenous Māori were made full British citizens. In addition, the British government promised to supervise any future land transactions, keeping the Māoris' best interests at heart. Of course, as the Crown's best intentions were conceptualized more than twelve thousand miles away, but enforced locally, as with indigenous peoples elsewhere, the Māori continued to be hoodwinked, cheated, and deprived of vast tracts of their lands.

After leaving Warkworth, toward this region with its rich history, I headed. I paused that afternoon at the Pukorokonoro Miranda Shorebird Centre along the way and spent the night in a quiet hotel in Turangi. The next morning I drove south in heavy rain. The windshield wipers barely beat back the drops such that I could see the road. Eyes fixed on the broken white line, it took hours to reach the great Te Urewera. Comprised of several ranges, this mountainous region, roughly one hundred miles east to west and thirty miles north to south, is the largest tract of wilderness left on North Island. It is also the home of the Māori Ngai Tuhoe tribe, known as "Children of the Mist." The area's lush, craggy mountaintops surround deep valleys wreathed with low clouds, and the sound of running water is pervasive. The steep slopes are covered with a broadleaf forest dominated by the Tawa, a magnolia-like tree, the Pukatea, of the same family, and the Kohekohe, which is similar to a mahogany.[11] Occasional stands of the conifer Rob cut, the kahikatea, are mixed in. Called a white pine locally, the kahikatea looks like a huge and ancient cedar tree. Each one I saw was covered in swarms of epiphytes, some as big as pineapple plants while others you could fit in your hand. Underneath this soaring canopy is a seemingly endless shrub layer of gorgeous tree ferns, a plant whose aesthetics are unparalleled. In the forest, the ever-present din of falling water is periodically punctuated by beautiful bell-like calls or ventriloquil "zzzttts" of the island's native birds. For nearly sixty years Te Urewera was a national park, then awakening to their citizenship and newfound political self-realization, the Māori pushed back and, citing the Treaty of Waitangi, their legal pact with the Crown, had it disestablished. Now this jewel, while still in most ways a national park, is in fact administered by a board comprised of Ngai Tuhoe and Crown members. New Zealand is still immersed in growing pains.

Entering Te Urewera south of Turangi on Route 38, the rain stopped just as I crossed the Huiarau Range under lingering dark clouds. I drove on a hair-raising gravel road through this incredible ecosystem. Generally following the Waiau River, the narrow road curved through tight turns up and down steep gorges. I drove slowly, but after several hours I began to feel completely isolated and then rather apprehensive. With a flat I might be stuck for hours, with a missed turn I might plunge, unbeknownst to anyone, far down into a gorge. I began to wonder if I was even on the right road. Thankfully I had filled up with gas in Murupara and after five hours, and with deep relief, at last I came to Lake Waikaremoana. There I took a break and some Motrin to ease the tension that gripped my back and neck and had left me with white knuckles. I hiked for a couple of miles on a well-maintained gravel trail to Lake Whakamarino, a smaller lake that feeds the great one. As I hiked along, my being relaxed, zen returned. Soon I realized that every other arboreal giant seemed to have a bellbird lurking in its midst calling out to the world. Shining cuckoos, newly returned from their winter home in the Solomon Islands and resplendent in their emerald coats, were quarrelling with each other for territories. I paused frequently along the trail to gaze up in admiration at the spectacular dripping verdant canopy. Flashing fantails, a small warbler-sized bird with a spectacular tail, displayed and entertained me. Supported by massive trunks, the forest giants formed an ancient ecological temple. I was captivated by the sheer beauty of the forest; and struck by the ironic contrast that it was the very type of forest that Rob dedicated several years of his life to cutting down.

An hour or so later, I was back in the car wending my way down to the lower slopes to my second intersection with Rob in New Zealand. Alongside the road, the various streams converged to form Waiau River, and together we descended toward Frasertown. To step back; I knew from Rob's description that a few miles up the Wairoa River from Hawke's Bay, lay the town of Wairoa. Here Rob and his unnamed Scottish partner and wife had met and taken direction from William Lockwood and the Māori chief Paora te Apatu, alias Paul Argeri, before heading to their assigned logging location a few more miles upstream at the first tributary: Waiau River. The junction where the Waiau joins the Wairoa is where Frasertown stands today, and it was my first stop.

I paused here again, now in pouring rain, where the two muddy streams converge, where a muddy gravel road crosses a stout cement bridge, and where several dozen little houses lay scattered in a village that might be almost anywhere on earth. I immersed myself for the moment in the place. Rob had lived and worked here for two-plus years. The site neatly matched Rob's description; the floodplain is flat and true surrounding the stream itself, and the land rises nearby into rolling hills, now covered with long grasses. In the distance, behind me and to the north, the great ranges of the Te Urewera, from which I had just come, loomed. That day, the Waiau was frothing madly, fresh from the rain I had driven through. Filled with grayish clay-sized sediment, the water swirled downstream with an opaque silvery hue, colored like glacial outwash. The hills around were crisscrossed with low barbwire fences and each section was filled with sheep or lowing cattle, while the only trees near at hand were a dozen huge weeping willows lining the streambank.

The great visual discontinuity in time, between the forest that had been on the site in Rob's day and the cleared pastures now, didn't really matter, for I was here; today. I had returned along his path to a fairly precise spot, 160 years after he left. I felt his presence in the cold rain then, standing beside me. I pictured him thinking it an imprudent mission, a solipsistic goal, but then I knew he would have cracked a smile, chuckled at my audacity, and mostly been moved that someone still cared. I broke out my stashed bottle of Laphroaig, sat on a fence line in the pouring rain, and hoisted a peaty toast to him. I drank to his life, to his run in the great game, and to his progeny. Then I hoisted a second, with respect to all the roads, trepidations, and dreams we both sorted through to be here, my success in an epic ten-thousand-mile mission to find him, and our convergence in time and space. The rain eased, and as the sun popped out just above the western horizon, I went down the road to Wairoa itself, where I spent the night in a nice quiet motel.

When the first cock crowed, I hastily scrambled in the predawn light to walk over to the bridge that crosses the Wairoa River in the center of town. Downstream, to the east, under the timid glare of the rising sun, the swirling, gray-hued waters headed to the sea. Behind me, there was Lockwood Point on the south bank of the river, marked by several great Norfolk Island Pines and a new corrugated steel building used by a local boating club. On the north side of the river, just across the river, stood Takitimu Marae, a historic Māori temple. While Lockwood Point had been the home of Rob's trader friend, and the one who introduced him to Paora te Apatu, Takitimu Marae was built on the site where Paora te Apatu and his cochief, Topu, lived and had erected their pa. That morning, the tall meetinghouse, white on the outside with great dark red carved columns bracketing its front, soared in the morning's lemon light amid a great meadow shiny with dew.

From fairly decent records[12] I gleaned a number of facts regarding both the Māoris and the first pakehas in the region. One of the four Māori tribes, or iwis, in Hawke's Bay was led by an ancient warrior, Te Apatu. Descended from Kahungunu and Ruatapuwahine, Te Apatu was famous for a dramatic escape in a canoe sometime in the 1820s during the Musket Wars. Then as early as 1837, a trader, Joel Polack, noted that a horse previously brought to the region by a pakeha was then in possession of Chief Apatu of Wairoa. Te Apatu was also known to have had at least two children, a daughter Rawinia, and a son Paora, called Paul by the pakehas. Then just two years before Rob's arrival, Chief Te Apatu died by drowning in 1853. Allegedly his trading vessel got caught on the sandbar entering the river and he was lost.

When Rob arrived in Wairoa in 1855, Te Apatu's son, now a young chief, was also a trader and was the commander of the *Tere*, a small trading vessel that "supplied Napier dinner tables with apples, peaches, pears and watermelons," all of which makes sense in context of his relationship with Lockwood and dealings with Rob. From other sources, we also know that in 1855, the two leading chiefs in the district, Pitihera Kopu and Paroa Te Apatu, chose a Christianized Māori, Tamihana Huata, to teach them the new religion, Christianity. We also know that years later, the Takitimu Marae, the marae I gazed upon from the bridge in Wairoa, was built on the site where they resided. Māori recollections have it that the first marae was erected at their pa, Te Hatepe. Then after the unrest in the 1860s, the marae was abandonded and mysteriously burnt to the ground. Years later elders encouraged the re-erection of the meetinghouse and in 1926 one leader, Hata Tipoki, took charge of the construction. So today, the elaborate carvings of Takitimu Marae stand on that spot and tell the history of the Ngati Kahungunu.

A decade after Rob's departure, records show Paora te Apatu facilitating a series of land deals in the late 1860s and mid-1870s with Donald McLean and the Crown, and indeed he is credited, or perhaps reviled, with selling the land on which Wairoa now stands in 1866. Paora then sided with the pakehas and stood up against the rebellious Māoris during the "troubles," but along the way and perhaps due to his close relationships with pakehas, he apparently lost his influence, for in the campaign against the rebel leader Te Kooti in 1868, Paora could muster only twenty-five warriors. After that he recedes in history, though he supposedly died in October 1875.[13] We also know that Paul's older sister, Rawinia, married a pakeha whaler, William Christy, and her close ties with pakehas were reflected in her obituary. She was allegedly over a hundred years old when she died in 1909. The papers recognized that "her many deeds of kindness to the early settlers do not die with her, for they live in the memories of some now living here, who knew her well and appreciated her deeds."[14] Sadly though, it is clear from Rawinia's obituary that neither she nor Paul had any children, for she was listed as the last of her line.

Regarding the pakehas, we know that Captain John Harris is credited with being the first to settle in Hawke's Bay. He arrived in 1831 on his trading schooner in the midst of the Musket Wars. Like the Pilgrims landing amid a decimated Patuxet village, as his party was armed they inherently conferred protection on their new Māori neighbors, and so were welcomed. Harris established a trading post in Wairoa where trading for flax was paramount. We also know that more flax traders began to trickle into the area in the early 1840s, paying the Māoris for their boarding and transportation with blankets, shirts, and tobacco.[15] At the same time, while other missionaries had stopped by, Reverend James Hamlin and his wife were the first to settle in Wairoa, and they came to stay in 1844.

In his tale, Rob thought William Lockwood arrived in Wairoa around 1842 or so. He was known as *Wiremu Piriwhirri Taura*, roughly translated as "William who makes rope." Whether Lockwood was Harris's agent or a competitor is unknown, but in reminisces about Wairoa given in 1936, an old-timer recollected, "The first settlers in Wairoa were the Lockwoods, the Spooners and the Coopers, who traded with the Māoris and sold them moleskin trousers, monkey coats (i.e. short coats) and American shirts."[16] I could not actually find him documented until 1851, when Lockwood is mentioned in a legal claim against him for a share of whaling profits.[17] It appears apart from being a trader, Lockwood supplemented his income as a part-time whaler on a boat based on the Mahia Peninsula. He then appears for years in the Electoral Rolls, through the 1860s. By then, William Lockwood has a "freehold" house on an acre of land in Wairoa, a wife, and two children. Lockwood's house and trading post were presumably near what is today still known as Lockwood's Point on the west side of town. After Rob's departure, sometime in the 1860s, Lockwood appears to have moved south to Napier, and a few years later, upon his death in 1869, he is listed as having been a boatbuilder by Napier's curator of estates.

Rob's arrival in Wairoa late in 1853 also coincided with the arrival and rise of Donald McLean in the region.[18] Donald McLean had come to New Zealand in 1840, via Australia, from his home in Scotland. He initially cut timber and managed a trading schooner on the Waihou River, south of Auckland. There he learned Māori and immersed himself in their culture. As a forester, he was comfortable in the bush, and with his language skills he was soon recognized for his ability to sensitively "arrange" matters between Māoris and settlers. In 1844 he was appointed to the Protectorate of Aborigines and achieved considerable success in resolving a number of conflicts. When that political office was eradicated, given his talents, he was then appointed police inspector in Taranaki, a town one hundred miles east of Hawke's Bay. Over time, McLean was recognized for administering firm and fair justice, as he identified closely with hardworking bush settlers but was contemptuous of the "drunken blackguards" who offended his Scottish morality. His career prospered, and by 1848, a few years before Rob's arrival, he returned to the Hawke's Bay region to lead land purchase negotiations for the government.

Visiting Wairoa in January 1851, McLean described the land as "rich and fertile," and later as "well suited for pasture and agriculture." He observed there were about two thousand Māori in the area, and that they were in favor of selling some land. However, because of "the numerous tribes on the river," he wanted to purchase only one side of the river, for he was concerned about not leaving sufficient land for Māori. He hoped to minimize future problems "as our cattle and sheep would destroy their crops, creating trouble." In order to avoid future difficulties he informed the pakehas there of his intention to purchase only one side of the Wairoa River and ascertained that the southern bank could "be easily purchased."[19] All of which matches the fact that today downtown Wairoa and Lockwood Point lie on the south bank of the river, while the Māoris' marae is on the north side.

By Rob's arrival in 1853 Donald McLean was the chief land purchase commissioner. As McLean was Scottish, focused on Hawke's Bay, and worked closely with the Māoris, he likely was a linchpin in setting up Rob and his unnamed Scottish friend and wife with Lockwood and Paora te Apatu. Later, well after Rob's departure from the area in 1857, McLean rose higher in the government to become a minister, though his record is now viewed with mixed feelings. On one hand, for all his land deals he has been credited as being one of the most honest pakehas and a friend to the Māoris, while on the other hand, the volume of these deals has also been blamed in part for the Māori revolt in the 1860s.

In the quiet of the early hour, gazing up river, contemplations of Rob's journey were reflected in the river. Like Pooh sticks they swept past, untarnished by the rising sun. With the marae marking Paora te

Apatu's homesite to the right, and Lockwood Point to the left, Rob's historical reality welled up within. For a moment I again felt his luminous presence and was transmogrified by the act of accomplishing something that I never actually thought would happen. On one hand I did realize my trip was a rather self-absorbent act, a rationalization for a reason to visit a distant place, but on the other, I felt a deep connection. Standing on the bridge, straddling two universes, I appreciated the tangible elements of the moment. I heard my sister then; she, one who has always believed in the afterlife and spirits, encouraging me to accept a familial contact from another dimension. I could hear her telling me that I was at a special intersection, like a wormhole in time and space, and that I should embrace the moment and accept my intersection with our great-great-grandfather, such as it was.

The sun then moved above the horizon and its glare erased the mood. I drove into town, and after a desperately needed coffee and two donuts from Osler's Bakery, I then wove my way slowly through the rest of Wairoa's sleepy streets. First, east along Marine Parade, the street paralleling the river, past an array of vaguely Victorian-style government-looking buildings, then turning south I followed the bend in the river down Kopu Road. At its end, marked by a dusty and littered turnaround, lay the mouth of the river. Here, exactly as Rob had described, two great bars of black volcanic sand emanated from each side of the river and reached out towards each other. Between the two sandbars, each shouldering a great array of tree trunks and debris, a narrow breach swirled as the river met flooding tidal waters. Gulls and terns flew above, calling, and I marveled again at the convergence of reality and Rob's manuscript.

CHAPTER 22

The Cannibals of Fiji

AFTER THREE YEARS OF LOGGING IN THE "BUSH," AND WITH SOME prodding from the Māoris, it was at last time for Rob to head home. Leaving Wairoa behind, Rob headed to Auckland in November 1857. Rob still had not left his demons behind, and he blamed himself for his inability to live as virtuously as he thought he ought. However, he still felt it was time to go. So after "wandering up and down the streets of Auckland in a most miserable state of mind," he shortly found himself outbound on the whaler *Isaac Howland* under Captain Reuben Hobbs.

Reuben Hobbs was born in Rhinebeck, New York, a small town on the lower Hudson River, in 1819 and grew up to be an inveterate sea dog.[1] It is evident from reading his log, how he handled his crew, and in his career later in life that he was a straightforward and stern person. When the *Isaac Howland* left Nantucket on this voyage, Reuben and his wife, Delia, had just had a baby girl, Ann. After the ship's return with Rob in June 1859, and poignantly characteristic of those times, Reuben spent little time at home. Instead he left on his next voyage just more than a year later in August 1860, going back to sea as captain of the ship *Norman*. While he was away this time, Delia died of diphtheria, and so for the next three and a half years, relatives brought up their daughter. When he returned in July 1865, Reuben wasted little time and soon married a forty-three-year-old widow, Susan Pease. She was the daughter of well-known Nantucketians Captain John Harper Pease and Mary Bunker Pease, and had been a mere twenty-two when she wed her first husband in 1844, the boatbuilder Allen Hinckley of Barnstable, Massachusetts.

Just a few years after they married, Allen suddenly died, leaving Susan with two young sons. After their marriage, Susan looked after her and Reuben's combined families until he retired from his life at sea in the 1870s. Thereafter, the family stayed on Nantucket; he worked in the lighthouse service as assistant keeper at Great Point Lighthouse, and later he was the keeper of the light at Polpis. He eventually passed away in their home on Union Street in 1905, at the ripe old age of eighty-six, and Susan followed the next year, aged eighty-four.

Fortunately, Captain Hobbs kept a log of his voyage on the *Isaac Howland*.[2] So, in parallel with Rob's remembrances of the trip home, Captain Hobbs's log confirmed a number of items and was used to embellish a few scenes from the return voyage. Picking up the tale as he interesects with Rob, on January 10, 1858, Captain Hobbs wrote that they had anchored off Tapeka Point in the Bay of Islands, where four crew members immediately deserted the ship. Several days later, as they were then in the harbor resupplying, seven more crew members were legitimately discharged. When the ship was almost ready to sail, three additional crew members, who were injured and in the hospital, were cut loose with $30 of pay each. So, to fill as many of these slots as he could, on January 15th, 1858, Captain Hobbs then shipped ten new crew members, including Rob. Given that there was a near mutiny on the outbound trip, and the high turnover in Auckland as noted, one might reasonably doubt Captain Hobbs's leadership capabilities.

Now aboard the *Isaac Howland*, they sailed north to whale among the line islands. In May 1858, Rob and the other crew members sight land ahead, which proves to be Cantab, one of the Fiji Islands, around which Captain Hobbs said they would spend most of their time for the remainder of the year. The newspaper *The Friend* confirms the timing as it reports the *Isaac Howland* as being off the "Feejees" in June 1858, forty-two months out and with 1,300 barrels of sperm oil on board.[3] While on Cantab, they learned "that our two Cantab islanders, who had jumped overboard, had actually succeeded in swimming to land, but not to their own island, and that in conformity with the custom of these islands, they were killed and eaten."

Rob's casual tone here makes it almost possible to skim over the two intertwined and truly horrific events that took place—events that certainly weren't unique among whalers. The stark truth is that after unhappy sailors deserted his ship, Captain Hobbs kidnapped two unwitting islanders and forced them aboard; a capital crime. Then, culturally isolated, their hair cut off, and made to undertake hard labor, they are of course totally terrified. After just twenty days, the Cantabians threw themselves overboard, gambling that they could swim an amazing distance to shore. They in fact survived a thirty-plus-mile swim, but were then killed and eaten because they had the bad luck to land on an island that wasn't their own. Cannibalism was still fairly common in the Fijis.

Much of what we know about the Fiji Islands at that time comes from the same graphic memoir by Mary Davis Wallis that we referenced earlier, based on her time amid her husband's large trading network around the islands.[4] Having heard in advance of the cannibalistic reputation of the Fijians, Mary wisely endeavored to keep her distance from them, yet she remained immersed enough in their society to report on it with considerable depth. She described the Fijians as "robust people with straight black hair, a broad forehead, and thick lips. The countenances of the men are much disfigured by their practice of tattooing. The females tattoo their lips only." Yet, she was still clearly taken by the inherent beauty of the people and described the wife of one of the chiefs as "Rather fleshy, but [she] has a fine eye and handsome features, her hair was nicely dressed and powdered with the ashes of the burnt bread fruit leaves."

A significant portion of Mary's book recounts harrowing stories of cannibalism, and her observations are testimony to Rob's hearsay. To her credit, Mary was astute enough to recognize that the horrible events she witnessed were ultimately about politics, tribal power, and personal intrigues. She wrote, "it is my wish to show the Feejeans as I found them and to record truly their several traits of character as they came under my own observation. Little has been known of this people, except that they are cannibals." However, after such a seemingly sensitive prelude, she unleashes with, "It is said that there is not one of the natives . . . over five years of age that has not eaten human flesh. The hands of the slain are given to the children to eat."

Ultimately, Mary realized that cannibalism was mostly practiced after a battle between villagers or as a consequence of some injustice. After a fight, some of the slain would be carried home by the victors and then cooked and distributed among the village as a symbol of power. At other times, individuals were slain in retribution for some societal affront and their fate was consumption, a political tactic no different than the gibbets and stakes of Medieval Europe, though admittedly with an odd gastronomic twist. Cannibalism of Westerners was usually in retribution for an awful deed. In one horrid case, four beachcombers, one of whom Mary had known, had killed a Fijian woman and then kidnapped her young daughter. A young chief, Otima, ultimately retrieved the girl through some political bartering. However, the beachcombers soon hunted down Otima, put him in chains, and pressured the village to return the young girl to them. After learning of this, a number of islanders united to help. Rowing swiftly across the lagoon, the islanders caught up with the four escaping beachcombers and surrounded their canoe. The Fijians told the kidnappers they would not be killed if they immediately handed the chief and the girl back to them. The sailors, realizing they were completely outnumbered, complied.

In fact, all had not been forgiven. Later that night, while the beachcombers slept offshore in their canoe, thinking they were safe, several Fijians silently swam out to the canoe and soundlessly pulled it to shore. When the canoe ground into the sand on the beach, the beachcombers jumped up in surprise as the islanders swiftly attacked. Three of the beachcombers were killed immediately, but the fourth, Harry, the one Mary Wallis had met, "was wounded in the leg and taken ashore with the bodies of his companions." "The next day he was obliged to witness the horrible feast and listen to the praises bestowed upon the flesh of his friends." Mary recounted; "The next day they took off his leg and obliged him to sit and see that devoured. On the third day they finished him. My heart sickens while I record these horrible truths." Papers in the region reported that the case was brought before the British consul in 1848, and he declined to pursue arrests or a court case against the islanders.

He wrote that "upon investigation, there was reason to believe that the foreigners had given some provocation which led to these tragical proceedings."[5]

Naturally, missionaries worked hard to halt this practice, but even as late as 1854 it was still occurring sporadically. One missionary wrote that, in their presence, "in defiance of British and American Sloops of War, in spite of our promises to enrich them, five of the most intelligent and lady-like women were strangled in honor of the old cannibal Tanoa! This has fearfully revived the horrid custom."[6] Fortunately, this was near the conclusion of the gruesome epicurean practice.

CHAPTER 23

Gales of Amundsen's Sea

AFTER FIJI, THE *ISAAC HOWLAND*'S NORTHWARD ARC DREW TO A CLOSE and Captain Hobbs turned her back toward New Zealand and then home. Sailing eastward across the wide Pacific, Rob wrote of the voyage, "Sometimes in good weather and with fair winds, at other times beating about against heavy seas and adverse gales." Oddly though, Rob glossed over most of the details of this long stretch, focusing instead on his epiphany. While Rob was preoccupied with his god, the *Isaac Howland* had a much tougher passage. Captain Hobbs's logbook sheds more light on this part of the journey.[1] When the captain declared they were "homeward bound" on February 12, 1859, the *Isaac Howland* was 520 miles northeast of Auckland, due south of Sunday Island. From that time onward, the ship never went north, nor paused to search for whales. Instead, the captain kept her far in the southern latitudes, sailing ten degrees south of the Tropic of Capricorn. He set course directly for Chile from New Zealand, and five weeks later, on March 23, when they saw some right whales they were 2,400 miles west of Santiago.

Things turned nasty as they edged evermore into the Amundsen Sea, and then toward Bellingshausen Sea off Antarctica's coast. On March 26, the captain noted the beginning of a "heavy gale" from the west, for which they took in all sails, except the double-reefed fore and main topsails. Later in the afternoon, the shrieking winds buried their rails in the whipped seas. Tossed by colossal rollers whose tops were a frothing spume, the captain's log, reflecting his terse style, noted it was difficult to "get enough grub down" at dinner—an observation you might expect from a greenhand, but not from a briny veteran. It must have been truly wretched.

The storm continued overnight. The next morning, Captain Hobbs observed the seas were "as heavy as she could possibly take." How the terrified men slept during such a pounding is painful to ponder; slamming against the ship's ribs in their bunks as waves swept the deck before pouring coldly down the hatches. At five bells, the seas tore off the starboard boat. The waist boat went next. Before dark, they were forced to close-reef the main topsail. What terror to ascend the ratlines then. The gale continued into the second night and well through the following morning, before finally moderating slightly. At this point, the captain ordered a reef taken out of the foresail and topsails. Too quickly, it would seem, for the wind soon "carried" the sails away and busted a stay, sending a tremor up the mainmast. The impact of this event is noticeable in Rob's preserved map, which depicts the ship's sudden southern declination then. On March 29, the winds at last gave way to a fog and drizzle, and for the next two days they continued east, now about a thousand miles from the Horn.

With barely a rest, another gale struck on April 1. In the afternoon, as the crew took in the foresail, another stay snapped. The howling winds then shredded a topsail. This storm continued through the next day. It broke several more stays, and the captain then had the crew reef nearly all the sails. Without sufficient stays, the masts would surely snap. While not getting blown backward, or luckily too far off course, the storm markedly slowed their progress. Driving the ship deeper south, the *Isaac Howland* rode out the storm, bow to the wind, the crews' hands likely clasped in prayer.

The ship enjoyed decent enough weather for the next few days so the crew could make some repairs and resume forward progress. Then, on April 8, when they were still 350 miles west of the Horn, essentially parallel to Punta Arenas, a third gale pummeled them. By noon that day they were in Force 10 winds and had taken in nearly all their sails. The captain brusquely reported "tremendous seas." Terrifying cobalt waves now rolled by high above the rails, their tops hissing off. This storm passed, too, and Captain Hobbs noted a "moderate breeze" at dawn by April 10. They rounded the Horn on April 13, and Captain Hobbs ecstatically marked the event with bold handwriting in his log's margin.

After gaining the Atlantic, the *Isaac Howland* steered northeast, straight for New Bedford. Skirting the Falklands well east, they saw fin whales almost every day, but the whales were too fast to bother with. Buoyed by strong breezes, they continued making good progress until five hundred miles south of Montevideo, when the captain's log recounted another heavy gale on April 21st. This one must have been one of the worst, for the captain noted the barometer dropped to a low of 28½ inches, roughly a Category 3 hurricane.

Near three bells, the wind switched directions instantly, as it does in the eye of a hurricane, causing the ship to nearly broach. As she heeled hard over in the raging seas, the bow slammed into a great wave and the forward-most sails plunged into the seas. With their bellies filled with water, and the sails' weight now at odds with their forward motion, the jibboom snapped and the fore-topsail boom was ripped off. With the jibboom being an extension of the bowsprit, to which a number of stays for the forward rigging were attached, chaos ensued. The *Isaac Howland* skewed amid the roaring breakers as the crew scrambled to pull in the tangled rigging. They finally managed to lash the shattered gear to the deck, and totally exhausted and soaked, the men slunk below to their bunks. Once the storm passed, the crew then spent the next two weeks making repairs as best they could. They jury-rigged the booms and re-spliced the severed stays as they slowly continued north.

At last, two months later on June 25, they picked up a pilot off New Bedford, and the next morning slipped into port. Before daylight, the "land sharks" were already on board in such numbers that "only with the greatest difficulty" could Rob's crew "get our sails clewed up and furled." By noon they were on shore, and Rob bid goodbye to the old ship that had been his home. After buying a decent suit of shore clothes, Rob and his friend Whitmarsh boarded at the house of Steven Spooner; likely the retired skipper of the pilot ship *Fawn*. He had a house at the intersection of School and Second Streets, where the Harborview Towers are today.

When Rob returned to the wharf in his new garb a few days later, after staying with Whitmarsh's family, he would have had to reckon with the ship's owners for his pay. Who, Michael Dyer, curator of the New Bedford Whaling Museum, noted did not include Isaac Howland Jr. himself anymore, for the family patriarch had died in 1834. However, he had built one of the most successful and storied whaling fleets in the city's history, and upon his passing the firm had been taken over by Thomas Mandell, a partner since 1819, Edward Mott Robinson, and Sylvia Ann Howland, the daughter of Isaac's original partner, Gideon Howland. By the time of Rob's return, the firm owned thirty-odd whaling ships, a large wharf in New Bedford, and an oil factory.[2] Yet Rob's yield, after ten years away, was but 21 cents, followed by a magnaminous gift of $5 to send him on his way.

CHAPTER 24

Fate of Rob's Ships

Neither of Rob's ships lasted long after he left them. The barque *Smyrna* perished in an incident on a distant island from what was likely just simple spite,[1] and the *Isaac Howland* was captured and burnt in the high Arctic.[2] In the middle of the Southern Atlantic is the island of Saint Helena, the site of Napoleon's exile. On the north side of the island, at the end of a steep and narrow dry valley, lies the harbor of Jamestown. Famous is its "wharf," which is just a natural rock face with a road on top. Carved into black volcanic cliffs, the "wharf" stands above what is called the town's "beach." The putative beach is just a submerged rock ledge that extends out roughly one hundred yards before a sheer drop into deeper water. There are no sheltering arms for this harbor, and no sand on the beach. A ship anchored offshore has very little to protect it from the great soaring waves that regularly roll south across an unimaginable stretch of the Atlantic. Visiting ships anchor a quarter-mile offshore and must daringly ride out any weather.

Whether it was due to the crackling sounds or the dancing light, scarcely five years after Rob left the *Smyrna* in New Zealand, a sailor hollered an alarm in St. Helena's harbor about 1 a.m. on November 3, 1864. The whaling ship *Smyrna*, now under Captain Reuben Kelly of New Bedford, was "on fire." The harbormaster immediately called for help, and the HMS *Rattlesnake*, a British man-of-war that happened to be nearby, responded. With the limited firefighting capabilities of the day, the crew of the *Rattlesnake* could do little more than wet down canvas sails to lay over the hatches and liberally pump water below. The goal was to simultaneously deprive the fire of oxygen and drown the flames.

For all their efforts, the fire could not be sufficiently checked. At six in the morning, with its innards still smoldering and great tendrils of smoke emanating from the portholes, several captains from nearby ships gathered. After a "survey," meaning a consultation among the harbormaster and the captains involved in fighting the fire, they determined the *Smyrna* was irreparably damaged. With the smoke curling up against the lemon-yellow sky at dawn in a scene as if by William Turner, the harbormaster directed that before the *Smyrna* sank and obstructed the anchorage, she should be towed onto the "beach" for salvage. The crews on the *Smyrna* and the *Rattlesnake* reboarded the charred and smoldering vessel, cut the stays and shrouds, pulled down the masts, and dismantled as much as they could. They then cut her loose from her anchors, and by two in the afternoon she was winched aground. Filled with an estimated seven feet of water and being rolled and slammed on the rocks by each large wave, the ship began to break up. As was customary at the time, far from any insurance investigator, the harbormaster and the consulting captains signed an agreement concurring on her doom, and the ship was then declared sunk.

Smyrna's 330 bbls. of sperm oil and 2,000 pounds of whalebone were removed, as were the recovered anchors, chains, and other hardware. The oil, bone, and hardware were sold within days at a hastily convened public auction. The crew, with nothing other than the clothes they swam ashore in, were taken in by the American consul and given three months' pay from the auction proceeds to help them get home. While the consul's final report lists the cause as "spontaneous combustion," local reports note this was only after one crew member, a Mr. Davis, had been detained and incarcerated on suspicion of having caused the fire. A steward hailing from Baltimore, he allegedly suffered abuse at the hands of a mate and was spiteful. However, without any evidence to sustain the charge, he was released the next day, and the case regarding the demise of the *Smyrna* was closed.

The *Isaac Howland* met a far more notorious fate a year later, in 1865. The *Isaac Howland* and the *Sophia Thornton*—the ship Rob noted they had "sistered" with in the South Pacific—were both propelled into Civil War history when they became among the last ships to be captured and burnt by a notorious Confederate raider. The CSS *Shenandoah*, under Captain James Waddell, captured and burned thirty-four whaling vessels in the Arctic nearly two and a half months after General Robert E. Lee formally surrendered at Appomattox. Captain Waddell's actions after the Confederacy's surrender legally made him a pirate, and the fact that he had been told that Dixie had been hauled down, but refused to accept it, tarnished his reputation forever.

A tall, thin, austere-looking Southerner, Waddell was described as looking like one of the Winthrops from Boston. He sported a short haircut, with a sharply defined part on the right side, and boasted a full handlebar mustache. He had acquired a limp while at the US Naval Academy in Annapolis after being shot in the hip during a duel. After graduating, Waddell initially embarked on an undistinguished career as a professor there. However, with the outbreak of the Civil War, as a native Tar Heel, he resigned his commission in the U.S. Navy and joined the Confederate cause. He saw no action during the first several years of the war, but opportunity came his way in the spring of 1863 when he was asked to go to Europe on behalf of the Confederate navy. The Confederacy had secretly purchased a sailing steamer named the *Sea King*. On the cusp of her times, she was unique for having engines in a sailing world, and this allowed her to cruise in the doldrums or head straight upwind.

Waddell took charge and converted her to a warship, staffed her, and set off on a cruise to the Pacific. Waddell's orders were to "greatly damage and disperse" the Union's whaling fleet, for the fleet was considered a source of revenue as well as a training ground for the Union's sailors. Refitted with guns and renamed the *Shenandoah*, Waddell headed off in late October 1864. Sailing south along Africa, she rounded the Cape of Good Hope and headed to the Pacific Ocean. Making port at Melbourne in January 1865 to repair a broken propeller, the *Shenandoah* reversed the "line," sailing east. Waddell finally captured four whalers, and most importantly, maps and charts that showed that the Union whaling fleet was then far north in the Bering Sea. The *Shenandoah* cruised north into the Sea of Okhotsk off Siberia at the beginning of June 1865.

Thousands of miles behind, the Confederate army had already surrendered. General Lee gave up his army on April 9 at Appomattox. Another 100,000 Confederates lay down their arms to General Sherman on April 26, and the Confederate generals Taylor and Smith, with their western armies, raised the white flag in New Orleans in May. By June, Jefferson Davis was already in a jail cell, and the war over. But not for the wrathful Waddell. The *Shenandoah* continued north on its ignominious mission. In the Barents Sea, a great storm energized the ice floes, which almost pierced the *Shenandoah's* hull, but the wind subsided. Flying a Russian flag of convenience on her scurrilous mission, Captain Waddell first captured and destroyed one of the largest whalers, the *William Thompson*, on June 22.

Even then after learning from the crew that Lincoln had been assassinated and Lee had surrendered, Waddell retorted it was all "a damned Northern lie." The next day, he found five whalers clustered around a pod of bowhead while in calm seas. One whaleboat even had an iron in a whale and was zipping across the placid ocean on a Nantucket sleighride. The first ship taken was the *Milo*, but instead of burning her, Waddell spared the ship in order to have a hull in which he could place captured crews. With her engines powering her in still airs, the *Shenandoah* next chased down the *Sophia Thornton* under Captain Moses Tucker. Tucker valiantly refused to stop until a cannonball was fired across her bow and another into her topgallant sail. At that, she hove to and surrendered. After being stripped, the *Sophia Thornton* was afire by nightfall. Moving on, Waddell captured and burned several more whalers over the course of as many days. Near the Diomede Islands, in the midst of the strait, the *Shenandoah* came upon another cluster of whalers. The previous evening, June 26, the whaler *Brunswick* had collided with pack ice and cracked several of her planks, and her exhausted crew had been pumping water madly all night just to survive. Raising the ship's flag upside down, the international signal of distress, the captain had called upon nearby whalers for help. After several responded, including the *Isaac Howland* now under Captain Jeremiah Ludlow, they concurred the *Brunswick* could not be saved. Just as this assembly surrounding the stricken ship set to divvy up its contents, the *Shenandoah* arrived. As it was dead calm again, none of the whalers could escape the steamer, and so, like all the rest, the *Isaac Howland* was emptied of her crew, stripped of her valuables, and torched. Her weary hull descended to the deep on June 28, 1865.

Either because Yankee prey was now scarce, or perhaps because he finally accepted that the South had indeed capitulated, Waddell soon ceased his piracy and turned his ship south. Sailing past San Francisco two months later in August, he intersected the English ship *Barracouta*, whose captain independently confirmed the war was over. Waddell was at last forced to recognize that he and the *Shenandoah* were outlaws, and so he ordered the *Shenandoah*'s cannons stowed and the ship repainted, hoping to camouflage himself as he ran for home. Sailing for the only port he thought might be safe, the *Shenandoah* arrived in Liverpool, England, five months later, on November 15, and Waddell formally surrendered to the authorities. Five years later he popped up in the United States, first as a steamboat captain in San Francisco and then in charge of oyster management for the state of Maryland. He died and was buried in Annapolis in 1886, a gray pariah in his time.

PART IV

CONTEMPLATIVE GURRY

Passions and Reflections

CHAPTER 25

The Evolution of God

FOR A MOMENT, LET US PUT THE TANGIBLE ELEMENTS OF ROB'S JOURNEY aside and all the things Rob saw and did, and examine the heart of his tale. Let us pause to contemplate the complicated aurora of Rob's epiphany, arguably the seminal event and zenith of his journey. It is when he finally understands his own potential, it is when he wrote his own gospel. At long last, on March 5, 1859, under the Southern Cross, still more than twelve thousand miles from home, Rob saw the light. The site is marked with a cross on his map. The cross marks the day when he prevailed over all the gods haunting his past and came to realize his god, his potential, had been there all along, like the magic of Dorothy's shoes. As Dorothy did, he finally came to understand that only he could forgive himself and find his way home, and that capacity was one he had always had.

In reflecting on Rob's spiritual journey through life, I found it difficult to understand, much less relate to, his religious paradigm. As I tried, I naturally began to ponder my beliefs, my own ideology, and those religious constructs that lay between us; the beliefs of my ancestors spanning the 160-year interlude. Occasionally while working on his manuscript, in the specious hope of gaining some insight into the whaler's thinking, I would turn from the text and stare at one of the few photographs of Rob I had managed to find, kept as a family treasure all these years. It came from the same cracked black leather trunk in which the manuscript had lain. Rob's picture was taken on the day of his grandson's baptism. My grandfather, G. Franklin Ludington, is perhaps a year old in the picture and surrounded by his parents and both sets of grandparents. Taken in

1896, the seven of them are stoically poised, with the elders seated, in front of the whaler's summer retreat in Mountain Lakes, Maryland.

An only child, my little grandfather looks straight ahead, staring in amazement at the photographer, his mouth and earnest eyes wide open. He is dressed in a flowing white baptism dress common to those times and wearing stiff black leather shoes. He sits on one grandmother's knee. Her husband, an oysterman, is next to them. To their left are Rob and his wife, Eudocia, and standing behind the four grandparents are my grandfather's parents, Minnie Armstrong and her husband, the last of the oystermen, George Ludington. Surprisingly to me, Eudocia is massive, a physical trait not apparently passed along. Dead within a year of the picture, she wears a low-collared but very stiff black Victorian dress made of crepe. Her graying hair is captured under a small, flowered teardrop hat. Like her grandson, Eudocia stares with intensity at the camera and no smile creases her face. Rob, the whaler, now looks like the vestryman he has become. He is in his Sunday best; a black suit with matching vest, a white shirt, and a floppy black bow tie. At sixty-eight, he still has a good mop of white hair and a full beard. He has a slight smile and looks kindly, but tired, perhaps a bit wary.

On the third floor of our house where I worked on Rob's manuscript, I would at times ease back in my chair, watch the dust motes drift in the shafts of sunlight, and wonder how Rob truly perceived his god, the numen he revered in his youth, wrestled with in the South Pacific, and finally glorified as he matured and became a patriarch. Losing his parents at an early age no doubt infused Rob with insecurity and left him bereft of direction. With apparently minimal emotional support or guidance from his uncles, he soon careened from a wealth of friends, a secure place in his community, and a promising career into a maelstrom of carousing around Baltimore. Managing to at least graduate from the dental college, though still ashamed of his own behavior, he left Baltimore with promises of restraint. He failed, and soon enough, the inveterate inebriate was publicly drunk and riding his horse during his dentistry rounds in Kentucky and then South Carolina. His promising career derailed. He succumbed to his weaknesses and was clearly party to additional shameful events that he alludes to, but wisely did not share. At last he lay, passed out and destitute, on the cobblestoned streets of New York. Feeling he had demeaned himself so completely that he had alienated all who cared for him—his professors, friends, and even his family—Rob believed he had nowhere else to turn, so he gave himself up to the sea. How lost and afraid he must have felt. How alone.

No one's life is easy. Every day, we hear about people around the world who suffer great deprivations, death, and unimaginable horrors. Even the luckiest among us experience hardships and losses. Against such pressing shadows of despair, I recognize that I am blessed never to have felt so lost and shamed that I felt as bereft of friends and family as Rob did. The emotions that motivated him to run away for ten years made me wonder about his perspective and the depth of his pain. How did he characterize his sins? What delineated the line, in his judgment, that he felt once crossed, prohibited him from returning? Were his sins really so great? Or was it that his times were so harsh? Without parents and a stronger community for emotional support, was he simply just insecure and lost? It seems he tried to substitute god as a surrogate for the parents whose guidance and love he sorely missed. And failed miserably. Staring at Rob's photograph in the afternoon's sunlight, I tried to walk in his shoes and understand what drove him.

I began searching Rob's text for deeper meanings, and then I explored other family papers in the old leather trunk. I hoped to crystallize my understanding of his notions of sin and foregiveness. But, as I probed for his perspective, I realized that, like a set of those Russian matryoshka dolls, Rob's god was historically linked, and only understood from an array of relogous spirituality stretching across several generations. His god was preceded by the beliefs of his grandparents and his parents and the church he was raised in. Moreover, from my distant perpective I knew any understanding I might achieve of Rob's persuasion would naturally be varnished by my own beliefs. In my quest to grasp my family's relationship with god over a century and a half, I ended up having to unearth Rob's uncle's god, Rob's gods, and even discover my grandfather's faith. Lastly, I looked at mine. While I had certainly never intended to examine my own beliefs when I first took Rob's manuscript from my mother's hands, this was ultimately necessary and fair as I dissected others'.

By the time Rob first boarded the *Smyrna* in New Bedford, he viewed himself as a troubled sinner. He clearly regretted his dependency on alcohol, his intemperate behavior, and the resulting job losses and alienation they engendered. He felt guilty about the shame his behavior brought to his uncles and the wasted chits they used to get him into dental school and land jobs thereafter. Rob appreciated that he had tarnished the family name, squandered his uncles' trust, and overtly flung their gifts of opportunity to the winds. As evidenced by how he was treated as a pariah on his return to Baltimore, even after ten years, Rob's actions before he left must have been public and atrocious. No doubt they were much worse than he shared, for witness the distance kept by his friends and family even when he returned. Like some alcoholics I have known, he was probably a sloppy drunk, rude, and embarrassing. He might have even been a liar or thief. Early in my life, I attributed such odious behavior—including that of some close friends—to a lack of self-discipline. Now I recognize there are sometimes deeper genetic, physiological, and psychological roots. Rob, however, attributed his drinking and its associated behaviors to his failure to remain connected with his god.

Rob's initial god appears defined by its antagonism, less by its grace and compassion. With respect to how Rob truly envisioned this god, in scouring the text I felt I was searching among shadows. While I could find little from Rob's text or any earlier writings about his actual religious beliefs, I took some time to dig into Methodist history and looked again at the "discourse" given at his uncle Thomas's funeral in 1869.[1] Together these proved to be a window through which I might appreciate the religious construct of Rob's youth.

American Methodism began shortly after the American Revolution, and it was a breakaway from John Wesley's Methodist Church in England. Central to the faith was a strong belief in education coupled with spiritual development. Expectations of the faithful in the early nineteenth century centered on modest dress, honest dealings, financial restraint, and sobriety. Adherents were encouraged to "converse sparingly and cautiously with young women," seek the abolishment of slavery, and in general follow a "stringent and oft-times abstemious social ethic."[2] Clearly Rob failed in his youth on a number of these points.

With that as background, I then turned to his uncle's funeral discourse. The minister, Reverend Stitt, presumably rendered the church's dogma at the time when he eulogized Uncle Thomas. The reverend framed Thomas as one who was pure of speech, regular in his prayers, careful in every action, rigorous in his honesty, and determinedly just to others. The reverend particularly noted that, when Thomas took over his father's grocery store, he immediately changed the business to focus on cloths, fabrics, and millinery accessories, shifting away from alcohol, which then was the profit leader in most grocery stores. Further along in the sermon, the reverend extolled that when a business acquaintance of his uncle's nearly bankrupted their store, Uncle Thomas "sacrificed almost everything he possessed" to clear the debt. It took many years, but Thomas "walked out of their (creditor's) house a poor but free man, and beginning the world anew, after having passed beyond the meridian of life, yet clear of any debt." In conclusion, the reverend credited Thomas with consistent generosity toward the church as well as having exceptional humility. He highlighted that, for more than sixty years, Thomas successfully ran several businesses in Baltimore, yet he sought no prominent position, was content to live without ornate trappings, and went to his grave with a spotless reputation.

My observation is that Uncle Thomas's god was transactional. The deity that Rob grew up with frowned upon drinking and sinning, but there was little mention of charity, love, or forgiveness. This god favored you if you remained financially sound, but was indifferent as you swept by the crippled and destitute on the city's streets. As Rob's story unfurled, I wondered if his church's transactional god was the one he still prayed to. I realized not, and that the heart of his tale was the evolution of his god. The god of Rob's youth, as was preached at the Light Street church, was probably that described in his uncle's treatise. While close to him for a while, Rob felt he had abandoned this god in his formative years as he foundered. Then, after three and a quarter years at sea, Rob set off into the forests of New Zealand for four and a half years. At last, Rob emerges from his wilderness, still railing against his god, and still lost after seven years of wandering. However, with his new Bible in hand, he again seeks to discover and delineate his god. Rob still didn't seem to appreciate what he was seeking, and he clearly did not yet perceive a god of grace. Still shrouded in doubt, he returns to the sea, on a path headed home. Still floundering spiritually, he continued his quest for enlightenment.

To understand the evolution of Rob's god, an ironic juxtaposition of a concept, I also purchased the book he repeatedly read on his journey home. This was the book Rob had acquired while gamming with other whaleships in April 1858: J. G. Pike's *Religion and Eternal Life: or, Irreligion and Perpetual Ruin, the Only Alternative for Mankind*. Not often read now, and certainly no breakthrough in religious philosophy, an 1835 edition in fine condition cost me only twenty-three dollars—a pittance for the connection it brought. Seen through the lens of Pike's book, this new god was more corporeal.[3] Pike depicts a god who is actively engaged in judging each individual's behavior. This god stands at the Pearly Gates and personally appraises each mortal as they approach, after having "watched over you by day and by night." Pike's god not only monitors your behavior on earth, but explicitly provides you with everything. "How many days of ease have you enjoyed! How many nights of security have you passed, when, sunk in sleep and insensibility, you had none to secure you but God! . . . Have you lived many years, and never for a day been destitute of needful food and decent clothing? God has supplied these needs."

I think it would be difficult to achieve absolution and find redemption with such a god. Pike observes, "Look at the creation, and you may exclaim, 'My Father made it all.' Look at the sun; it is darkness compared to His glory. Look at the world; it is the creature of a moment in His sight." Pike's god must be lionized for its great works yet is still so insecure as to demand each mortal's devotion. The covenant this god seeks is a transactional assessment of reflected valuation, not a glowing radiance of absolution and endless love.

At last though, Rob finds a new interpretation of god. With his epiphany that starry March night under the Southern Cross, still six months from home, Rob finally leaves the avaricious puritanical god of his youth behind and embraces a far different god. On that transformational night, Rob turns away from his uncle's transactional god and Pike's god of fire and brimstone and finally clasps a more loving and forgiving god, one that I was raised to think of as Jesus's father. Of that night, Rob wrote, "A Divine voice said to me 'Thy sins, which were many, are all forgiven thee,' and floods of joy and gladness swept my poor heart." This is a far more compassionate god than Pike's. This New Testament god accepts Rob's sins, appreciates him even with his failings, and gently and graciously brings peace to Rob's life. My inference is that the time it took to comprehend the difference between the two gods is what kept him away from home so long. He could not go home, until at last he was found. Rob finally appreciated a different god, one who spoke to him; the god from within. The evidence for this evolution is both in his manuscript as well as scribbled in the margins of his Bible. The notations throughout his Bible are passage numbers and the dates he reread them. These dates don't cover his time at sea, but rather range across the first few years when he was back in Baltimore. Tellingly, the passages marked are primarily from the New Testament and were particularly chosen to evoke humility, faith, and forgiveness. This redemptive god is at last the one that guided him home to Baltimore, and the one he evangelizes about the rest of his days.

I then turned to the fulcrum of this tale, my grandfather, G. Franklin Ludington. The person who lay equally between Rob and me in time and space. Astonishingly he had left reflections on god. Born in 1895, he was a toddler in the whaler's large household in Baltimore. Years later, after graduating from John Hopkins, he was drafted toward the end of World War I and assigned to the 48th Infantry Regiment of the U.S. Army. Luckily, though he worked on maps depicting the front along the Rhine, he was based at Camp Sevier in South Carolina. After the war, G. Franklin went to Harvard Law School, and from there he moved to New York, ultimately settling in to become a partner with the old law firm of Milbank & Tweed. His family remembers him for his intellect, diligence, and passion for collecting.

Throughout his life, he kept several scrapbooks filled with newspaper articles, small remembrances, poems, and pictures. Tucked in one of those was part of a term paper he composed while in law school.[4] Entirely focused on god and religion, he begins by noting that the Christ in the church's writings is a "synthetic" figure, crafted from a historical Jesus by theological administrators. The whaler's grandson then implored his reader to understand that "any true concept of his person and attributes must ultimately be determined by what he said, rather than by what others said of him." Next, referencing Matthew's story of the laborers in the vineyard and Luke's admonishments about loving your enemies,[5] he points out that Jesus did not preach about fairness and an equitable distribution of goods or money, but rather preached love. In stark contradiction to the god of Rob's uncle, the whaler's grandson notes "equity is of the essence of business, . . . but *quid pro quo* . . . has nothing to do with Christianity." He writes that Jesus's actions "make no demand; and offer no reward."

Further on, G. Franklin quotes the Light Street church's leader in the 1920s, Bishop Burns, who writes, "search the Gospel story from beginning to end, and you will not find one word of Jesus against social impurity, nor a word against drunkenness, . . . nor slavery, . . . nor war. He did not lift his voice, nor cry from the street corners. He did not rail against the evils of the day."[6] Instead, Jesus aimed to construct a new social order by rebuilding the human heart: "His new heaven and new earth were, first, new hearts and new minds."

In his summation, G. Franklin has his own and unique transcendental epiphany. He declares that, since the true gospels about Jesus must reflect an introspection of each human's relationship with him, the gospels must always be open to change, additions, and revisions. In recognizing that the only authentic gospel about Jesus are his words as captured by his apostles, the whaler's grandson proposes that each believer's personal experience is their "gospel." In other words, outside of conveying Jesus's actual words, Paul's epistles are no more or less important as gospels than your experience or mine. G. Franklin's epiphany sheds light on Rob's gospel; Rob's god was not contained in the Bible or any other book, but rather was the one who spoke to him that night sailing home across the Pacific.

As I read Rob's journal and then my grandfather's views, I tried to understand how their gods intersected with mine. Raised on the cynical streets of New York, and then pursuing a career as a biologist and conservationist, my views on Christianity are decidedly more secular than sacred. We went to church most Sundays in my youth, and I recall my eighth-grade confirmation, though less for the lessons and more for the abbey I stayed in during our retreat. As for belief in divine interventions and supernatural events, I prefer the celestial realm of observation, measurement, and experiment. I believe in facts, evidence, and the scientific method. Dubious and unproven claims of some god's involvement in human affairs fail to gain purchase in my mind. I had an out-of-body experience during open-heart surgery when I was fourteen. In Central America, I had a .45 pointed at my head and the trigger pulled. Twice, I nearly drowned or froze to death in wintertime boating incidents, and as a first responder, I was but several hundred yards from the first tower when it fell on 9/11. In none of these moments did I feel god, hear a voice from above, or think that any such entity might save me, and I certainly have never felt any type of hovering judgment, except my own and those of people around me. In line with this, to me the greatest value of religious faith has been the establishment of universally shared moral pillars and ethical constructs. I remain convinced that the only judgment is that experienced on earth. How you treat others through life will determine how they reciprocate, and whether on your passing, your community will cherish memories of you, or dispatch you to the oubliette of human history.

Nor will I ever believe that Christianity's god is any more certifiable than any other deity; even less so in recent times, given the cultural violence such assertions beget. I remain wholly unconvinced that Christians would have the only window into god's debatable presence on earth. But I haven't left the fold completely, and I am willing to entertain the notion of some divine intervention in the creation and metaphysics of the universe, including whatever force brought on the big bang, the spark of life, and the conscious ascendance of *Homo sapiens*.

However, at the crux of these thoughts, what I most decry is the hypocrisy of religious zealots with anthropocentric proclivities. If you truly believe in god, then one should recognize that the same entity also produced the resplendent biodiversity that characterizes Earth. If a being created us, it also created the gorgeous mosaic of species that are the biotic foundation of our planet. Our planet's myriad of species ultimately underlies the biogeochemical cycling, food webs, and ecological complexity that forms the ecological fabric of our planet; the warp and weft we humans will need in our run for eternity.

In the end though, from this religious inquiry, I might at least have found an answer to a question I long pondered when Rob wrote early in the tale that "as my story is an autobiography, and not an account of a whaling voyage, I will say some, but not too much, hereafter regarding the number of times when we saw whales, . . . but it is my intention, however, to omit most things of this nature, instead covering only such events as have a direct relation to the purpose of this narrative." For what this purpose was, he never made too clear, though near the end of his tale, he does return to the theme as he notes "I desire to say that while I am glad to write for my love ones this account of my wanderings, my principal purpose in telling the miserable story of my sin and shame is to exalt and honor Him."

Still rather obfuscating, I wondered what his real intentions were. Then in digging into Methodism, I found an insight that led me to the conclusion that perhaps his narrative was really an attempt to reframe his life, even if just to himself, in line with John Wesley's, the founder of the Methodist faith. A story Wesley often told was that "He had not [readily] found salvation. His entrance into the ministry and his living the disciplined life were not signs of new life in Christ, but were, instead, signs of his seeking to find God's acceptance by performing good works. . . . Finally, he learned that he did not have to save himself. That assurance, that he was already saved and so did not have to worry about his salvation, came on May 24, 1738. While hearing a reading of Luther's preface to the Epistle to the Romans, Wesley felt his heart strangely warmed and began to trust God for his salvation."[7] Commonly referred to as his "Aldersgate experience," it would appear that perhap Rob's tale was prepared as a parrallel story, one largely shaped to portray himself in the light of an epiphany and redemption, as his faith's founder experienced.

CHAPTER 26

In His Path

AFTER SPENDING SO MUCH TIME READING ROB'S WRITING AND researching his voyage, I developed a deep desire to tread in his path. I felt compelled to see some of what he saw, smell the tang of the ocean, feel the impact of great waves on a ship's bow; travel far from home. And while I might have sought to pick up his trail among the romantic palms of the South Pacific, amid his tale, Rob wrote "someone heaved a coconut shell overboard today, and it had scarcely touched the water before a bird of the petrel kind had lighted on it. There he was, a small sailor in a small frail barque alone on the heaving ocean." The image that Rob evoked pierced my soul and enwrapped my psyche. It connected me with a side of Rob I had not seen, and so instead I set my heart for somewhere quite different. Somewhere wilder.

In my youth, my zeal for birds had landed me a job volunteering in the American Museum of Natural History's ornithology department. I spent high school and college vacations physically rearranging bird specimens. In the early 1980s as academics began reexamining morphologically derived phylogenetic trees in light of molecular systematics and cladistics, the curators sought to realign the bird collection. So when research showed that storks were more closely related to vultures than herons, which they superficially resemble, I was delegated to move the specimens. Over several spring, Christmas, and summer vacations, I moved all the shrikes, storks, flycatchers, woodpeckers, old-world warblers, and barbets. In and out of monolithic gray steel cabinets, up one hall, down another, waiting impatiently for old clanking elevators, then hoisting twenty pounds of tray packed with specimens into a new location. Each day I was immersed in the smell of mothballs and my shoulders ached from the physical labor, but I loved every minute. In the hallways and the library, I walked among ornithological legends: Dean Amadon, Bud Lanyon, John Bull, Lester Short, Francois Vuilleumier, Walter Bock, Ernst Mayr, and others. Thursday afternoons were the best, for visiting scientists always gave a teatime lecture to the department.

Lunchtime was also special as I would wander the museum's endless halls, gazing at the great dioramas, visually caressing each mounted specimen. Robert Cushman Murphy's "Ship Followers" became my favorite. As a young naturalist, Murphy daringly sailed to the South Atlantic in 1912 aboard one of America's last wooden whaling ships, the *Daisy*. The ship spent nearly a year at sea around the Falklands, South Georgia Islands, and the Antarctic Peninsula. As the crew slaughtered whales and seals, he studied the seabirds.[1] Forty years later, as chairman of the Ornithology Department at the museum, he lobbied hard and raised the funds for the Whitney Hall of Oceanic Birds. The hall opened in 1953, and among all the dioramas, it was said he pushed hardest for the unusual but beguiling one titled "Ship Followers." The diorama depicts soaring pelagic seabirds over deep troughed green-hued seas from the perspective of a fictitious schooner off the southern coast of New Zealand; as far away from the museum as one might be, in the farthest wilds of the antipodes. In stark contrast to Holden Caulfield, who loved these same halls for their temporal cessation bringing him peace amid his juvenile angst,[2] as a youth I readily imagined the opposite. I knew the birds actually flew between my visits; they were all so alive to me. Once I left the hall, I was sure they resumed their endless quests across the tempestuous seas.

Thus, I became entranced by the idea of following in Rob's wake 'round the Horn, a place as wild and distant as could be, and a place where I might bask in my love for birds. Cape Horn looms as the northern pillar of Drake Passage and marks the five-hundred-mile strait between Antarctica and South America. The south end is delineated by the Southern Orkney Islands, just off the coast of Antarctica, including Elephant Island, where Maj. Ernest Shackleton's crew was marooned in 1916 after their ship the *Endurance* was crushed by ice. Luckily for them,

Shackleton made his infamous and epic voyage to a whaling station on South Georgia island to secure help. In the strait, the Pacific's ceaseless west winds push cold southern waters into the Atlantic, where they flow under the warm water pouring south from Brazil. The convergence sweeps nutrients to the surface, feeding plankton, which in turn attract fish and squid; a banquet for the South Atlantic's seabirds and whales. But the seas here are also the most dangerous on earth. Fomented by the katabatic winds blowing off Antarctica, the winds and seas fuse in a region with low barometric pressures to create a procession of storms that constantly sweep east through the strait. Vast, cream-topped cerulean rollers characterize these waters, which turn a dull, leaden green and heave higher when intense gale-force winds conspire to whip them up. In the southern winter, this dangerous mix escalates dramatically with the addition of blizzards, brash ice, and somnolent icebergs drifting north. One day, when I saw an online advertisement for such a trip, led by an extraordinary birder and at a reasonable rate, I jumped at the opportunity. It would be a twelve-day trip from Buenos Aires, south to the Falklands and the Antarctic Peninsula, and then north past Cape Horn and up the Humboldt Current in the Pacific to Santiago, Chile.

Cape Horn with its legendary waters, which Rob rounded twice, has also long enticed explorers and ornithologists. More than eighty scientific expeditions ventured to the area in the eighteenth and nineteenth centuries. Among those who visited were James Cook on the *Endeavour* in 1769, Charles Darwin on the *Beagle* in 1832, and Sir James Ross on the *Erebus* in late 1842. The last visits were just a few scant years before Rob first went 'round on the *Smyrna* in 1849. As an ornithologist, I avidly contemplated each mention of a bird in Rob's tale, and I mythically projected myself into his journey. As the *Smyrna* first sailed south, leaving New Bedford in winter, immediately offshore Rob would have seen alcids, a family of birds including razorbills, murres, and dovekies. These are northern convergent evolutionary equivalents of the penguins. He probably wouldn't have seen the first gannets, shearwaters, and petrels until farther south, off Cape Hatteras. Crossing the equator, the diversity would have increased, and east of Rio de Janeiro they likely would have encountered the first mollymawks, the smaller albatrosses. At that point, if he had known, Rob would have joined with Robert Cushman Murphy when he exalted, "I now belong to a higher cult of mortals, for I have seen the albatross!"[3] Offshore Buenos Aires, the *Smyrna's* crew would've begun seeing giant petrels and new and different shearwaters, but not until they were off the coast of Patagonia would they have likely spied the consummate South Atlantic species, the great wandering albatross, the larger storm-petrels, prions, and penguins. The latter were known to whalers as "woggins," nicknamed after "Jack Woggins," a captured king penguin that lived on a whaling ship in 1827 before dying several months later from a diet of salted beef.[4] Only perhaps on his way home, when the *Isaac Howland* deviated rather far south in the Bellingshausen Sea, might Rob have at last observed those species that Ernest Shackleton described near South Georgia, the "cape pigeons, whale-birds (prions), terns, mollymauks, nellies, sooty, and wandering albatrosses."[5]

With the longest wingspan of any bird, in some individuals almost twelve feet from tip to tip, and with the most graceful flight pattern, the royal and wandering albatrosses are the talismans of the southern oceans. They are members of a loosely identified group of birds called pelagics, more an ecological collection than a phylogenetic one. Pelagics include species from several different bird families: penguins, skuas and jaegers, alcids, tropicbirds, albatrosses, storm-petrels, petrels, shearwaters, frigatebirds, and boobies, as well as a few gulls and terns. Their shared superficial trait is that they essentially spend their life at sea, theoretically only returning to land in order to nest.

Within the pelagics, the albatrosses are the headline members of the Procellariiformes order, or "tubenoses," as they are colloquially known. The group includes the families of the albatrosses, shearwaters, storm-petrels, and petrels. The tubenoses are the most effortless aviators of all the pelagics, and at sea they exhibit a beautiful-to-behold flight pattern consisting of characteristic soaring swoops and gravity-fed glides.[6] From a distance they look like they're sailing along a scallop's edge. To facilitate their life at sea, the tubenoses have evolved unique adaptations. They can desalinize seawater, minimize the strain on their wings for their lengthy journeys, and "sleep" while flying. Named for the nasal salt gland above their eyes, tubenoses extract salt from their bloodstream and excrete it through a pair of tubes running down the top of their bill. They also have a "tendon lock," whereby a tendon in their upper wing can lock the wing's horizontal orientation in place, thus alleviating the strain on their muscles in flight. This allows them to fly for extended periods and in gale-force winds without becoming energetically exhausted.[7] Amazingly a third trait is that they can rest half their brain while flying, thus getting some neurological respite as they quasi-sleep. Finally, like vultures, a number of species have also developed extraordinary olfactory capabilities,[8] which allows them to find fish or squid near the ocean's surface even in the dead of night.[9]

In Rob's time, as well as today, the presence of albatrosses and other seabirds far offshore evoked warm feelings, and for reason. One whaler observed "I had the two o'clock masthead. I had not been there long before two of the prettiest little birds, a kind of seagull, . . . came and stood with me on the top-gallant yard. . . . They had been there off and on for about an hour when, sure enough, I raised a school of sperm whales."[10] To a greenhand, the empty ocean often appears to be an ecological desert. Yet to birds that have spent millions of years learning its mysteries, they know to forage where eddies swirl, where upwellings bring plankton to the surface; where the krill and squid gather. Pelagic seabirds and whales commingle at such feeding sites, thus to those on the lookout, the visible presence of such seabirds is a good sign.

In particular, the great albatrosses were considered omens of good luck to sailors wary of the doldrums, for they are the harbingers of wind. Given their large size, albatrosses need consistent and strong winds for lift. When winds are less than ten or fifteen miles per hour, they tend to rest on the water. So, for sailors whose passage across the ocean is dependent upon stretched canvas, seeing an albatross soar across the waves is auspicious, and while perhaps unaware of the reality underpinning their mutualistic relationship based on wind and whales, sailors have always considered catching or killing an albatross loutish behavior. The long-standing cultural relationship is celebrated by Samuel Coleridge's epic poem of 1798, *The Rime of the Ancient Mariner*.[11] Metaphorically reflecting the link between god and the ocean's winds, Coleridge's albatross was a good Christian soul that had been helping the ancient mariner's ship escape the clutches of the southern oceans. The bird was leading his ship home on a path through icebergs until the ancient mariner thoughtlessly slew it. Upon the albatross's death, the winds die and the ship is beset by the doldrums. Soon the ancient mariner's fellow sailors begin perishing from thirst while the ship drifts. With the dead albatross now hanging from the mariner's arrogant neck, he is humbled, but eventually comes to an epiphany about nature and god. In the final part of the tale, in my favorite paean to biodiversity, the ancient mariner observes:

> *He prayeth best, who loveth best*
> *All things both great and small;*
> *For the dear God who loveth us,*
> *He made and loveth all.*

In my first endeavor to follow in Rob's wake, in January 2020 I flew to Buenos Aires to join a group organized by the birding travel agency Wings and led by Steve Howell. Surprisingly, I met him literally upon landing at the airport as we both looked for our bags on the carousel. Tall and red-cheeked, with a scruffy beard and wild unkempt hair, he still has strong traces of a lovely Welsh accent. He will tell you he has been birding his entire life; his skill set would seem to corroborate that. After university, Steve headed across the Atlantic to escape the potentially stultifying British life he dreaded. He spent several years as a nomad, mostly traveling around the United States and Mexico. A fascination with seabirds moved him to periodically weave in time aboard fishing trawlers and other ships during his wanderings. After accumulating the equivalent of more than four years at sea, Steve has acquired an encyclopedic knowledge of pelagic seabirds and boasts of having seen more than 95 percent of the world's tubenose species. Also at the airport was his sidekick for this occasion, young Luke Seitz. A birder from Connecticut, now living in Ithaca, New York, he proved to be one of the best birders with a spotting scope I ever met.

I awoke early on January 23, our first full day at sea. There was but a thin strip of gray light on the eastern horizon as I showered and dressed.

We were well offshore, just on the edge of the continental shelf, hundreds of miles east of Buenos Aires and traversing depths of several thousand feet. It was cold outside at 5:30 a.m., and thoughtfully I put on several layers of clothes, for the winds buffeted across the ship's deck at thirty to forty miles per hour. In the numinous pink of the dawn, hundreds of greater shearwaters were flying by, and mixed among them were a couple of cory and manx shearwaters. These species are common off the coast of New England in summer, but they head south during our winter. Sunrise brought little warmth, but at least the dull gray seas shifted to a brighter blue and I could see they were now flecked with foam. Not soon after, a large black-and-white bird crested a wave several hundred yards off the bow. Steve hollered "Yellow-nose!" and we all rushed to the rail as he pointed at my first albatross. The large bird swept by, nary a flap, arcing up against the sky and then gliding deep into a wave trough. The seas closed around it, and it was gone. A little later, quivering from the excitement, and a bit from rising at such an early hour, I went to get a cup of coffee. Alone for a moment in the stairwell of our small cruise ship, clasping the hot mug in hand, I paused briefly to exult that I had at last, with Rob, joined the brotherhood of Robert Cushman Murphy.

As we sailed ever southward, the mix of species shifted. Over the next several days we saw several yellow-nosed albatrosses, hundreds of black-browed albatrosses, and our first wandering albatross. We also spotted a number of other tubenoses, including giant petrels, dozens of Atlantic petrels, soft-plumage petrels, white-chinned petrels, and at least two spectacled petrels. The parade even included small flocks of black-bellied storm-petrels and Wilson's storm-petrels. Soon enough I was hard struck by the realization that, having gone to sea for more than fifty years with the hopes of one day seeing an albatross, after just a few days well offshore in the Southern Seas, I had seen thousands.

Late one night, as the ship took a solid pounding punching through storm-driven swells, I closed my book and lay back in my bunk and considered my voyage in contrast to Rob's. He sailed with twenty-three others on a one-hundred-foot ship. They slept packed into tiny berths or curled up in swaying hammocks. He worked from dawn to dusk and suffered through a shift in the dead of night as well. The food was at best indescribably awful. While perhaps fast for its time, the *Smyrna* was ponderously slow by any measure today. In the leg of her journey from the Falklands to the 45° parallel off Chile, the *Smyrna* averaged just fifty miles a day, about two miles per hour. The *Isaac Howland* was a bit faster, and heading home she covered fourteen thousand miles in 130 days, or roughly four miles per hour. I, on the other hand, was sailing in a small cruise ship, speeding along at twenty miles an hour, and I didn't have any assigned task other than to watch birds. Cosseted in a reasonably large cabin with a comfortable bed, I could even watch television or movies at night, and my ship came with an array of food options; from three-course sit-down meals to an endless buffet of good grub. Rob's ship wallowed or smashed through rough seas, and it would have been dwarfed by mine, which sailed along as serenely as a commuter train. Letting late-night thoughts get away, I wrestled with some guilt over my fortune to live in a different era, to have not fallen as far into sin and despair as Rob did, and to have had the chance to have pursued an interesting career while earning enough to afford this trip. As his product, I was also incredibly appreciative that Rob survived his trip and ultimately settled down. At an even deeper level, given that my grandfather, Rob's grandson, died quite early, in his fifties and well before my current age, I also recognized how fortunate I was to have a wonderful family and great friends, and to have lived long enough to follow my passions. At last I went to sleep lulled by the booming bass drumbeat as great swaths of spray broke upon the bow.

Over the course of our voyage we visited the Falklands, cruised the Antarctic Peninsula, and then turned north to Cape Horn and the Beagle Channel, finally sweeping up the Humboldt Current to disembark at Santiago, Chile. I appreciated every moment at sea. One morning, we were well into the South Atlantic, far offshore in Drake Passage. Light winds from the southwest enveloped us, yet it was quite cold as I cupped my coffee. As the sun rose, a few sooty shearwaters flew across our bow, as well as several white-chinned shearwaters, but the numbers now belonged to the prions, an achingly beautiful, small, blue and gray petrel. Also called "whalebirds," their coloration is amazing camouflage against the backdrop of the seas. Indeed, the plumage of these birds inspired the blue, gray, black, and white camouflage patterns seen on World War II naval ships operating in Arctic waters. A bit larger than purple martins, prions fly just as gracefully. These tubenoses are swift but delicate in their movements, flitting up and down oceanic canyons and prancing across wave faces fifty times their size. Their acrobatics made my heart skip as I watched them twist and turn in midair. They swooped up from the wave troughs, shot out the curls, then amazingly disappeared before my eyes, so perfectly blending in, they vanished in an instant against the seething blue seas. Although seldom seen given their distribution, prions are considered one of the most abundant of all seabirds. They often congregate in flocks of thousands, especially around feeding whales, hence their nickname "whalebirds." That morning, we watched them fly past us in an endless stream. At one point, counting a steady trickle of one or two prions spread out every hundred yards parading down both sides of our ship, I let my mind wander quantitatively, and approximated this out. I saw our ship sailing through a celestial constellation, a sparkling net of prions, all hovering just above the waves; millions of them. I imagined the prions as stars and we a cosmic spaceship accelerating through them.

As we continued south, the sun rose higher, and the largest albatrosses appeared more regularly. Amid the constant flow of black-browed albatrosses, a wandering or royal albatross leaves no doubt of its identity; they are almost double in size; a bomber to a fighter. The black-browed albatross can almost be mistaken for the familiar black-backed gull of the North Atlantic, but the wandering albatross's enormous wingspan and its trait of serenely sailing along above the waves makes them unmistakable. Here and there, in great contrast, diminutive diving petrels skittered across the water before the bow of our ship. Trying to take off, but usually failing, they would run for fifty yards across the sea with their wings flapping madly, and then with a splash and thump, immediately plunge beneath the surface. Since they appeared to swim faster than they could fly, an underwater escape from a beast as great as our ship was probably a smart move.

Passing rafts of ruddy-brown kelp, we saw a few hovering gray-backed storm-petrels. These were perhaps the most particular and elusive birds of the trip. Like the prions, gray-backed storm-petrels are found in only a very limited southern range: off the Falklands, south of New Zealand,

and near a few Indian Ocean islands. Given their small size, nondescript gray backs, and usually solitary existence, they're also extraordinarily difficult to spot among the waves. However, as they are inevitably found hovering near kelp, I scrupulously watched for such floating cinnamon clumps, while trying to fathom the ecological pressures exerted on these storm-petrels over the millennia that shaped their evolution. Clearly specialized to feed on creatures found hiding in the floating masses of kelp, they are for some reason limited to just the southern oceans. Moreover, as these birds nest on only a few islands, their continued existence is precarious.

Approaching Antartica, we sailed over Shackleton's Fracture Zone and the South Shetland Trench, which lay almost 15,000 feet below. The seabed was as far down as Mount Whitney in California is up. Cloaked in fog, we approached the continent, and luckily we had radar instead of "rope-yarn guns." The air was freezing, and the ongoing thick fog still enveloped us. Contemplating for a moment, I again thanked science and technology for my layers of polyester fleece, GORE-TEX, eiderdown, and my bright red, waterproof Helly Hansen smock with neoprene cuffs and collar. I winced as I thought about the tattered and threadbare garb, and likely bare feet, that Rob must have suffered in while crossing the Southern reaches. That morning the sky slowly lightened, and visibility extended about a half-mile from our ship. The bird life shifted again. We encountered our first Cape petrels, also known as pintado petrels. Appearing like a conjurer's trick, this large petrel with broad wings has a startling camouflage pattern consisting of large cinnamon blotches against a white background. It is the most striking pelagic I'd ever seen, and clearly evolved to blend with the snow-strewn brown cliffs they nest on. I was entranced, but as much by the emotions they evoked. I couldn't help but remember my first sight of Cape petrels; for they were the stars in the "Ship Followers." Due to that diorama, Cape petrels have always epitomized the mythic southern oceans to me; a place far beyond my reach, a legendary oceanic setting at the end of the earth brimming with obscure species. Beautiful to behold, that morning's flock of Cape petrels soared up from just under the ship's bow as if on some unseen thermal.

Their appearance reinforced my decision to follow in Rob's track and provided a tangible assurance that, a century or more later, one might still breathtakingly experience something as it once was. After they circled the ship a half-dozen times, without a sound or apparent cue, they merged back into the fog. Silently. Gone.

As the ocean's depth beneath us rose to a thousand feet, whales, sea lions, swimming penguins, and soaring pelagics reappeared. In one fifteen-minute interval I counted eighteen Cape petrels, three black-browed albatrosses, two giant petrels, seven Wilson's storm-petrels, and an Antarctic tern. Sadly, the fog closed in, and an alabaster mist again obscured distant views. We were back to just quick glimpses of swimming penguins or silhouetted birds fleeing our ship. Occasionally we could hear whales blowing and the eerie cries from some unknown seabird, but the creatures were largely veiled from our sight. However, every once in a while some cool bird would sweep into view, crossing close under our bow before veering off. In this way, I saw my first light-mantled sooty albatross. As the fog slowly shifted to a light rain, the type of weather the Basque call an *xirimiri*, this rare gray ghost appeared off the bow, quartering toward us. A medium-sized albatross with an alluring smoky-brown body, it has an ashen cap and a bold white eyelid. Not ship followers as many other albatrosses are, the light-mantled sooty albatross follows its own path, low over the water. It flies with an ethereal grace. Increasingly rare, their numbers have been plummeting as they are frequent victims of long-line fishing, unable to resist diving underwater to grab a baited hook. As it disappeared back into the misty rain, our small group was silent in awe.

While this swing by the Antarctic Peninsula was intriguing, I longed to return to the open ocean, to immerse myself in Rob's great "billows" and to watch for pelagic seabirds that he might have seen from the decks of the *Smyrna* or *Isaac Howland*. Thankfully, after three days along the peninsula we headed back across Drake Passage, and the continent's roiled slate-colored waters receded in our wake. They were soon replaced by currents sweeping in from the Pacific, a clearer cerulean blue. The wind picked up, and soon the tops of the waves were ripped off and the ship's rigging began to shriek. The waters off Cape Horn were as advertised. So far from land, the birdlife had again become truly pelagic. Several wandering and a royal albatross were following our ship. Both black-browed and gray-headed albatrosses appeared. The small prions were largely gone, and instead we saw thousands of sooty shearwaters and blue petrels. The blue petrels are hard to tell apart from prions; they are distinguished only by a darker cap and buffy tip on the tail. At one point, we saw a group of Magellanic penguins, and I was deeply struck by their precarious plight. The flock was hundreds of miles from land in waters thousands of feet deep, migrating north ahead of the impending Antarctic winter. In their own way, like the northern songbirds who fly south out over the Atlantic each fall, these penguins were perilously swimming a great distance in seas too deep to feed and far from any haven should a predator appear. I felt for them, so vulnerable in the huge breaking waves. I was moved to ponder that their biannual migration across this five-hundred-mile strait had been recurring for millions of years, and so too it would in the future. But then again I realized, that under the still unknown future impacts of climate change, perhaps not.

Suddenly, a buzz moved through the ship, a brown haze was on the horizon, and everyone emerged on deck. We were approaching Cabo de Hornos, the southernmost bluff on an island just south of Tierra del Fuego. It appeared hardly different from the nondescript brown and greenish hills behind it, but as we closed in, one edge resolved itself. Cape Horn's predominate great gray cliff face with jagged teeth was a bit farther south than all the others. Stretching back northward from the cliff were two sage-green shrub-covered shoulders, each a mile or so in length. It was the first terrestrial plant life we had seen in a week. On the island's eastern spine was a huge sheet of standing steel, a giant cookie cutout whose inside shape was an albatross in flight. Placed there thirty years ago, the statue honors the "end of the world"; the confluence of the two greatest oceans and the turning point for so many voyages. It is also a monument to the lost lives of a multitude of sailors. Gazing at it, I experienced an upwelling of emotion as I thought about Rob making his way past this place . . . twice. Below the sculpture, Chilean poet Sara Vial's inscription translates to:

I am the albatross that waits you At the end of the world.
I am the forgotten souls of dead mariners
Who passed Cape Horn
From all the oceans of the world.
But they did not die
In the furious waves.
Today they sail on my wings
Toward eternity,
In the last crack
Of Antarctic winds.[12]

After circling and passing back under the cliffs of Cape Horn, we turned north into Beagle Channel. Two days later, passing one of the most remote and forlorn lighthouses in the world, Faro Evangelistas, we sailed straight into a brawling Pacific storm. With no immediate way farther north among the tangled islands off Chile, and the clock ticking toward our set arrival time, the captain could not delay to allow the storm's passing. We were soon enveloped in the huge rollers. Staggering the ship, towering waves surged past the main deck. Some were at least thirty-five feet from trough to crest, and their foaming tops were simply shorn off. The crew barred the doors to the decks and forbade anyone from going outside. Everyone grasped at handrails and wobbled on unsteady feet, and more than a few passengers stumbled by, greenish-hued, heading to their cabins. At one point I sneaked out onto the deck at last light and clung to an inner railing for a few minutes. I imagined Rob's ship in these seas. It would have completely disappeared in the troughs between any of these swells; its survival highly doubtful.

At first light the next day, we were on deck and in the midst of the Humboldt Current. This great oceanic flow sweeps cool waters two thousand miles north from Chile to Peru. The resulting upwelling close to the shore makes the coast off Peru one of the most productive marine habitats in the world. The sea was once again a mesmerizing cobalt blue. The storm's vestigial whitecaps writhed across the ocean's surface, creating a bold damask effect. We were also wreathed in birds. The pelagics had shifted to a strong Pacific flavor: pink-footed shearwaters instead of the

Atlantic's greater shearwaters, Salvin's instead of gray-headed albatrosses, royal albatrosses outnumbered wanderers, and the smallish Stejneger's and Juan Fernandez petrels became increasingly frequent. The entire day was the most wonderful, unbridled, pelagic trip ever. It surpassed my wildest ornithological aspirations as seabird after seabird soared by, many of them new to me. I especially loved the latter two petrels, the Stejneger's and Juan Fernandez, who zipped and soared among the waves like spitfires. Amid this flurry of oceanic life, I felt jealous of all of Rob's time at sea.

Cupping my coffee that morning, with the end of our voyage approaching, I paused to appreciate my twelve-day journey in Rob's wake. I had savored pelagic seabirds from two oceans as well as Drake's Passage. I had seen eight species of albatross, eighteen different shearwaters and large petrels, three storm-petrels, and five penguins. By an ecologist's Venn diagram, their niches overlapped but did not exclude. As these phylogenetic relatives sailed over the southern seas, selection pressures from competition, predation, and other factors had endowed each species with its unique plumage, various morphological traits, and habits that significantly differentiated them. I had witnessed a splendid window into our planet's biodiversity at its subtle best, with all the birds' variations reflecting millions of years of procreation and selection on our only home; Earth.

Later, as the evening closed in, and we were far west of Isla Mocha off Chile, a pod of sperm whales surfaced just off the port rail. Their timely appearance at this late point in the voyage prompted me again to think of Rob, but in a melancholy light. Aside from his battle to find god, I wondered what he had thought about as he crossed these very waters, first outbound, then back; trepidation going, anxiety in returning? What fears had he carried into the unknown each time he rounded Cape Horn? On his return nine years later, Rob was no doubt wiser and more mature, but as I knew from his tale, still deeply conflicted about his self-control and moral standing. Watching the whales, basking in the birds, and thinking about Rob, I was deeply grateful. However, I could not help but look back at his life and begin to judge him. Yet, my secular and analytical side reminded me that any judgment would be unfair, as it would necessarily be skewed by historical context, biased by modern moralities, and ingracious to say the least. As Matthew pointed out: "Why do you look at the speck of sawdust in your brother's eye and pay no attention to the plank in your own eye?"[13]

I settled with the notion that he was a good man. Even though Rob lost his parents early, in his youth he worked hard in his community and went on to graduate with a solid professional degree. He also seems to have had a solid moral compass. For while he never explicitly reveals his views on race, a key topic of his and these times, his early connection with Alfred Cookman and later his overt acceptance of islanders, even comfortably sleeping with a man of color, rare for his era, would seem to confirm his abolitionist bent. Rob's embrace of the poor, orphans, disabled, and others of a different color later in life indicate the depth of his heart, and he also deserves credit for finding the strength to break free. After falling into drink and repeatedly losing his self-control, Rob knew enough to change his field of play. So he set off on a decade-long trip across the South Pacific, surely whaling was in essence the wilderness of his day. In such light, I admire him for his ability to, ultimately, find himself. Even with setbacks, he regained his courage and tremulously rebuilt his pride. He rejoiced in January 1852 when he "crossed the fore-topgallant yard!" He embraced the hard work of sawing in New Zealand, "crying in pain through his whole first night," and soon enough his pride is evident as he revels in making bread, "sweet and palatable." Then between lumbering jobs in New Zealand, while on the *Dolores* amid the horrendous storm that was undoubtedly a typhoon, he coolly takes the wheel. His character reemerges, a discernable revenant rising from the "accursed drink." Returning to Baltimore, Rob at last found redemption, in his mind and in his community. He came to the self-realization that his future rested solely in his own hands, on his own efforts; and he finally reclaimed his dignity.

In the end, given the planks in my eye, and the fact that without him I would not be, I wisely pushed aside all my judgments and decided to bask instead in the gracious light of his complicated being, grateful for his time on earth and the seeds he sowed. So with night closing in and at the end of my short voyage, I felt renewed by my quest to find my great-great-grandfather, and I felt as spiritually connected as thought I might ever be. With these lingering thoughts, I was the last to leave the forward deck then, only going below when the black silhouettes of the last shearwaters over the Pacific faded to naught, soaring against a sea turning a deep purple.

CHAPTER 27

"A Fruitful Vine"

IMMEDIATELY UPON HIS RETURN TO BALTIMORE, ROB MOVED BACK into his uncle Thomas's house at 73 North Paca Street.[1] Thomas's first wife, Frances Crawford, had died in 1856 while Rob was away; and he had quickly remarried Pamela, twenty years his junior. After several months of reacclimating himself, demonstrating his sobriety, and beseeching others for work, Rob landed his first job at a grocer's, J. O. Dugan's. Then, after a few more months, he was hired as a salesclerk at his uncle's large and well-known millinery store, Armstrong & Cator. By then Uncle Thomas had retired and sold his shares to his partners, but apparently he still had some pull. When he started working on February 11, 1860, Rob was ecstatic, but he naively credited his god, not his uncle, for coming through:

> *At last, He came to my aid! He has enabled me to overcome every solicitation to indulge in my old propensity of drink, and He raised up friends for me on the right hand and the left, securing for me congenial employment.*

Meanwhile, down the street, Rob's other uncle, Robert G. Armstrong, managed his thriving bookstore, and with his wife, Achsay, had two grown children, Rebecca, age twenty-four, and Dorsey, age twenty-two. Their home was at 14 North Eutaw Street. An interesting lacuna is that, while compatriots in age, Rob never once mentions his first cousins, much as he never mentioned his grandmother. Perhaps some grevious schism?

Anyway, a year and a half after his return, on December 9, 1860, he celebrated his thirty-second birthday with the wish: "May the Lord help me to keep the resolution I have this day formed to serve him the remainder of my days, be they many or few." Then on January 4, 1861, as the prospect of a Civil War loomed, Rob recorded the day as one "appointed by the president for fasting, humiliation, and prayer." As Lincoln wasn't to be president for another two weeks, it was actually the lame duck, President Buchanan, who declared it a holiday, saying "Let us with deep reverence beseech him to restore the friendship and good will which prevailed in former days among the people of several states; and, above all, to save us from the horrors of civil war." In fact, at the time many viewed his act contemptuously, including Frederick Douglass, who caustically noted Buchanan's Dred Scott decision and support of Kansas's proslavery constitution.[2]

Time rolled onward, and with his growing self-confidence Rob became more involved in both his church and its Sunday school. His demonstrated sobriety and reengagement with his community began to bear fruit. "With such help from God, I was gratified to find that little by little I was painting a more favorable standing of myself in the community and rising in the regard of the firm as was evidenced by the increase of my salary from year to year," he wrote. By this point Rob's autobiographical account has shifted to more of a sporadic diary. Occasionally, though, he was still inspired to capture his thoughts, and in December 1863 as Rob celebrated his thirty-fifth birthday, he reflected on his achievements. Most critical to him, he was still sober, employed, and had survived his ten-year odyssey.

As one who has reached the summit of a high mountain turns to look back from the turnings and windings of his devious journey, so on the occurrence of this day, I look back with wonder at all through which the Lord my God had led me.

In fact, he was not only at peace, but happy and hopeful about the future. By then Rob had met a young woman, Eudocia Muller, age eighteen, and fallen in love. The Mullers were an established middle-class family of Baltimore. Her father, Louis, was from Pennsylvania, but early in his life he had moved to Baltimore and learned the upholstery trade. By 1849, just as Rob left South Carolina, Louis had opened a store on Frederick Street that offered furniture repair but also sold wallpaper, rugs, and window drapes. Eudocia's mother, also Eudocia, owned and managed her own hat store. In the 1860s she was a frequent customer at Armstrong & Cator, and this is evident in Rob's logbook, which was used in these years to record store sales. Louis's obituary provided some further details regarding their family of four sons and three daughters, listing one son as a fire commissioner, another as a school commissioner, a third as a reverend, and one of the three daughters as a renowned organist.

Shortly after their marriage in 1865, Rob and Eudocia moved to 76 Lexington Street to begin their own family, and in 1868, the year Uncle Thomas died, and perhaps with a financial boost from him, they established their own millinery store at 237 West Baltimore Street. A few years later the store shifted to 128 Lexington Street, and in 1888 the store shifted to a larger location at 209 West Lexington Street, where it remained for a number of years. When I last visited Baltimore, the site was still a large store, albeit abandoned and boarded up with rusted roll-down steel shutters sadly covered in graffiti. Just across the street lies the "Meadow," a quiet public park with benches and sunshades set among some native grasses. During this period of their lives, Eudocia increasingly appears to have fully assumed the store's management. Rob has again put dentistry behind him and is simply listed as a salesman, then a few years later as bookkeeper. Clearly she became the tour de force, and advertisements at that time portrayed Eudocia as "having enlarged her establishment . . . she is now prepared to exhibit a handsome assortment of round hats and bonnets in the very latest styles." The couple appear to have done reasonably well, and by 1892 Rob and Eudocia are residing in two three-story attached residences at 2000 Mt. Royal Terrace, which had been combined to make one large home. The house still stands today, almost exactly two miles due north of the Inner Harbor, in a gracious tree-lined neighborhood.

The depth of Rob's love for his wife and joy at their large brood is evident in what he wrote at the end of his tale . . .

"Now nearly thirty years have passed, and Eudocia Muller has for many years proved to be a help mate indeed to me. With her I have abundantly realized Solomon's proverb. We at once established a family altar in our house, and He has verified in our home the larger part of Psalm 128." From the beginning of the Song of Ascents;

Blessed are all who fear the Lord,
who walk in obedience to him.
You will eat the fruit of your labor;
blessings and prosperity will be yours.
Your wife will be like a fruitful vine
within your house;
your children will be like olive shoots
around your table.[3]

Their first child, Minnie, from whom I am descended, was born in 1866, a year after they married. Minnie ultimately married George F. Ludington, an oysterman. In the old photograph he sports a truly weird haircut, and he has big ears and a funny-looking mustache. His father, John Bliss Ludington, looking distinguished, was also an oysterman. He had moved to Baltimore from New Haven, Connecticut. George followed his father into the business of packing oysters in Baltimore, but he cleverly expanded into canning and broadened their business to include fruits and vegetables. In 1895, George and Minnie had one child, called G. Franklin, who was my grandfather.

Minnie was followed by Adelaide, born in 1868. Known as Ada, she stayed with her family until late in life. After Eudocia's untimely early demise, Ada managed the household, her younger siblings, and even her father in his dotage. In 1914, well after Rob's death, she married a Robert Devine, age fifty-one, of North Dakota, but sadly he died not long after, and Ada returned to Baltimore. William, the next child, was born in 1872. In one family photograph, when he appears to be in his twenties, he is jauntily perched atop a racy bike with a funky hat on his head. William grew to become a rather successful lawyer in Baltimore, litigating divorces and bringing suits against companies and the city of Baltimore for employee accidents and malfeasance. He was married to Mary Church, and they had two children. From newspapers later in that era, it appears that William spent almost all his free time raising dogs and hunting; he even served as a deputy game warden. At one point, William was featured in the papers for helping to apprehend some poachers by bravely using his finger extended inside his pocket and pretending it was a gun.[4]

The next child, Louis, was born in the Grand Central Hotel of New York City in 1875. There must be a story in that. Growing up in Baltimore with the rest, he earned his medical degree at the University of Maryland and started his career at Bay View Hospital in Baltimore. Louis then moved out to Breckinridge, Minnesota, to serve as a doctor for the Great Northern Railway Company and be a surgeon at Franciscan Hospital. In Breckinridge, he married Louise Hyser, and together they had two children, Robert and Margaret. After ten years in Minnesota, the family then moved to Danville, Indiana, where Louis built his own very successful private practice.

Another son, Robert, was born in 1879, but sadly he died at age five. Next came Jennie, who according to my mother was my grandfather's favorite aunt. Born in 1883, she was also apparently the heart and soul of the family, allegedly keeping communications among the siblings going through the years. Roughly eight years after Rob died, during an agonizing heat wave she visited a friend living in Anderson, Indiana. There she met a young man, Wade Free, whom she shortly married in 1911, at the age of twenty-eight. After the ceremony in Baltimore, a small reception was held in Minnie's house before Jennie and Wade returned to Anderson. They ultimately had two children, Wade Free Jr. and Louise Armstrong Free. Wade Jr. went on to become a highly decorated soldier in WW II, and upon returning from the war he married Mary McNeely.

It was she, Jenny's daughter-in-law Mary, who near the end of her life gave Rob's logbooks to the New Bedford Whaling Museum.

The whaler's second-to-last child, Harry, was born in 1886. He remained in and around Baltimore for many years and worked for the Campbell Metal Window Corporation. He was an assistant manager when the company was bought by Truscon Steel, and so he and his family moved to Youngstown, Ohio. Married to Elizabeth Murray, they had two children, Harry J. Armstrong Jr. and Elizabeth Armstrong, later Elizabeth Finn. Finally, Gelston, the family's baby, was born in 1888 when Eudocia was age forty-one and Rob sixty. Gelston was only eleven when his mother died, and seventeen when his father passed. Largely raised by Ada, in his teens he appears to have been taken under Jennie's wing, for he moved out with her to Indiana in 1911 when she married. He ultimately became an electrical engineer and worked in Pittsburgh for a while with the Carnegie Corporation. At some point he moved back near Jennie and was introduced to Louis's wife's sister. He married her, Harriet Hyser, and they had two sons, John E. Armstrong and Robert Gelston Armstrong. Their second son, Robert Gelston Armstrong, is worthy of his own book.

Robert Gelston Armstrong, named after his grandfather, was born in Danville, Indiana, in 1917. Extraordinarily adept at languages, he studied at Miami University in Ohio and became intellectually fascinated by Marxism and pacificism in the face of the looming crisis of World War II in Europe. He then attended the University of Chicago, where his interest in socioeconomic theory pulled him into graduate studies in cultural anthropology. He was also an active member of the campus antiwar movement. Called up for service, he joined the army in 1942 and was given a succession of assignments, ultimately as squad leader in a line company. Soon he was engaged in battles at the Ardennes Forest, the Ludendorff Bridge, and the Ruhr Pocket. When the war ended, his language skills were in great demand, and he was transferred to the army's Monuments, Fine Arts & Archives Program in Berlin, where he worked alongside famed Monuments Man, Captain Bernard D. Burks. Returning to the United States in 1946, Robert Gelston reenrolled in the PhD program of the University of Chicago and became involved in the Civil

Rights Movement. However, McCarthyism targeted Robert Gelston for his interests, and the FBI blackballed him in academia. In an effort to escape the government's harassment, he moved to Nigeria, and there he rose to be chairman of his department at the University of Ibadan. Much honored for his work in Nigeria, yet alienated from his own country, he never returned to the United States and died alone in Lagos in May 1987.[5] I wish I had known.

Anyway, as Rob and Eudocia managed their store and their "fruitful vine," Rob settled ever more deeply into the community. He immersed himself in his church, rising in the ranks to join the vestry and teaching Sunday school until age seventy-two. His faith and apparent open-mindedness also connected him to a number of charities in the city, and in 1898 he was appointed by the state of Maryland to oversee the Industrial Home for Colored Girls. It was also during this period of his life, sometime around 1895, in his late sixties, that he decided to consult his logs and write an autobiographical account of his time at sea.

Sadly, in September 1899, when she was just fifty-three, Eudocia died from appendicitis. This is when their daughter, Ada, stepped up to manage the bustling household and help finish raising the younger children. With Rob as the patriarch, the 1900 Census shows those living in the Mt. Royal house included George and Minnie Ludington and their 1-year-old son G. Franklin Ludington, as well as 31-year-old Ada Armstrong, 27-year-old William just starting his law practice, 24-year-old Louis in medical school, 17-year-old Jennie, 14-year-old Harry, and 11-year-old Gelston, plus two paid helpers. Then, just three years after Eudocia passed away, in 1902, Rob the whaler died from a heart ailment at age 74.

Rob's redemption and civil connectedness were reflected in his will.[6] With his estate valued at $81,476, Rob first set aside funds to cover Gelston's future education, a gift to Ada for her selfless help in recent years, and a small gift to my grandfather, G. Franklin. A tithe, or one tenth of the rest, was then to be first allocated among a slew of charities, with the remainder of the estate to be equally split among the surviving children. The charities he picked were a mix of Methodist Church organizations and those supporting the needy, including homes for "Colored

Girls," "Fallen and Friendless Women," "Orphans," "Incurables," and the "Hospital for Consumptives," as well as the "Indigent Sick Society of Baltimore."

Today, Rob peacefully lies next to Eudocia in the Mt. Olivet Cemetery in Baltimore. I visited Mt. Olivet recently on a cloudy chilly late autumn day. After much tramping in the wet grass, I found Rob and Eudocia side by side near the crest of a hill. Rob's tombstone notes that "He was a good man, and full of the holy ghost and of faith." Adjacent lie Minnie and George F. Ludington. Together they all enjoy a splendid view of Baltimore, and from their plot one can see the city's tallest buildings as well as the great loading docks along the harbor to the east. Just over a small knoll, Rob's mother and father are buried in a plot alongside Rob's uncle Thomas and his two wives. Next to them lie Rob's grandparents, William and Jane Armstrong. Under encroaching sod, their gravestone was half-buried and covered in leaves. I paused that morning and, with a plastic spoon that came with my coffee, I knelt to sweep the stone clean and scrape it free of moss . . . and wondered if anyone else ever would again.

CHAPTER 28

The Infinite Abyss

SOMETIMES NOW, I CLOSE MY EYES AND THINK OF ROB'S, AND THEN MY, trip around Cape Horn and my subsequent journey to the Southern Galapagos off New Zealand. I imagine surging cerulean rollers, hear howling winds, and envision soaring seabirds set against a horizon as atmospheric as William Turner's impasto might beget. I merge the times and images and visualize Rob braced against the stays in the "Ship Followers," while looking out for a flight of whalebirds. In parallel I recollect leaning over the polished rail of my ship to watch the Cape petrels rising from Antarctica's mists to grace my journey. Perhaps after all this reflection, on family history and the fate of our planet, I am in too deep. Perhaps my wishful green ethos has pulled me from the boundaries of our human reality. Absorbed in a swirl of melancholy thoughts regarding our future, I wonder if we humans are in our twilight, or can we yet find a way to a new dawn in human ecology.

For the moment, the wandering albatross still soar in great arcs across the boisterous seas of Drake Passage, prions flit around the Snares, and sperm whales slide under the cobalt waves that roll north with the Humboldt Current. Our cetaceans and tubenosed birds remain some of the most tangible biotic markers of our planet. For those lucky enough to see whales in the wild today, it's awe-inspiring to watch their colossal bodies course through the seas with fluid grace, breaching, or surging to the surface with their jaws agape. We are fortunate now that with fifty years of respite from man's savage hand, if you journey to places such as Stellwagen Bank off Cape Cod, Monterey Bay in California, or off the coasts of Alaska and Maui, you may see them rise near your boat, blow, and then ease back into the deep. Majestic and knowing, they are magnificent creatures. So too, are the great wandering albatrosses, prions, and all the other pelagics that soar on the oceans' winds, nest on the few remaining uninhabited islands, and snatch krill or squid from the sea's mercurial surface.

Yet, I think we all recognize that human society now stands on the edge; a precipice that will determine our, and our planet's future. Collectively, we are at the point where we must intellectually and ethically grapple with our relationship with other life-forms on earth. We must appraise ourselves, our future needs, and candidly evaluate our capabilities in managing the planet's ecology. We need to assess the planet's carrying capacity, and our interactions with our biological partners on this our one and only home, Earth. Herman Melville understood this more than 170 years ago when, in *Moby-Dick*, he wondered "whether Leviathan can long endure so wide a chase, and so remorseless a havoc; whether he must not at last be exterminated from the waters, and the last whale, like the last man, smoke his last pipe, and then himself evaporate in the final puff."[1] Robert Cushman Murphy, in pushing to open the Whitney Hall of Oceanic Birds in the heart of New York City just seventy years ago, recognized the soaring albatross was deeply symbolic of clean oceans and still-wild places. It is now time that we, Hominids of the Holocene, must face up to our apparently unquenchable appetite to dominate the planet and monopolize every resource. We must recognize that even our current self-appraisals are skewed by modern technology and twisted by imbedded historical anthropocentrism, and that the clock is ticking on our fate.

Our oceanic ecosystems cover 71 percent of the world. The continued presence of the great pelagics in the Southern Oceans reflect an ecosystem of still relatively clean waters, abundant krill, and uninhabited islands. Yet the evidence points toward a contrary trend. Even with the cessation of large-scale commercial whaling in the 1960s and the current population rebound, extinction looms for nearly all whales. At present, blue whales still barely hover above extinction levels from historical overhunting. The near-extinguishment of the Amazon's pink dolphins, vaquitas, a diminutive porpoise in Baja California, and numerous other species highlights overfishing and a failure of regional regulation. The decline of killer whales off Seattle and around the world is due to competition with humans, toxic effluents, and ship traffic. The Atlantic and Pacific right whales are nearly extinct as well, with only a few hundred remaining. The right whales I watched off Cape Cod so long ago are now dying at an unprecedented rate from entanglements with lobster traps and collisions with ships. The last right whales are disappearing simply so ships at sea can go a bit faster and humans can enjoy cheaper lobsters culled from greater depths. Even this past year, Maine's elected delegation anthropocentrically inserted a provision in a spending bill to deny whales the additional protections they need.[2]

If we are honest, we know that we humans are poor at restraint and worse at sharing. The oceans' species that we do not harvest directly for food, we are killing with toxic chemicals, an infinite cavalcade of plastic, warming seas, or by our unfettered competition. All large animals inevitably compete with us for resources, and thus until we shift our paradigm and even the scales of environmental justice, whales and pelagic seabirds will be forever endangered. The reign of such animals will most likely be quietly brought to a sad conclusion in the next century as certain nations increase the unregulated harvest of our oceans' krill. Whales and seabirds do not have to be harpooned or shot to die; starvation works equally well. And frankly, if we humans must now harvest the oceans' krill and squid at the rate we do, the truth is we have already placed ourselves in a precarious position with respect to our future; for we are clearly living beyond our means.

Besides directly outcompeting our fellow species on earth, we also display a great tendency to destroy the biotic fabric of the landscapes we dominate. We have already usurped and now poorly manage most of our planet's grassy plains, fertile valleys, and verdant forests. Daily the evidence lies before us, for in our hubris we have managed to burn rivers with pollution, cut off species from critical breeding sites and migration routes, engulf our forests in flames from mismanagement, and ceaselessly expand the monocultural crop production that leads to ecologically depauperate landscapes. New Zealand is a classic example, for one must travel to offshore islands to see most of the native bird species, as the mainland has been overrun with invasive species. In the United States, large animals are rare, and even monarch butterflies and an infinite number of lesser-known insects are vanishing for lack of vegetative diversity and indiscriminate applications of pesticides. As the World Wildlife Fund well knows, the large wild mammals from around the world that we love as plushy toys all teeter on the brink of extinction. The rain forests from Borneo to the Amazon are disappearing, old growth is nearly gone, our rivers are drying up, and now even the ice caps and glaciers are shrinking. The more we humans put our hands on the controls, the more precarious these ecosystems become. We do not manage the Earth very well, and our hubris clouds our judgment.

In parallel we continue to delude ourselves, for modern technology has to a large degree sucked the air from public support for the preservation of parks, marine sanctuaries, and endangered species. In the past two decades, lavish audiovisual presentations have derailed our participation in and real appreciation for our imperiled ecosystems. We have, to a great extent, been lulled into a vortex of believing that the natural world has now been successfully and forever preserved by the work of David Attenborough, PBS, Wikipedia, and a host of other movies, shows, and podcasts. At the same time, seeing the real thing has become expensive, underrated in comparison, and increasingly unappreciated. Not only is it hard, time-consuming, and expensive to journey to remote tropical forests, high mountain plateaus, or distant oceans, but such trips can be disappointing after having watched movies or television specials. In situ, lions on kills are rare, pandas are rather boring as they chew bamboo, and humpbacks don't breach that often. Shortly, we will have but zoos, some cloaked and labeled as national parks, but most the small, simple breeding enclosures we know. The fate of individuals is also not often fairly recognized. It is rare for people to actually witness the last tiger in a forest, a right whale entangled, or an albatross hooked and drifting lifeless beneath the waves. When they do, they act, but of course by then it is usually too late.

As critically, across the globe the religious and political ideological warfare of the current era has obscured, if not distracted us from the infinitely more necessary goal of a sustainable and biologically diverse planet. From scientists and conservationists to government officials, the politically active already seem to have accepted a vision of a future Earth with pint-sized nature preserves and zoos augmented with cryonic preservation; some nations not even that. Unceasing population growth and commensurate development are apparently foregone conclusions, politically too intractable to tackle; the ultimate "tragedy of the commons." Propelled by extremes in politics, overwhelmed by religious fervor, the conservation agenda has buckled from its focus on biodiversity and ecosystem preservation. We have capitulated from a vision of a future where humans would sustainably exist alongside our fellow species on Earth, to one of unchecked human dominance. Moreover, even in the conservation-minded nations, an enthusiasm for climate change has become the meme of the moment. Deep concerns for the planet's ecological fabric and biodiversity now feel pushed aside as political attention has swerved to metaphysical topics such as carbon offsets, pooling emissions, risk management, and green investment strategies. Conservation today has become largely anthropocentric and transactional, as though we might all wish to live with just each other.

The Amazon is burning, the Serengeti is shrinking, and the clarity of our oceans is diminishing. Every ecosystem is imperiled. The resplendent array of the world's flora and fauna is shrinking; in their numbers, their interactions, and certainly in their ethical parity with us. Like the lynx in the classic ecological paradigm, we may well eat the last hare without appreciating its impact on our own future; our own extinction. The last Atlantic right whale will likely drown alone somewhere off the coast of New England, tangled with a lobster pot. The remaining gray-backed storm-petrels swirling out over the South Atlantic will disappear as their food web is overwhelmed by plastic, or their kelp extinguished by the rising water temperatures. The reflective light in the eyes of the penultimate light-mantled sooty albatross will wink out in the gloom of the dark waters as it futilely battles a long-line's hook beneath the surface of the sea.

While Rob prayed for his own salvation, I pray for ours. I pray that our species will collectively find a way to extend our ethical and spiritual benevolence to all creatures, great and small. I pray we broaden our morality and religious dogmas to encompass the ecological pageantry that is the essential biotic fabric of our only home, Earth. The intrepid Abbe Armand David, the nineteenth-century French missionary and naturalist, observed: "It is a real pity that the education of the human species did not develop in time to save the irremediable destruction of so many species which the Creator placed on the earth to live beside man, not merely for beauty but also to fulfill an important role in the economy of the whole."[3]

In the twilight of our once wild planet, I continue to pray that we will broaden our humanity to protect the last great places on land, in the ocean, and under the sky. I pray we will learn to better manage our planet and maintain the niches and the minimum critical populations needed for each species. I pray that we will redouble our efforts to save the rarest ones before it's too late, especially those that most of us will never see. I pray we will collectively raise our voices in crying out against extinction. Losses, if we're not vigilant, that we may never know. Without a substantive change in our collective hearts, the departure of species largely unseen, such as the snow leopard or light-mantled sooty albatross, will likely be but a silent slip into the infinite abyss of extinction.

Notes

1. Coleridge, Samuel Taylor. 1834. *The Rime of the Ancient Mariner*, in *The Poetical Works of S. T. Coleridge*, ed. Henry Nelson Coleridge. London: W. Pickering.

Chapter 1

1. Stellwagen Bank bubble feeding informed by: Wiley, David, Colin Ware, Alessandro Bocconcelli, Danielle Cholewiak, Ari Friedlaender, Michael Thompson, and Mason Weinrich. 2011. "Underwater Components of Humpback Whale Bubble-net Feeding Behaviour." *Behaviour*, vol. 148, no. 5/6:575–602; Allen, Jenny, and Mason Weinrich, Will Hoppitt, and Luke R. 2013. "Network-Based Diffusion Analysis Reveals Cultural Transmission of Lobtail Feeding in Humpback Whales." *Science*, vol. 340:485–488; Norris, Scott. 2002. "Creatures of Culture? Making the Case for Cultural Systems in Whales and Dolphins." *BioScience*, vol. 52, no. 1:9–14; and Schmicker, Kristen M. 2015. "Humpback Whale Distribution on Stellwagen Bank." *Journal of Aquaculture & Marine Biology*, vol. 2, no. 1:00014. DOI: 10.15406/jamb.2015.02.00014.

2. Whitehead, Hal, M. Dillon, S. Dufault, L. Weilgart, and J. Wright. 1998. "Non-Geographically Based Population Structure of South Pacific Sperm Whales; Dialects, Fluke-markings and Genetics." *Journal of Animal Ecology* 67:253–262; and Whitehead, Hal, and L. Rendell. 2004. "Movements, Habitat Use and Feeding Success of Cultural Clans of South Pacific Sperm Whales." *Journal of Animal Ecology* 73:190–196.

3. Garland, Ellen C., Luke Rendell, Luca Lamoni, M. Michael Poole, and Michael J. Noad. 2017. "Song Hybridization Events during Revolutionary Song Change Provide Insights into Cultural Transmission in Humpback Whales." *Proceedings of the National Academy of Sciences of the United States of America*, vol. 114, no. 30 (July 25, 2017), pp. 7822–7829.

4. Armstrong, Robert W. 1865. Autobiography. 100 pgs. (to be deposited at New Bedford Whaling Museum; hereafter NBWM)

5. Armstrong, Robert W. 1849–1859. Logbooks (two, one original, one a copy). Deposited at NBWM; NBW #1267.

6. Armstrong, Robert W. Unk. Polyglot Bible. (his copy; front pages missing; to be deposited at NBWM)

7. Armstrong, Robert W. 1865. Autobiography. 100 pgs. (to be deposited at NBWM)

CHAPTER 2

1. Hartmann, William, and Ron Miller. 1991. *The History of Earth.* Workman Publishing Co. New York, N.Y. 261 pgs.

2. Cetacean evolution compliled from: Arnason, Ulfur, F. Lammers, V. Kuma, M. Nilsson, and A. Janke. 2018. "Whole-Genome Sequencing of the Blue Whale and Other Rorquals Finds Signatures for Introgressive Gene Flow." *Science Advances,* vol. 4, no. 4 (Apr. 4, 2018). [science.org/doi/10.1126/scieadv.aap9873]; and Gingerich, Philip D. 2003. "Land-to-Sea Transition in Early Whales: Evolution of Eocene Archaeoceti (Cetacea) in Relation to Skeletal Proportions and Locomotion of Living Semiaquatic Mammals." *Paleobiology,* vol. 29, no. 3:429–454; Gingerich, Philip D. 2012. "Evolution of Whales from Land to Sea." *Proceedings of the American Philosophical Society,* vol. 156, no. 3:309–323.; and Mackintosh, N. A. 1972. "Biology of the Populations of Large Whales." *Science in Progress,* vol. 60, no. 240:449–464. Science Reviews 2000 Ltd.

3. Wong, Kate. 2002. "The Mammals That Conquered the Seas." *Scientific American,* vol. 286, no. 5:70–79.

4. Gingerich, Philip D. 2012. "Evolution of Whales from Land to Sea." *Proceedings of the American Philosophical Society,* vol. 156, no. 3:309–323; and Gingerich, Philip D. 2003. "Land-to-Sea Transition in Early Whales: Evolution of Eocene Archaeoceti (Cetacea) in Relation to Skeletal Proportions and Locomotion of Living Semiaquatic Mammals." *Paleobiology,* vol. 29, no. 3:429–454.

5. Sasaki, T., M. Nikaido, H. Hamilton, M. Goto, H. Kato, N. Kanda, L. A. Pastene, Y. Cao, R. E. Fordyce, M. Hasegawa, and N. Okada. 2005. "Mitochondrial Phylogenetics and Evolution of Mysticete Whales." *Systematic Biology,* vol. 54, no. 1:77–90.

6. Shoemaker, Nancy. 2005. "Whale Meat in American History." *Environmental History,* vol. 10, no. 2:269–294. Oxford University Press. Henry Frowde. London, England; and Whitridge, Peter. 1999. "The Prehistory of Inuit and Yupik Whale Use." *Revista De Arqueología Americana,* no. 16:99–154. Accessed April 10, 2020. www.jstor.org/stable/27768424.

7. This section, the "Primer," is largely based on: True, Frederick W. 1904. "The Whalebone Whales of the Western North Atlantic." *Smithsonian Contributions to Knowledge,* vol. 33:27–464. Washington, D.C. (from the Library of the University of California); Starbuck, Alexander. 1878. *History of the American Whale Fisher from Its Earliest Inception to the Year 1876.* Published by the Author. Waltham, Mass. Kessinger Legacy Reprints. 763 pgs.; and Hohman, Elmo P. 1928. *The American Whaleman.* Augustus M. Kelley, Publ. Clifton, N.J. 355 pgs.

8. True, Frederick W. 1904. "The Whalebone Whales of the Western North Atlantic." *Smithsonian Contributions to Knowledge,* vol. 33:27–464. Washington, D.C. (from the Library of the University of California)

9. Cheever, Henry T. 1850. *The Whale and His Captors; or, The Whalemen's Adventures, and the Whale's Biography as Gathered on the Homeward Cruise of the* Commodore Preble. Harper & Brothers, Publ. New York, N.Y. 314 pgs.

10. True, Frederick W. 1904. "The Whalebone Whales of the Western North Atlantic." *Smithsonian Contributions to Knowledge,* vol. 33:27–464. Washington, D.C. (from the Library of the University of California)

11. Hohman, Elmo P. 1928. *The American Whaleman.* Augustus M. Kelley, Publ. Clifton, N.J. 355 pgs.

12. Macy, Silvanus J. 1868. *Genealogy of the Macy Family from 1635–1868.* Joel Munsell. Albany, N.Y. 563 pgs.

13. Hohman, Elmo P. 1928. *The American Whaleman.* Longmans, Green & Co. New York, N.Y. Reprinted 1972. Economic Classics. Augustus M. Kelley Publishers. Clifton, N.J. 355 pgs.

14. Davis, Lance E., R. E. Gallman, and T. D. Hutchins. 1988. "The Decline of U.S. Whaling: Was the Stock of Whales Running Out?" *Business History Review.* Harvard Business School. Cambridge, Mass., pgs. 569–595.

15. This section covering the last gasp of whaling is compiled from: McHugh, J. L. 1977. "Rise and Fall of World Whaling: The Tragedy of the Commons Illustrated." *Journal of International Affairs,* vol. 31, no. 1:23–33; McVay, Scott. 1966. "The Last of the Great Whales." *Scientific American,* vol. 215, no. 2:13–21; and Whitehead, Hal, J. Christal, and S. Dufault. 1997. "Past and Distant Whaling and the Rapid Decline of Sperm Whales off the Galapagos Islands." *Conservation Biology,* vol. 11, no. 6:1387–1396.

16. McHugh, J. L. 1977. "Rise and Fall of World Whaling: The Tragedy of the Commons Illustrated." *Journal of International Affairs,* vol. 31, no. 1:23–33.

17. Andrews, Roy Chapman. 1954. *All About Whales.* Allabout Books, Random House, New York, N.Y. 148 pgs.

18. McVay, Scott. 1966. "The Last of the Great Whales." *Scientific American,* vol. 215, no. 2:13–21.

CHAPTER 3

1. Armstrong, James L., Ed. 1902. *Chronicles of the Armstrongs.* Marion Press. New York, N.Y. 497 pgs. [https://archive.org/details/chroniclesofarms00arms/page/405/mode/2up]

2. Armstrongs. Armstrong Clan History. [https://www.armstrongclan.info/clan-history.html]

3. Fraser, George MacDonald. 1971. *The Steel Bonnets.* Barrie & Jenkins. London. 398 pgs.

4. Stitt, Rev. J. B. 1869. *Discourse Delivered on the Occasion of the Funeral Services Held in the Memory of the Late Thomas Armstrong, Esq. in the Light Street Church.* Kelly, Piet & Co. Publ. Baltimore, Md. 26 pgs. (to be deposited at NBWM)

5. Much of this section, and the one later in the book on the Armstrongs, was put together by creating a full ancestry analysis and then tracking each name through both their addresses in Baltimore as well as posted advertisements in the city directories. All Armstrong addresses and relevant Baltimore addresses were taken from: Baltimore City Directories (Matchett's). 1752– 1900. From Baltimore City Archives. [https://msa.maryland.gov/bca/baltimore-city-directories/index.html]; R. L. Polks and Wood's 1820s–1880s (available at the Internet Archive—https://archive.org/); and a short biography by Glenn, Grovsenor R. 1915. "Armstrong, Cator & Co., Baltimore Biographical." In *The Illustrated Milliner.* January, 1915. The Illustrated Milliner Co. New York, N.Y. Pgs. 54–60.

6. Armstrong, James L., Ed. 1902. Ibid.

7. Saffell, Charles C. "The Citizen Soldiers at the North Point and Fort McHenry, September 12 & 13, 1814." From Brock University Library—SPCL E 356 B2 N37.

8. Glenn, Grovsenor R. 1915. "Armstrong, Cator & Co., Baltimore Biographical." In *The Illustrated Milliner*. January, 1915. The Illustrated Milliner Co. New York, N.Y. Pgs. 54–60.

9. Taylor, Alan. 2021. *American Republics: A Continental History of the United States, 1783–1850*. W. W. Norton & Co. New York, N.Y.

10. A dive into understanding Baltimore in Rob's era came from: Scharf, J. Thomas. 1881. *History of Baltimore City and County*. Louis H. Everts, J. B. Lippincott & Co. Philadelphia. 947 pgs.; and Mayer, Brantz. 1871. *Baltimore: Past and Present*. Richardson & Bennett, Baltimore, Md. Allen Co. Public Library Genealogy Center. [Openlibrary_edition OL23703690M]

11. Norman, Joseph Gary. 1987. "Eighteenth Century Wharf Construction in Baltimore, Maryland." Thesis presented to the faculty of the Department of Anthropology, the College of William and Mary, Virginia. [https://core.ac.uk/download/pdf/235409017 .pdf]

12. Reamy, Bill, and Martha Reamy, Eds. 1987. *1860 Census of Baltimore City*: Vol. 1: 1st and 2nd Wards, and Vol. 2: 3rd and 4th Wards. Family Line Publications. Silver Spring, Md.

13. Shane, Scott. 1999. "The Secret History of the City Slave Trade." *Baltimore Sun*. June 20.

14. Douglass, Frederick. 1881. *Life and Times of Frederick Douglass, His Early Life as a Slave, His Escape from Bondage, and His Complete History to the Present Time*. Park Publishing Co.

15. [S:0 - BS, 1875] Edgar Allan Poe Society of Baltimore—A Poe Bookshelf—The Poet Edgar Allan Poe. (Anonymous, 1875) [https://www.eapoe.org/works]

CHAPTER 4

1. The last verse of "Highland Mary" by Robert Burns (1792) was written inside Armstrong's logbook: Armstrong, Robert W. 1849–1859. Logbooks (two, one original, one a copy). Deposited at NBWM; NBW #1267.

CHAPTER 10

1. Likely just before the gale that swept Bass Strait, May 28th, 1855; from Callaghan, Jeff, and Peter Helman. 2008. *Severe Storms on the East Coast of Australia*. Griffith Centre for Coastal Management. Griffith University, Queensland, Aus. ISBN 978-1-921291-50-0

CHAPTER 15

1. Anonymous. 1891. Obituary of Samuel Kramer. *Baltimore Sun*, August 17.

2. Smithson, Christopher T. 2014. Maryland Society of the Sons of the American Revolution 125th Anniversary/Annual Meeting April 20, 1889–April 20, 2014, Westminster,

Md.; and Anonymous. Sailors Union Church in Historical Marker Database. [https://www.hmdb.org/m.asp?m=7076]

3. Douglass, Frederick. 2003. *My Bondage and My Freedom*. Penguin Classics. 370 pgs.

4. Robinson, Robb. 2010. *Far Horizons: From Hull to the Ends of the Earth*. Maritime Historical Studies Centre. [https://citeseerx.ist.psu.edu/viewdoc/download?doi=10.1.1.737.6510&rep=rep1&type=pdf]

5. Ridgeway, Henry B. 1874. *The Life of The Rev. Alfred Cookman*. Nelson & Phillips, Harper & Bros. New York, N.Y.

6. Ridgeway, Henry B. 1874. *The Life of The Rev. Alfred Cookman*. Nelson & Phillips, Harper & Bros. New York, N.Y.

7. Anonymous. Dr. Chapin Harris. In Pierre Fauchard Academy. [https://www.fauchard.org/publications/12-dr-chapin-a-harris]

8. Anonymous. 1880. Obituary in the *True Kentuckian*, Paris, Ky. December 15, pg. 3.

9. Anonymous. 1899. *Bourbon News*, Nov. 10, and Bourbon Co. Obituaries [https://bourboncoky.info/Obituaries.html]; Ancestry. [https://www.ancestry.com/mediaui-viewer/collection/1030/tree/17761021/person/952545782/media/8270eebc-fbb6-43a5-b135-9ea53671ca73?_phsrc=GOd8&_phstart=successSource]

10. Raymond, Ida. 1870. *Southland Writers: Biographical and Critical Sketches of the Living F Writers of the South*. Vol 2. Claxton, Remsen, & Haffelfinger. Philadelphia, Pa. 973 pgs.

CHAPTER 16

1. Tobey, R. B., and C. H. Pope. 1905. Tobey Genealogy. Charles Pope Publisher. Boston, Mass. 365 pgs. [https://archive.org/details/tobeytobietobyge00tobe/page/n389/mode/2up]

2. Ford, Herbert. 2012. *Pitcairn Island as a Port of Call*. McFarland & Co. Publishers. Jefferson, N.C.

3. Macy, Silvanus J. 1868. *Genealogy of the Macy Family from 1635–1868*. Joel Munsell. Albany, N.Y. 563 pgs.

4. Dyer, Michael P. Undated Draft. *A Pal of the World: The Observations and Illustrations of the American Whaleman at Home and Abroad, 1817–1900*.

5. Whaling ship details compiled from: Starbuck, Alexander. 1878. *History of the American Whale Fishery from Its Earliest Inception to the Year 1876*. Published by the Author. Waltham, Mass. Kessinger Legacy Reprints. 763 pgs.; Hohman, Elmo P. 1928. *The American Whaleman*. Longmans, Green & Co. New York, N.Y. Reprinted 1972. Economic Classics. Augustus M. Kelley Publishers. Clifton, N.J. 355 pgs.; and Palmer, Horace L., and Virginia A. Palmer. 1971. "A Wisconsin Whaler: The Letters and Diary of Horace L. Palmer." *Wisconsin Magazine of History*, vol. 54, no. 2:86–118.

6. Palmer, Horace L., and Virginia A. Palmer. 1971. "A Wisconsin Whaler: The Letters and Diary of Horace L. Palmer." *Wisconsin Magazine of History*, vol. 54, no. 2:86–118.

7. Paddack, William C. 1893. *Life on the Ocean; or Thirty-Five Years at Sea*. Riverside Press. Cambridge, Mass. 242 pgs.

8. Whitman, Walt. "My Tribute to Four Poets." In *Rivulets of Prose*. Carolyn Wells and Alfred F. Goldsmith, eds. Philadelphia: Greenberg Press, 1928. Freeport, N.Y.: Books for Libraries Press, 1969, pgs. 31–33.

9. Darwin, Charles. 1931. "The *Beagle* Starts Her Voyage." *Science News Letter*, vol. 20, no. 558:394–396.

CHAPTER 17

1. Much of this section on whale capture, cutting, and trying is from: Hohman, Elmo P. 1928. *The American Whaleman*. Longmans, Green & Co. New York, N.Y. Reprinted 1972. Economic Classics. Augustus M. Kelley Publishers. Clifton, N.J. 355 pgs.; and Whaling details from: Starbuck, Alexander. 1878. *History of the American Whale Fisher from Its Earliest Inception to the Year 1876*. Published by the Author. Waltham, Mass. Kessinger Legacy Reprints. 763 pgs.; and Palmer, Horace L., and Virginia A. Palmer. 1971. "A Wisconsin Whaler: The Letters and Diary of Horace L. Palmer." *Wisconsin Magazine of History*, vol. 54, no. 2:86–118.

2. Koopman, H. N., and Z. P. Zahorodny. 2008. "Life History Constrains Biochemical Development in the Highly Specialized Odontocete Echolocation System." *Proceedings of the Royal Society*, vol. 275:2327–2334; and McKenna, Megan, T. W. Cranford, A. Berta, and N. D. Pyenson. 2011. "Morphology of the Odontocete Melon and its Implications for Acoustic Function." *Marine Mammal Science*, vol. 28, no. 4:690–713.

3. Cheever, Henry T. 1850. *The Whale and His Captors; or, The Whalemen's Adventures, and the Whale's Biography as Gathered on the Homeward Cruise of the* Commodore Preble. Harper & Brothers. New York, N.Y. 314 pgs.

4. Hobbs, Reuben A. 1854–1859. Logbook of the Ship *Isaac Howland*. Collection of the Nantucket Historical Association. 228 pgs.

CHAPTER 18

1. Keynes, Richard D. 2003. "Charles Darwin's Findings on the *Beagle*." *Proceedings of the American Philosophical Society*, vol. 147, no. 2:103–127.

2. Townsend, Charles H. 1925. "The Whaler and the Tortoise." *Scientific Monthly*, vol. 21, no. 2:166–172.

3. Bauer, G. 1889. "The Gigantic Land Tortoises of the Galapagos Islands." *The American Naturalist*, vol. 23, no. 276:1039–1057.

4. Townsend. 1925.

5. Paddack, William C. 1893. *Life On The Ocean*. Cambridge. Printed at the Riverside Press, H. O. Houghton & Co. (from the Library of the University of California, Internet Archive). 242 pgs.

6. Townsend, Charles H. 1925. "The Whaler and the Tortoise." *Scientific Monthly*, vol. 21, no. 2:166–172.

7. Bauer, G. 1889. "The Gigantic Land Tortoises of the Galapagos Islands."
The American Naturalist, vol. 23, no. 276:1039–1057.

8. Townsend, Charles H. 1925. "The Whaler and the Tortoise." *Scientific Monthly*, vol. 21, no. 2:166–172; and Townsend, Charles Haskins. 1926. "The Galapagos Tortoises in

their Relation to the Whaling Industry." *Zoologica*, vol. IV, no. 3. The New York Aquarium Nature Series, New York Zoological Society. New York, N.Y. 137 pgs. [https://mysite.du .edu/~ttyler/ploughboy/townsendgaltort.htm]

9. Townsend, Charles Haskins. 1926. "The Galapagos Tortoises in their Relation to the Whaling Industry." *Zoologica*, vol. IV, no. 3. The New York Aquarium Nature Series, New York Zoological Society. New York, N.Y. 137 pgs. [https://mysite.du.edu/~ttyler/ ploughboy/townsendgaltort.htm]

10. Caccone, A., J. P. Gibbs, V. Ketmaler, E. Suatoni, and J. R. Powell. 1999. "Origin and Evolutionary Relationships of Giant Galapagos Tortoises." *Proceedings of the National Academy of Sciences*, vol. 96, no. 23:13223–13228.

CHAPTER 19

1. Gulick's lectures well describe the Kingsmills at the time: Gulick, Rev. Luther H. 1944 (reprinted from 1860–1861). "Lectures on Micronesia." In *Fifty-Second Annual Report of the Hawaiian Historical Society for the Year 1943*. Honolulu, Hawaii. Pgs. 7–55.

2. Rouleau, Brian. 2010. "Maritime Destiny as Manifest Destiny: American Commercial Expansionism and the Idea of the Indian." *Journal of the Early Republic*, vol. 30, no. 3:377–411.

3. Woodford, C. M. 1895. "The Gilbert Islands." *The Geographical Journal*, vol. VI, no. 4:325–350. Royal Geographical Society. William Clowes & Sons, Ltd. London. Also good desription in Rossier, W. H. 1870. "Kingsmill Archiplelago." Pgs. 254–268 in *North Pacific Pilot: Part II. The Seaman's Guide to the Islands of the North Pacific.* James Imray and Son, Savill, Edwards and Co. Printers, London. Transportation Library VK 917 R83.

4. Paddack. Ibid.

5. Wilkes, Charles. 1845. *United States Exploring Expedition (1838–1842). Narrative of the United States Exploring Expedition during the years 1838, 1839, 1840, 1841, 1842.* Philadelphia: Lea and Blanchard. [https://catalog.hathitrust.org/Record/001983708]

6. Maude, H. E., and Ida Leeson. 1965. "The Coconut Oil Trade of the Gilbert Islands." *Journal of the Polynesian Society*, vol. 74, no. 4:396–437.

7. Maude, H. E. 1964. "Beachcombers and Castaways." *Journal of the Polynesian Society*, vol. 73, no. 3:254–293.

8. Hayes, Floyd E., H. Douglas Pratt, and Carlos J. Cianchi. 2016. "The Avifauna of Kosrae, Micronesia; History, Status and Taxonomy." *Pacific Science*, vol. 70, no. 1. University of Hawaii Press.

9. Most of the Hussey story was drawn from his nephew's book: Paddack, William C. 1893. *Life on the Ocean.* Cambridge. Printed at the Riverside Press, H. O. Houghton & Co. (from the Library of the University of California, Internet Archive) 242 pgs. Though corroboration was also from: Anonymous. 1853. "Mutiny on Board the *William Penn*— Murder of Isaac P. Hussey." *The Friend*, April 3, 1853: 10, 31, 2.

10. Maude, H. E. 1964. "Beachcombers and Castaways." *Journal of the Polynesian Society*, vol. 73, no. 3:254–293.

11. Anonymous. *Baltimore Sun* vol. LXXL, no. 118. Pg. 4. Oct. 2, 1872; and Anonymous. *Chicago Tribune.* Sept. 16, 1872. Pg. 5.

12. Maude, H. E. 1964. "Beachcombers and Castaways." *Journal of the Polynesian Society*, vol. 73, no. 3:254–293.

13. Maude, H. E. 1981. *Slavers in Paradise*. Australian National University Press & Stanford University Press. ISBN 0 7081 1607 8. 266 pgs.

14. Wallis, Mary Davis. 1851. *Life in Feejee, or Five Years among the Cannibals*. William Heath, Publ. Boston, Mass.; and Wallis, Mary. 1994. *The Fiji and New Caledonia Journals of Mary Wallis, 1851–1853*. Institute of Pacific Studies, Suva & Peabody Essex Museum, Salem, Mass. SNP Printing. ISBN 982-02-0095-4.

15. Mahlmann, John James. 1918. "Reminisces of an Ancient Mariner." *Japan Gazette*, Yokohama, Japan.

16. Most of the details regarding the Wilkes Expedition were from: Reynolds, William. 2004. *The Private Journal of William Reynolds, United States Exploring Expedition 1838–1842*. Penguin Books, London, England. 269 pgs; though some fact-checking came from Wilkes, Charles. 1845. *United States Exploring Expedition (1838–1842), Narrative of the United States Exploring Expedition during the years 1838, 1839, 1840, 1841, 1842*. Philadelphia: Lea and Blanchard.

17. While William Reynold was somewhat cynical to begin with, an even clearer insight has been provided by: Coleman, Kenneth Robert. "'Dangerous Subjects': James D. Saules and the Enforcement of the Color Line in Oregon" (2014). Dissertations and Theses. Paper 1845. [https://pdxscholar.library.pdx.edu/cgi/viewcontent.cgi?article=2845 &context=open_access_etds]

18. Rennie, Sandra J. 1985. "In Search of Souls: The Cultural Interaction between Hiram Bingham, Jr., the Hawaiians and the Gilbertese through Mission Contact 1857–1903. Thesis. Australian National University. Canberra, Australia.

19. Anonymous. "Important Information (Wrecks off the Kingsmills)." *The Friend*. May 1853, pg. 38.

20. Spencer, Capt. Thomas. "Of the Events Attending the Massacre of Part of the Crew Belonging to the Whaleship *Triton* of New Bedford." *The Friend*. Sept. 1848, pgs. 70–72, and Oct. 1848, pgs. 73–74; Anonymous. 1848. "Massacre at Sydenham's Island." *Polynesian* (Hawaiian newspaper). Mar. 25, 1848; and Young, Peter T. 2017. *Triton. Polynesian* (Honolulu newspaper). March 25, 1848, pg. 2. In Images of Old Hawai'i. [https://imagesofoldhawaii.com/triton/]

21. Maude, H. E., and Ida Leeson. 1965. "The Coconut Oil Trade of the Gilbert Islands." *Journal of the Polynesian Society*, vol. 74, no. 4:396–437; and Gulick, Rev. L. H. In *Nautical Magazine and Naval Chronicle for 1862*, no. 4, vol. XXXI. Simpkin, Marshal and Co. Stationer's Hall Court, London. Pgs 169–417 (intermittent chapters).

22. Maude, H. E., and Ida Leeson. 1965. "The Coconut Oil Trade of the Gilbert Islands." *Journal of the Polynesian Society*, vol. 74, no. 4:396–437.

23. Haley, Nelson C. 1990. *Whale Hunt: The Narrative of a Voyage*. Mystic Seaport Museum. Mystic, Conn. 304 pgs.

24. Fisher, Capt. Alfred. "Destruction of a Vessel and Murder of Her Crew." *The Friend*. Nov. 1853, pg. 85.

25. Anonymous. 1852. "Loss of the Ship *Ontario* of New Bedford." *The Friend*. October 1852, pg. 68.

26. Maude, H. E., and Ida Leeson. 1965. "The Coconut Oil Trade of the Gilbert Islands." *Journal of the Polynesian Society*, vol. 74, no. 4:396–437.

27. Anonymous. 1852. "Loss of the Ship *Ontario* of New Bedford." *The Friend*. October 1852, pg. 68.

28. Sacramento *Daily Union*, vol. V, no. 653. April 27, 1853. Published by E. G., Jefferis & Co.

Nauru 11. *The Daily Mercury*. April 20, 1853. 32, 2, 2. New Bedford, Mass. NBWM Lib.; and Gulick, Rev. L. H. "Intelligence from Micronesia." *The Friend*. July 1853, pg. 98. Whaleman's Shipping List.

29. Anonymous. 1853. "Late Whaling Intelligence (Brig *Inga*)." *Daily Mercury*. Apr. 20, 1853: 32, 2, 2.

30. Gulick, Rev. L. H. 1853. "Intelligence from Micronesia (*Inga* and Hussey Affairs)." *The Friend*. July 1853, pgs. 53–54.

CHAPTER 20

1. Little, Elizabeth. 1994. "The Female Sailor on the *Christopher Mitchell*: Fact or Fantasy." *American Neptune* 54:252–256.

2. The Hussey affair was largely compiled from Paddack's book (who was Hussey's nephew): Paddack, William C. 1893. *Life On The Ocean*. Cambridge. Printed at the Riverside Press, H. O. Houghton & Co. (from the Library of the University of California, Internet Archive) 242 pgs.; but also corroborated with other accounts; Anonymous. 1853. "Mutiny on Board the *William Penn*—Murder of Isaac P. Hussey." *The Friend*. April 3, 1853:10, 31, 2; Gulick, Rev. L. H. 1853. "Intelligence from Micronesia (*Inga* and Hussey Affairs)." *The Friend*. July 1853, pgs. 53–54; and "Late Whaling Intelligence." *Daily Mercury*. Apr. 20, 1853: 32. 2. 2. New Bedford, Mass.

3. Anonymous. 1849. *Salem Gazette*. Dec. 18, 1849, 3, 2, 6 NBWM Lib.; and Anonymous. 1849. *Daily Evening Transcript*. Dec. 15, 1849, 20, 2, 5 Boston, Mass. NBWM Lib.; and of course Paddack, William C. 1893. *Life on the Ocean; or Thirty Five Years at Sea*. Riverside Press. Cambridge, Mass. 242 pgs.

4. Hezel, Francis X. 1983. *The First Taint of Civilization: A History of the Caroline and Marshall Islands in Pre-Colonial Days*. Pacific Islands Monograph Series, No. 1. University of Hawaii Press, Honolulu, Hawaii. 412 pgs.

5. Starr, J. B. 1850. "Brig *William Penn* at Auction." *Marine News*, Sacramento Traanscript, vol. 1, no. 108, Sept. 5.

6. Browning, Mary A. *Traders in the Marshalls*. In *Micronesian Reporter*, Pacific Digital Library. 48 pgs.

7. Gulick, Rev. L. H. 1853. "Intelligence from Micronesia (*Inga* and Hussey Affairs)." *The Friend*. July 1853, pgs. 53–54.

8. *The Friend*. April 1, 1853. 10, 31, 2. Honolulu, Hawaii NBWM Lib.

9. The story of the *Ann Alexander* comes largely from: Sawtell, Capt. Isaac F. 1846–1849. Ledger of Ship *Ann Alexander*. In Nicholson Whaling Collection. Providence Public Library, R.I. And Whalemen's Shipping List. Vol. IX, No. 36. Nov. 4, 1851; though the ship's logbook was also used to corroborate some facts (i.e., crew names,

dates); also: Kaplan, Sidney. 1952. "Can a Whale Sink a Ship?" *New York History*, vol. 33, no. 2:159–163.

10. Sawtell, Clement C. 1962. "The Ship *Ann Alexander* of New Bedford 1805–1851." The Marine Historical Association. No. 40. Mystic, Conn. 103 pgs.; and Anonymous. "Thrilling Account of the Destruction of a Whaling Ship by a Sperm Whale in Whalemen's Shipping List." Vol. IX, no. 36. Nov. 4, 1851. New Bedford, Mass.

11. Anonymous. 1854. "Taken at Last (Killing of *Ann Alexander* Whale)." *The Friend*. May 1854, pg. 36.

12. Settling Sunday Island is compiled from: Wollenberg, Ken R. 2000. *Bottom of the Map*. Xlibris Corp. ISBN # 978-0-7388-8866-8; Gunn, John. 1888. "The Kermadec Islands." *Scottish Geographical Magazine*, vol. IV:599–604. T. and A. Constable Printers. Edinburgh, Scotland.

13. The *Rosa y Carmen*'s voyage across the South Pacific is from: Maude, H. E. 1981. *Slavers in Paradise*. Australian National University Press & Stanford University Press. ISBN 0 7081 1607 8; and Anonymous. 1884. Appendix to the Journals of the House of Representatives. Vol. 1, pgs. 62–66. New Zealand. 266 pgs.

CHAPTER 21

1. Anonymous. *New Zealander*, volume 12, no. 1061, June 18, 1856, pg. 2 [https://paperspast.natlib.govt.nz/newspapers/NZ18560618.2.3]; and [http://www.newzealandgenweb.org/index.php/regions/auckland/44-source-records-auckland/38-passenger-ships-part-1].

2. Anonymous. 1853. London Lloyd's List. Aug. 23, 1853, pg. 22.

3. Anonymous. 1853. May 31, 1853, pg. 98. Whaleman's Shipping List.

4. Anonymous. 1895. "Monument to Hooker." *Boston Globe*, July 23.

5. Erickson, Lori. "The Sacred Trees of New Zealand." In *Spiritual Travels*. [https://www.spiritualtravels.info/spiritual-sites-around-the-world/new-zealand/sacred-kauri-trees-of-new-zealand/]

6. Armstrong, Robert W. Unk. Polyglot Bible. (his copy; front pages missing; to be deposited at NBWM)

7. Wilson, J. G. 1951. *The Founding of Hawke's Bay*. The Daily Telegraph Co. Napier, New Zealand. 36 pgs.

8. Mackay, Joseph Angus. 1949. "Historic Poverty Bay and the East Coast, N.I., N.Z." Electronic Text Collection Wellington, New Zealand. DU 436 AM 153 H.

9. Māori historical perspective derived from: Aginsky, Bernard Willard, and Te Rangi Hiroa (Peter H. Buck). 1940. "Interacting Forces in the Maori Family." *American Anthropologist*, New Series, vol. 42, no. 2, part 1:195–210; and Best, Elsdon. 1899. "Notes on Maori Mythology." *Journal of the Polynesian Society*, vol. 8, no. 2:93–121; and Kayser, M., and S. Brauer, R. Cordaux, A. Casto, O. Lao, L. A. Zhivotovsky, C. Moyse-Faurie, R. B. Rutledge, W. Schiefenhoevel, D Gil, A. A Lin, P. A. Underhill, P. J. Oefner, R. J. Trent, and M. Stoneking. 2006. "Melanesian and Asian Origins of Polynesians: mtDNA and Y Chromosome Gradients across the Pacific." *Mol. Biol. Evol.* 23 (11):2234–2244; Meijl, Toon Van. 1996. "Historicising Maoritanga Colonial Ethnography and the Reification of Maori Traditions." *Journal of the Polynesian Society*, vol. 105, no. 3:311–346;

and Middleton, Angela. 2003. "Maori and European Landscapes at Te Puna, Bay of Islands, New Zealand, 1805–1850." *Archaeology in Oceania*, vol. 38, no. 2, Case Studies in the Archaeology of Cross-Cultural Interaction:110–124; and Mutch, Nicola. "Voyage of Rediscovery (Maori Origins)." *Otago Magazine*, issue 34. University of Otago, New Zealand; and Thompson, Christina A. 1997. "A Dangerous People Whose Only Occupation Is War: Maori and Pakeha in 19th-Century New Zealand." *Journal of Pacific History*, vol. 32, no. 1:109–119; and Webster, Steven. 1998. "Maori Hapu as a Whole Way of Struggle: 1840s–50s before the Land Wars." *Oceania*, vol. 69, no. 1, Anthropology, Maori Tradition and Colonial Process:4–35; and Wilmshurst, Janet M., Atholl J. Anderson, Thomas F. G. Higham, and Trevor H. Worthy. 2008. "Dating the Late Prehistoric Dispersal of Polynesians to New Zealand Using the Commensal Pacific Rat." *Proceedings of the National Academy of Sciences of the United States of America*, vol. 105, no. 22:7676–7680.

10. Māori happenings in Hawke's Bay area compiled from: Hippolite, Joy. 1996. Wairoa. Waitangi Tiribunal Rangahaua Whanui Series. Working Paper: First Release. Wai 894 #A110 Waitangi Tribunal, PO Box 5022, Wellington, New Zealand; and Wilson, J. G. 1951. *The Founding of Hawke's Bay*. The Daily Telegraph Co. Napier, New Zealand. 36 pgs.

11. Nicholls, J. L. 1976. "A Revised Classification of the North Island Indigenous Forests." *New Zealand Journal of Forestry*, vol. 21, no. 1:105–132.

12. Wilson, J. G. and others. 1939. "History of Hawke's Bay." The Hawke's Bay Centennial Committee. A. H. and A. W. Reed, Dunedin & Wellington, New Zealand. 468 pgs.

13. Scholefield, G. H. 1940. *A Dictionary of New Zealand Biography*. Vol 1: A–L. Department of Internal Affairs. Wellington, New Zealand. 511 pages. [https://nzhistory .govt.nz/files/documents/dnzb-1940/scholefield-dnzb-v1.pdf]

14. https://www.facebook.com/groups/274423839327902/permalink /447496605353957/

15. Wilson, J. G. 1939. "Early Hawke's Bay." In "History of Hawke's Bay," J. G. Wilson and others, Eds. A. H. and A. W. Reed. Dunedin and Wellington, New Zealand. 468 pgs.

16. Lambert. 1936. *Pioneering Reminiscences of Old Wairoa*. Thomas Avery and Sons Limited. New Plymouth. The New Zealand Provincial Histories Collection [http://nzetc .victoria.ac.nz/tm/scholarly/tei-LamPion-t1-body-d26.html]; and Hippolite, Joy. 1996. Wairoa. Rangahaua Whanui District 11C. Working Paper—First Release. Waitangi Tribunal.

17. Druett, Joan. Unk. "William Lockwood—Wairoa River, New Zealand." [http:// newzealandgenweb.org/hawkes_bay/hbmisc/whalers.html]

18. Ward, Alan. Donald McLean biography. First published in the *Dictionary of New Zealand Biography* in 1990; reprinted in the *Te Ara, Dictionary of New Zealand Biography*. [https://teara.govt.nz/en/biographies/1m38/mclean-donald]

19. Hippolite, Joy. 1996. Wairoa. Waitangi Tiribunal Rangahaua Whanui Series. Working Paper: First Release. Wai 894 #A110 Waitangi Tribunal, PO Box 5022, Wellington, New Zealand.

Chapter 22

1. Levy, Paula Lundy, Ed. Historical Information about Persons Interred at Prospect Hill Cemetery, Nantucket, Mass. [https://www.prospecthillcemetery.com/milestones]

2. Hobbs, Reuben A. 1854–1859. Logbook of the Ship *Isaac Howland*. Nantucket Historical Association. 228 pgs.

3. Anonymous. 1858. "Memoranda (*Isaac Howland* in Feejee)." *The Friend*. October, pg. 80.

4. Wallis, Mary Davis. 1851. *Life in Feejee, or Five Years among the Cannibals.* William Heath, Publ. Boston, Mass.; also Seeman, Berthold. 1862. *Viti: An Account of a Government Mission to the Vitian or Fijian Islands in the Years 1860–1861.* Cambridge: Macmillan & Co. London. 448 pgs.

5. Pritchard, George. 1849. Letter from the British Consulate. Feb. 1849. *The Friend*. Dec. 20, 1849.

6. Anonymous. 1853. "Feejee Islands—No. III. (Recounting cannibalism in 1849.)" *The Friend*. December, pg. 92.

Chapter 23

1. Hobbs, Reuben A. 1854–1859. Logbook of the Ship *Isaac Howland*. Nantucket Historical Association. 228 pgs.

2. Dyer, Michael (Maritime Curator, New Bedford Whaling Museum). *A Pal of the World: The Observations and Illustrations of the American Whaleman at Home and Abroad, 1817–1900.* Unpublished Manuscript.

Chapter 24

1. The whaling ship *Smyrna*, now under Captain Reuben Kelly of New Bedford, was "on fire": Letter from George Gerard, Consul of the U.S.A. in St. Helena, to Hon. William Seward, Sec. of State. Sent Nov. 18th, 1864. From the collection at NBWM.

2. Songini, Marc. 2007. *The Lost Fleet*. St. Martin's Press; and Mawer, Granville A. 1999. *Ahab's Trade: The Saga of South Sea Whaling*. St. Martin's Press (pgs. 258–288).

Chapter 25

1. Stitt, Rev. J. B. 1869. *Discourse Delivered on the Occasion of the Funeral Services Held in the Memory of the Late Thomas Armstrong, Esq. in the Light Street Church.* Kelly, Piet & Co. Publ. Baltimore, Md. 26 pgs. (to be deposited at NBWM)

2. Stein, K. James. 1984. "Baltimore 1784—Historical—Theological—Ecclesiastical." *Methodist History* (periodical) 23:1; see also Stein, K. James. 2010. "The Expansion of Methodism in the Early 19th Century," a book review in *Methodist History*, June 15, 2010 (and the book he reviewed: *America's God: From Jonathan Edwards to Abraham Lincoln* by Mark A. Noll).

3. Pike, J. G. 1835. *Religion and Eternal Life: or, Irreligion and Perpetual Ruin, the Only Alternative for Mankind.* Leavitt, Lord, & Co. New York, N.Y. 216 pgs.; and Pike, John Gregory. 1862. *The Works of Rev. J. G. Pike with a Biographical Sketch.* Simpkin, Marshall & Co. Stationers Hall Court. London. 58 pgs.

4. Ludington, George F. 1920s. Essay on Christ. Unpl. (to be deposited at NBWM)

5. Matthew (20:1–16); and Luke (6:20–38) in King James Version. Unk. *The Holy Bible. The S. S. Teacher's Edition*. Oxford University Press. Henry Frowde. London, England. Oxford Fascimile Series No. 5. 462 pgs. (Minnie Armstrong's Bible, to be deposited at NBWM)

6. Burns, Bishop. March 8, 1928. The Christian Advocate; quoted in Ludington above.

7. Burnett, Ivan Jr. 1975. "Methodist Origins: John Wesley and Alcohol." *Methodist History*. July 7, pg. 5.

CHAPTER 26

1. Murphy, Robert Cushman. 1914. "Observations on Birds of the South Atlantic." *The Auk*, vol. 31, no. 4:439–457; and Murphy, Robert Cushman. 1914. "Cruising in the South Atlantic: From the Equatorial Island of Fernando Noronha to South Georgia on the Threshold of the Antarctic; An Account of the Museum's Recent Expedition to the Far South." *Brooklyn Museum Quarterly*, vol. 1, no. 2:83–110; and summed up in Murphy, Robert Cushman. 1947. *Logbook for Grace; Whaling Brig* Daisy. R. C. Murphy became chairman of the AMNH'S Ornithology Dept., raised the funds for the Hall of Oceanic Birds, and later was a leader in the fight to stop Robert Moses from paving Fire Island, New York.

2. Salinger, J. D. 1951. *Catcher in the Rye*. Little, Brown and Co. 234 pgs.

3. Murphy, Rob Cushman. 1947. *Logbook for Grace; Whaling Brig* Daisy *1912–1913*. MacMillan Co. Reprinted 1965. Time Reading Program, Special Edition. Time Life Books. New York, N.Y. 372 pgs.

4. Leavitt, Joshua, Editor. 1831. *Sailors Magazine and Naval Journal*, vol III, pg. 28. Rev. New York, N.Y.

5. Shackleton, Ernest Henry. 1982 (from a 1919 edition). South Century Publishing, London, England. ISBN 0-7126-0111-2.

6. Weimerskirch, H., T. Guionnet, J. Martin, S. A. Shaffer, and D. P. Costa. "Fast and Fuel Efficient? Optimal Use of Wind by Flying Albatrosses." *Proceedings: Biological Sciences* 267, no. 1455 (2000):1869–1874. Accessed April 11, 2020. www.jstor.org/stable /2665767.

7. Weimerskirch, H., T. Guionnet, J. Martin, S. A. Shaffer, and D. P. Costa. "Fast and Fuel Efficient? Optimal Use of Wind by Flying Albatrosses." *Proceedings: Biological Sciences* 267, no. 1455 (2000):1869–1874. Accessed April 11, 2020. www.jstor.org/stable /2665767.

8. Verheyden, Christophe, and Pierre Jouventin. 1994. "Olfactory Behavior of Foraging Procellariiforms." *The Auk* 111, no. 2:285–291. Accessed April 12, 2020. DOI:10.2307/4088593.

9. The olfactory capabilities of tubenoses is from: Nevitt, Gabrielle A., Marcel Losekoot, and Henri Weimerskirch. 2008. "Evidence for Olfactory Search in Wandering Albatross, Diomedea Exulans." *Proceedings of the National Academy of Sciences of the United States of America*, vol. 105, no. 12:4576–4581; and Phalan, Ben, Richard A. Phillips, Janet R. D. Silk, Vsevolod Afanasyev, Akira Fukuda, James Fox, Paulo Catry, Hiroyoshi Higuchi, and John P. Croxall. 2007. "Foraging Behaviour of Four Albatross Species by Night

and Day." Marine Ecology Progress Series vol. 340:271–286. Accessed April 12, 2020. www.jstor.org/stable/24871817.

10. Palmer, Horace L., and Virginia A. Palmer. 1971. "A Wisconsin Whaler: The Letters and Diary of Horace L. Palmer." *Wisconsin Magazine of History*, vol. 54, no. 2:86–118.

11. Coleridge, Samuel Taylor. 1834. *The Rime of the Ancient Mariner*, in *The Poetical Works of S. T. Coleridge*, ed. Henry Nelson Coleridge. London: W. Pickering.

12. https://library.princeton.edu/visual_materials/maps/websites/pacific/magellan -strait/cape-horn.html

12. https://library.princeton.edu/visual_materials/maps/websites/pacific/magellan -strait/cape-horn.html

13. King James Version. Unk. *The Holy Bible. The S. S. Teacher's Edition*. Oxford University Press. Henry Frowde. London, England. Oxford Fascimile Series No. 5. 462 pgs. (Minnie Armstrong's Bible, to be deposited at NBWM)

CHAPTER 27

1. Armstrong family details compiled from Rob's autobiography, a careful review of Baltimore City Directories (Baltimore City Directories; R. L. Polks and Wood's 1820s–1880s. At the Internet Archive [https://archive.org/]; and Baltimore City Directories (Matchett's), 1752–1900. From Baltimore City Archives [https://msa.maryland .gov/bca/baltimore-city-directories/index.html]), and a review of the US Census data in the period (via Ancestry.com).

2. Douglass, Frederick. 1864. *New York Tribune*. Speech given January 13, 1864, before the Woman's Loyal League at the Cooper Institute in New York City. [https://www .blackpast.org/african-american-history/1864-frederick-douglass-mission-war/]

3. Not precisely sure which version of this Psalm he read, but this is an older Methodist version from the Holston Conference of the United Methodist Church. [https://www .holston.org/devodetail/march-10-2020-15254772]

4. Anonymous. 1905. "Chasing Purse-Netters." *Baltimore Sun*. July 24, 1905, pg. 8.

5. Stocking, George W. Jr., and Robert Gelston Armstrong. (2002). "Society, Matter, and Human Nature: Robert Gelston Armstrong and Marxist Anthropology at the University of Chicago, 1950." *History of Anthropology Newsletter*, vol. 29, no. 1, article 3. Available at: https://repository.upenn.edu/han/vol29/iss1/3; and Anonymous. 1989. Robert Gelston Armstrong 1917–1987. Obituary in *Africa* 59 (4). [https://www.cambridge.org /core/services/aop-cambridge-core/content/view/FC4301ED759F396E53FAD8B7FE CDA512/S0001972000051561a.pdf/robert_gelston_armstrong_191787.pdf]

6. Armstrong, Robert W. 1902. Last Will and Testament of Robert Armstrong. (copy thereof; to be deposited at NBWM)

CHAPTER 28

1. Melville, Herman. 1851 (Reprinted 2016). *Moby-Dick*. Macmillan's Collector Library. 768 pgs.

2. Joselow, Maxine. "To Protect Lobstermen, Spending Bill May Speed Whales' Extinction, Activists Say." *Washington Post*. Dec. 20, 2022.

3. David, Abbe Armand. 1949. *Abbe David's Diary: An Account of the French Naturalist's Journeys and Observations in China in the Years 1866 to 1869.* Translated and edited by Helen M. Fox. Harvard University Press. Cambridge, Mass. 285 pgs.

Consulted Works & Citations

Anonymous. 1884. Appendix to the Journals of the House of Representatives. Vol. 1, pgs. 62–66. New Zealand. 266 pgs.

Anonymous. 1891. Obituary of Samuel Kramer. *Baltimore Sun*, August 17.

Anonymous. 1895. "Monument to Hooker." *Boston Globe*, July 23.

Anonymous. 1899. *Bourbon News*. Nov. 10.

Anonymous. 1905. "Chasing Purse-Netters." *Baltimore Sun*. July 24, 1905, pg. 8.

Anonymous. Bourbon Co. Obituaries [https://bourboncoky.info/Obituaries.html]; Ancestry [https://www.ancestry.com/mediaui-viewer/collection/1030/tree /17761021/person/952545782/media/8270eebc-fbb6-43a5-b135-9ea53671ca73 ?_phsrc=GOd8&_phstart=successSource].

Anonymous. 1989. Robert Gelston Armstrong 1917–1987. Obituary in *Africa* 59 (4). [https://www.cambridge.org/core/services/aop-cambridge-core/content/view/ FC4301ED759F396E53FAD8B7FECDA512/S0001972000051561a.pdf/robert _gelston_armstrong_191787.pdf]

Anonymous. 2020. *The Mysterious Death of Edgar Allan Poe*. Edgar Allan Poe Society of Baltimore. [Eapoe.org]

Anonymous. 1880. Obituary in the *True Kentuckian*, Paris, Ky. December 15, pg. 3.

Anonymous. 2022. https://www.facebook.com/groups/274423839327902/permalink /447496605353957/

Anonymous. Sailors Union Church in Historical Marker Database. [https://www.hmdb .org/m.asp?m=7076]

Anonymous. Dr. Chapin Harris. In Pierre Fauchard Academy. [https://www.fauchard.org /publications/12-dr-chapin-a-harris]

Armstrong, James L., Ed. 1902. *Chronicles of the Armstrongs*. Marion Press. New York, N.Y. 497 pgs. [https://archive.org/details/chroniclesofarms00arms/page/405/mode /2up]

Armstrong, Robert W. 1849–1859. Logbooks (two, one original, one a copy). Deposited at New Bedford Whaling Museum; hereafter NBWM; NBW #1267.

Armstrong, Robert W. 1865. Autobiography. 100 pgs. (to be deposited at NBWM)

Armstrong, Robert W. 1902. Last Will and Testament of Robert Armstrong. (copy thereof; to be deposited at NBWM)

Armstrong, Robert W. Unk. Polyglot Bible. (his copy; front pages missing; to be deposited at NBWM)

Armstrongs. Armstrong Clan History. [https://www.armstrongclan.info/clan-history .html]

Arnason, Ulfur, F. Lammers, V. Kuma, M. Nilsson, and A. Janke. 2018. "Whole-Genome Sequencing of the Blue Whale and Other Rorquals Finds Signatures for Introgressive Gene Flow." *Science Advances*, vol. 4, no. 4 (Apr. 4, 2018). [science.org/ doi/10.1126/scieadv.aap9873]

Ashley, Clifford. 1926 (1991 Reprint). "Glossary of Whaling Terms." *The Yankee Whaler*. Dover Publications. New York, N.Y. 156 pgs.

Baltimore City Directories; R. L. Polks and Wood's 1820s–1880s. At the Internet Archive. [https://archive.org/]

Baltimore City Directories (Matchett's). 1752–1900. From Baltimore City Archives. [https://msa.maryland.gov/bca/baltimore-city-directories/index.html]

Bauer, G. 1889. "The Gigantic Land Tortoises of the Galapagos Islands." *The American Naturalist*, vol. 23, no. 276:1039–1057.

Best, Elsdon. 1899. "Notes on Maori Mythology." *Journal of the Polynesian Society*, vol. 8, no. 2:93–121.

Browning, Mary A. *Traders in the Marshalls*. In *Micronesian Reporter*, Pacific Digital Library. 48 pgs. [https://pacificdigitallibrary.org/cgi-bin/pdl?e=d-000off-pdl--00 -2--0--010-TE--4-------0-1l--10en-50---20-fullsize-Kayangel--00-3-1-00bySR -0-0-000utfZz-8-00&a=d&cl=search&d=HASH015d0fc9266148e22363e4e9.35]

Brundage, B. C. 1948. "The Early American Whale Fishery." *The Historian*, vol. 11, no. 1:54–72.

Burnett, Ivan Jr. 1975. "Methodist Origins: John Wesley and Alcohol." *Methodist History*. July 7, pg 5.

Caccone, A., J. P. Gibbs, V. Ketmaler, E. Suatoni, and J. R. Powell. 1999. "Origin and Evolutionary Relationships of Giant Galapagos Tortoises." *Proceedings of the National Academy of Sciences*, vol. 96, no. 23:13223–13228.

Callaghan, Jeff, and Peter Helman. 2008. *Severe Storms on the East Coast of Australia*. Griffith Centre for Coastal Management. Griffith University, Queensland, Aus. ISBN 978-1-921291-50-0.

Cheever, Henry T. 1850. *The Whale and His Captors; or, The Whalemen's Adventures, and the Whale's Biography as Gathered on the Homeward Cruise of the* Commodore Preble. Harper & Brothers. New York, N.Y. 314 pgs.

Coleman, Kenneth Robert. "'Dangerous Subjects': James D. Saules and the Enforcement of the Color Line in Oregon" (2014). Dissertations and Theses. Paper 1845. [https: //pdxscholar.library.pdx.edu/cgi/viewcontent.cgi?article=2845&context=open _access_etds]

Coleridge, Samuel Taylor. 1834. *The Rime of the Ancient Mariner*, in *The Poetical Works of S. T. Coleridge*, ed. Henry Nelson Coleridge. London: W. Pickering.

Coleridge, Samuel Taylor. 1925. *Coleridge Poetry & Prose*. Oxford, at the Clarendon Press. 184 pgs. [https://archive.org/details/coleridgepoetryp00cole/mode/2up]

Creighton, Margaret S. 1990. "Fraternity in the American Forecastle, 1830–1870." *The New England Quarterly*, vol. 63, no. 4:531–557.

Damon, Rev. S. C. "Ship *Harriet* and Brig *Waverly*." *The Friend*. Nov. 1854, pgs. 82–83.

Dana, Richard Henry Jr. 1941. *Two Years before the Mast.* The Heritage Press, New York, N.Y. 347 pgs.

Darwin, Charles. 1931. "The *Beagle* Starts Her Voyage." *Science News Letter,* vol. 20, no. 558:394–396.

David, Abbe Armand. 1949. *Abbe David's Diary: An Account of the French Naturalist's Journeys and Observations in China in the Years 1866 to 1869.* Translated and edited by Helen M. Fox. Harvard University Press. Cambridge, Mass. 285 pgs.

David, Mrs. Edgeworth. 1899. *Funafuti: Or Three Months on a Coral Island.* John Murray, Albemarle St., London. In Library of Congress. DU590 D2. 377 pgs.

Davis, Lance E., R. E. Gallman, and T. D. Hutchins. 1988. "The Decline of U.S. Whaling: Was the Stock of Whales Running Out?" *Business History Review.* Harvard Business School. Cambridge, Mass., pgs. 569–595.

Davis, Lance E., R. E. Gallman, and K. Gleiter. 1997. "Agents, Captains, and Owners." Pgs. 381–422 in *In Pursuit of Leviathan: Technology, Institutions, Productivity and Profits in American Whaling.* L. Davis, R. Gallamn, K. Gleiter, Eds. University of Chicago Press. [nber.org/books/davi97-1]

Douglass, Frederick. 1881. *Life and Times of Frederick Douglass, His Early Life as a Slave, His Escape from Bondage, and His Complete History to the Present Time.* Park Publishing Co.

Douglass, Frederick. 2003. *My Bondage and My Freedom.* Penguin Classics. 370 pgs.

Druett, Joan. Unk. "William Lockwood—Wairoa River, New Zealand." [http://newzealandgenweb.org/hawkes_bay/hbmisc/whalers.html]

Dyer, Michael P. Undated Draft. *A Pal of the World: The Observations and Illustrations of the American Whaleman at Home and Abroad, 1817–1900.* New Bedford Whaling Museum.

Edwards, Everett J., and Jeannette Edwards Ratray. 1932. *"Whale Off!"; The Story of American Shore Whaling.* Frederick A. Stokes Co. New York, N.Y. 285 pgs.

Erickson, Lori. "The Sacred Trees of New Zealand." In *Spiritual Travels.* [https://www.spiritualtravels.info/spiritual-sites-around-the-world/new-zealand/sacred-kauri-trees-of-new-zealand/]

Fisher, Capt. Alfred. "Destruction of a Vessel and Murder of her Crew (Rudolph in Kingsmills)." *The Friend.* Nov. 1853, pg. 85.

Ford, Herbert. 2012. *Pitcairn Island as a Port of Call.* McFarland & Co. Publishers. Jefferson, N.C.

Fraser, George MacDonald. 1971. *The Steel Bonnets.* Barrie & Jenkins. London. 398 pgs.

Friend, The. *The Friend* (1843–1910); South Pacific newspaper, available at Hawaiian Mission Houses Digital Collections. [https://hmha.missionhouses.org/newspapers-and-periodicals-collections]

Garland, Ellen C., L. Rendell, L. Lamoni, M. M. Poole, and M. J. Noad. 2017. "Song Hybridization Events during Revolutionary Song Change Provide Insights into Cultural Transmission in Humpback Whales." *Proceedings of the National Academy of Sciences of the United States of America,* vol. 114, no. 30:7822–7829.

Gerard, George. 1864. Letter from George Gerard, Consul of the U.S.A. in St. Helena, to Hon. William Seward, Sec. of State. Sent Nov. 18th, 1864. From the archives at NBWM.

Gingerich, Philip D. 2003. "Land-to-Sea Transition in Early Whales: Evolution of Eocene Archaeoceti (Cetacea) in Relation to Skeletal Proportions and Locomotion of Living Semiaquatic Mammals." *Paleobiology*, vol. 29, no. 3:429–454.

Gingerich, Philip D. 2012. "Evolution of Whales from Land to Sea." *Proceedings of the American Philosophical Society*, vol. 156, no. 3:309–323.

Glenn, Grovsenor R. 1915. "Armstrong, Cator & Co., Baltimore Biographical." In *The Illustrated Milliner*. January 1915. The Illustrated Milliner Co. New York, N.Y. Pgs. 54–60.

Gould, Stephen J. 1983. "Darwin at Sea." *Natural History*, vol. 92, no. 9:14–20.

Grant, Peter R., and Nicola Grant. 1983. "The Origin of a Species." *Natural History*, vol. 92, no. 9:76–81.

Gulick, Rev. L. H. 1853. "Intelligence from Micronesia (*Inga* and Hussey Affairs)." *The Friend*. July 1853, pgs. 53–54.

Gulick, Rev. L. H. 1862. In *Nautical Magazine and Naval Chronicle for 1862*, no. 4, vol. XXXI. Simpkin, Marshall and Co. Stationer's Hall Court, London. Pgs. 169–417 (intermittently).

Gulick, Rev. Luther H. 1944 (reprinted from 1860–1861). "Lectures on Micronesia." In *Fifty-Second Annual Report of the Hawaiian Historical Society for the Year 1943*. Honolulu, Hawaii. Pgs. 7–55.

Gunn, John. 1888. "The Kermadec Islands." *Scottish Geographical Magazine*, vol. IV:599–604. T. and A. Constable Printers. Edinburgh, Scotland.

Haley, Nelson C. 1990. *Whale Hunt: The Narrative of a Voyage* (re: *Charles W. Morgan*). Mystic Seaport Museum. Mystic, Conn. 304 pgs.

Hartmann, William, and Ron Miller. 1991. *The History of Earth*. Workman Publishing Co. New York, N.Y. 261 pgs.

Hayes, Floyd E., H. Douglas Pratt. and Carlos J. Cianchi. 2016. "The Avifauna of Kosrae, Micronesia; History, Status and Taxonomy." *Pacific Science*, vol. 70, no. 1. University of Hawaii Press.

Herman, Louis M., A. A. Pack, S. S. Spitz, E. Y. K. Herman, K. Rose, S. Hakala, and M. H. Deakos. 2013. "Humpback Whale Song: Who Sings?" *Behavioral Ecology and Sociobiology*, vol. 67, no. 10:1653–1663.

Hezel, Francis X. 1983. *The First Taint of Civilization: A History of the Caroline and Marshall Islands in Pre-Colonial Days*. Pacific Islands Monograph Series, No. 1. University of Hawaii Press, Honolulu, Hawaii. 412 pgs.

Hippolite, Joy. 1996. Wairoa. Waitangi Tiribunal Rangahaua Whanui Series. Working Paper: First Release. Wai 894 #A110 Waitangi Tribunal, PO Box 5022, Wellington, New Zealand.

Hobbs, Reuben A. 1854–1859. Logbook of the Ship *Isaac Howland*. Collection of the Nantucket Historical Association. 228 pgs.

Hohman, Elmo P. 1928. *The American Whaleman*. Longmans, Green & Co. New York, N.Y. Reprinted 1972. Economic Classics. Augustus M. Kelley Publishers. Clifton, N.J. 355 pgs.

Kaplan, Sidney. 1952. "Can a Whale Sink a Ship?" *New York History*, vol. 33, no. 2:159–163.

Kayser, M., S. Brauer, R. Cordaux, A. Casto, O. Lao, L. A. Zhivotovsky, C. Moyse-Faurie, R. B. Rutledge, W. Schiefenhoevel, D. Gil, A. A. Lin, P. A. Underhill, P. J. Oefner, R. J. Trent, and M. Stoneking. 2006. "Melanesian and Asian Origins of Polynesians: mtDNA and Y Chromosome Gradients across the Pacific." *Mol. Biol. Evol.* 23 (11):2234–2244.

Keynes, Richard D. 2003. "Charles Darwin's Findings on the *Beagle*." *Proceedings of the American Philosophical Society*, vol. 147, no. 2:103–127.

King James Version. Unk. The Holy Bible. The S. S. Teacher's Edition. Oxford University Press. Oxford Fascimile Series No. 5. 462 pgs. (Minnie Armstrong's Bible, to be deposited at NBWM)

Kirsch, Adam. 2020. "The Abyss of Freedom. Soren Kierkegaard's Struggle with Himself." *The New Yorker*. [newyorker.com/magazine/2020/05/11/soren-kierkegaards-struggle-with-himself]

Koopman, H. N., and Z. P. Zahorodny. 2008. "Life History Constrains Biochemical Development in the Highly Specialized Odontocete Echolocation System." *Proceedings of the Royal Society*, vol. 275:2327–2334.

Lambert, 1936. *Pioneering Reminiscences of Old Wairoa*. Thomas Avery and Sons Limited. New Plymouth. The New Zealand Provincial Histories Collection. [http://nzetc .victoria.ac.nz/tm/scholarly/tei-LamPion-t1-body-d26.html]

Leavktt, Rev. Joshua, Ed. 1831. *Sailors Magazine and Naval Journal*, vol III, pg. 28. New York, N.Y.

Levy, Paula Lundy, Ed. Historical Information about Persons Interred at Prospect Hill Cemetery, Nantucket, Mass. [https://www.prospecthillcemetery.com/milestones]

Little, Elizabeth. 1994. "The Female Sailor on the *Christopher Mitchell*: Fact or Fantasy." *American Neptune* 54:252–256.

Ludington, George F. 1920s. Essay on Christ. Unpl. (to be deposited at NBWM)

Lyrholm, Thomas, and U. Gyllensten. 1998. "Global Matrilineal Population Structure in Sperm Whales as Indicated by Mitochondrial DNA Sequences." *Proceedings: Biological Sciences*, vol. 265, no. 1406:1679–1684.

Mackay, Joseph Angus. 1949. "Historic Poverty Bay and the East Coast, N.I., N.Z." Electronic Text Collection Wellington, New Zealand. DU 436 AM 153 H.

Mackintosh, N.A. 1972. "Biology of the Populations of Large Whales." *Science in Progress*, vol. 60, no. 240:449–464. Science Reviews 2000 Ltd.

Macy, Silvanus J. 1868. *Genealogy of the Macy Family from 1635–1868*. Joel Munsell. Albany, N.Y. 563 pgs.

Mahlmann, John James. 1918. "Reminisces of an Ancient Mariner." *Japan Gazette*, Yokohama, Japan.

Maude, H. E. 1964. "Beachcombers and Castaways." *Journal of the Polynesian Society*, vol. 73, no. 3:254–293.

Maude, H. E., and Ida Leeson. 1965. "The Coconut Oil Trade of the Gilbert Islands." *Journal of the Polynesian Society*, vol. 74, no. 4:396–437.

Maude, H. E. 1981. *Slavers in Paradise*. Australian National University Press & Stanford University Press. ISBN 0 7081 1607 8. 266 pgs.

Mawer, Granville A. 1999 *Ahab's Trade: The Saga of South Sea Whaling*. St. Martin's Press (pgs 258–288).

Mayer, Brantz. 1871. *Baltimore: Past and Present*. Richardson & Bennett, Baltimore, Md. Allen Co. Public Library Genealogy Center. [Openlibrary_edition OL23703690M]

McHugh, J. L. 1977. "Rise and Fall of World Whaling: The Tragedy of the Commons Illustrated." *Journal of International Affairs*, vol. 31, no. 1:23–33.

Mckenna, Megan, T. W. Cranford, A. Berta, and N. D. Pyenson. 2011. "Morphology of the Odontocete Melon and its Implications for Acoustic Function." *Marine Mammal Science*, vol. 28, no. 4:690–713.

McVay, Scott. 1966. "The Last of the Great Whales." *Scientific American*, vol. 215, no. 2:13–21.

Meiburg, Jonathan. 2013. "Inside the American Museum of Natural History's Hidden Masterpiece." In The Appendix. *Out Loud*, vol. 1, no. 3. [theappendix.net]

Meijl, Toon Van. 1996. "Historicising Maoritanga Colonial Ethnography and the Reification of Maori Traditions." *Journal of the Polynesian Society*, vol. 105, no. 3:311–346.

Melville, Herman. 1851 (Reprinted 2016). *Moby Dick*. MacMillan's Collector Library. 768 pgs.

Middleton, Angela. 2003. "Maori and European Landscapes at Te Puna, Bay of Islands, New Zealand, 1805–1850." *Archaeology in Oceania*, vol. 38, no. 2, Case Studies in the Archaeology of Cross-Cultural Interaction:110–124.

Murphy, Robert Cushman. 1914. "Observations on Birds of the South Atlantic." *The Auk*, vol. 31, no. 4:439–457.

Murphy, Robert Cushman. 1914. "Cruising in the South Atlantic: From the Equatorial Island of Fernando Noronha to South Georgia on the Threshold of the Antarctic; An Account of the Museum's Recent Expedition to the Far South." *Brooklyn Museum Quarterly*, vol. 1, no. 2:83–110.

Murphy, Rob Cushman. 1947. *Logbook for* Grace; *Whaling Brig* Daisy *1912–1913*. MacMillan Co. Reprinted 1965. Time Reading Program, Special Edition. Time Life Books. New York, N.Y. 372 pgs.

Mutch, Nicola. "Voyage of Rediscovery (Maori Origins)." *Otago Magazine*, issue 34. University of Otago, New Zealand.

Nevitt, Gabrielle A., Marcel Losekoot, and Henri Weimerskirch. 2008 "Evidence for Olfactory Search in Wandering Albatross, Diomedea Exulans." *Proceedings of the National Academy of Sciences of the United States of America*, vol. 105, no. 12:4576–4581.

Norman, Joseph Gary. 1987. "Eighteenth Century Wharf Construction in Baltimore, Maryland." Thesis presented to the faculty of the Department of Anthropology, the College of William and Mary, Virginia.

Norris, Scott. 2002. "Creatures of Culture? Making the Case for Cultural Systems in Whales and Dolphins." *BioScience*, vol. 52, no. 1:9–14.

Paddack, William C. 1893. *Life On The Ocean*. Cambridge. Printed at the Riverside Press, H. O. Houghton & Co. (from the Library of the University of California, Internet Archive) 242 pgs.

Palmer, Horace L., and Virginia A. Palmer. 1971. "A Wisconsin Whaler: The Letters and Diary of Horace L. Palmer." *Wisconsin Magazine of History*, vol. 54, no. 2:86–118.

Payne, Roger S., and Scott McVay. 1971. "Songs of Humpback Whales." *Science*, vol. 173, no. 3997:585–597.

Phalan, Ben, Richard A. Phillips, Janet R. D. Silk, Vsevolod Afanasyev, Akira Fukuda, James Fox, Paulo Catry, Hiroyoshi Higuchi, and John P. Croxall. 2007. "Foraging Behaviour of Four Albatross Species by Night and Day." Marine Ecology Progress Series vol. 340:271–286.

Pike, J. G. 1835. *Religion and Eternal Life: or, Irreligion and Perpetual Ruin, the Only Alternative for Mankind*. Leavitt, Lord, & Co. New York, N.Y. 216 pgs.

Pike, John Gregory. 1862. *The Works of Rev. J. G. Pike with a Biographical Sketch*. Simpkin, Marshall & Co. Stationers Hall Court. London. 58 pgs.

Preston, Douglas. 2019. "The Day the Dinosaurs Died." *New Yorker*. March 29.

Rannie, Douglas. 1912. *My Adventures among South Sea Cannibals*. Seeley, Service & Co. LTD. 38 Great Russell St., London. 408 pgs. DU 510 R3.

Raymond, Ida. 1870. *Southland Writers: Biographical and Critical Sketches of the Living F Writers of the South*. Vol 2. Claxton, Remsen, & Haffelfinger. Philadelphia, Pa. 973 pgs.

Reamy, Bill, and Martha Reamy, Eds. 1987. *1860 Census of Baltimore City*: Vol. 1: 1st and 2nd Wards, and Vol. 2: 3rd and 4th Wards. Family Line Publications. Silver Spring, Md.

Rennie, Sandra J. 1985. "In Search of Souls: The Cultural Interaction between Hiram Bingham, Jr., the Hawaiians and the Gilbertese through Mission Contact 1857–1903."

Thesis. Australian National University. Canberra, Austraila. [https://archive.org/details/myadventuresamon00rann/page/n9/mode/2up?view=theater]

Reynolds, William. 2004. *The Private Journal of William Reynolds, United States Exploring Expedition 1838–1842*. Penguin Books, London, England. 269 pgs.

Ridgeway, Henry B. 1874. *The Life of The Rev. Alfred Cookman*. Nelson & Phillips, Harper & Bros. New York, N.Y.

Robinson, Robb. *Far Horizons: From Hull to the Ends of the Earth*. Maritime Historical Studies Centre. [https://citeseerx.ist.psu.edu/viewdoc/download?doi=10.1.1.737.6510&rep=rep1&type=pdf]

Rossier, W. H. 1870. "Kingsmill Archipelago." Pgs. 254–268 in *North Pacific Pilot: Part II. The Seaman's Guide to the Islands of the North Pacific*. James Imray and Son, Savill, Edwards and Co. Printers, London. Transportation Library VK 917 R83.

Rouleau, Brian. 2010. "Maritime Destiny as Manifest Destiny: American Commercial Expansionism and the Idea of the Indian." *Journal of the Early Republic*, vol. 30, no. 3:377–411.

Salinger, J. D. 1951. *Catcher in the Rye*. Little, Brown and Co. 234 pgs.

Sawtell, Capt. Isaac F. 1846–1849. Log of Ship *Ann Alexander*. Courtesy of Nicholson Whaling Collection. Providence Public Library, R.I.

Sawtell, Clement Cleveland. 1962. The Ship *Ann Alexander* of New Bedford. 1805–1851. The Marine Historical Association, Inc., Mystic, Conn. No. 40. Reynolds Printing Co. New Bedford, Mass. 105 pgs.

Scharf, J. Thomas. 1881. *History of Baltimore City and County*. Louis H. Everts, J. B. Lippincott & Co. Philadelphia. 947 pgs.

Schmicker, Kristen M. 2015. "Humpback Whale Distribution on Stellwagen Bank." *Journal of Aquaculture & Marine Biology*, vol. 2, no. 1:00014. DOI: 10.15406/jamb.2015.02.00014.

Scholefield, G. H. 1940. APATU, PAORA (?-1875) In *A Dictionary of New Zealand Biography*. Vol 1: A–L. Department of Internal Affairs. Wellington, New Zealand. 511 pages. [https://nzhistory.govt.nz/files/documents/dnzb-1940/scholefield-dnzb-v1.pdf]

Seeman, Berthold. 1862. *Viti: An Account of a Government Mission to the Vitian or Fijian Islands in the Years 1860–1861*. Cambridge: Macmillan & Co. London. 448 pgs. [https://books.google.com/books?id=JEPh0OnFsiQC&pg=PA225&lpg=PA225&dq=Chief+Fiji+Islands+mudwater&source=bl&ots=6xApFZ-vuY&sig=G_nPfoR3qvOYNencL0Pt6H4BFt4&hl=en&sa=X&ved=0ahUKEwjyjKDIvqnQAhVM4YMKHdseBnkQ6AEIQjAD#v=onepage&q&f=false]

Shackleton, Ernest Henry. 2012 (from a 1919 edition). Duke Classics.

Shane, Scott. 1999. "The Secret History of the City Slave Trade." *Baltimore Sun*. June 20.

Sheperd, Henry E. History of Baltimore, Maryland, From Its Founding as a Town to the Current Year, 1729–1898. [http://www.ebooksread.com/authors-eng/henry-e-henry-elliot-shepherd/history-of-baltimore-maryland-from-its-founding-as-a-town-to-the-current-year-peh.shtml]

Shoemaker, Nancy. 2005. "Whale Meat in American History." *Environmental History*, vol. 10, no. 2:269–294. Oxford University Press. Henry Frowde. London, England.

Smithson, Christopher T. 2014. Maryland Society of the Sons of the American Revolution 125th Anniversary/Annual Meeting April 20, 1889–April 20, 2014, Westminster, Md. [https://www.mdssar.org/sites/default/files/archives/125th%20Anniversary%20of%20the%20MDSSAR_0.pdf]

Songini, Marc. 2007. *The Lost Fleet*. St. Martin's Press.

Spencer, Capt. Thomas. "Of the Events Attending the Massacre of Part of the Crew Belonging to the Whaleship *Triton* of New Bedford." *The Friend*. Sept. 1848, pgs. 70–72, and Oct. 1848, pgs. 73–74.

Starbuck, Alexander. 1878. *History of the American Whale Fishery from Its Earliest Inception to the Year 1876*. Published by the Author. Waltham, Mass. Kessinger Legacy Reprints. 763 pgs.

Starr, J. B. 1850. "Brig *William Penn* at Auction." *Marine News*, Sacramento Traanscript, vol. 1, no. 108, Sept. 5.

Stein, K. James. 1984. "Baltimore 1784—Historical—Theological—Ecclesiastical." *Methodist History*, vol. 23, no. 1, October.

Stein, K. James. 2010. "The Expansion of Methodism in the Early 19th Century," a book review in *Methodist History*, June 15, 2010 (and the book he reviewed: *America's God: From Jonathan Edwards to Abraham Lincoln* by Mark A. Noll).

Stitt, Rev. J. B. 1869. *Discourse Delivered on the Occasion of the Funeral Services Held in the Memory of the Late Thomas Armstrong, Esq. in the Light Street Church.* Kelly, Piet & Co. Publ. Baltimore, Md. 26 pgs. (to be deposited at NBWM)

Stocking, George W. Jr., and Robert Gelston Armstrong. 2002. "Society, Matter, and Human Nature: Robert Gelston Armstrong and Marxist Anthropology at the University of Chicago, 1950." *History of Anthropology Newsletter*, vol. 29, no. 1, article 3. Available at: https://repository.upenn.edu/han/vol29/iss1/3.

Taylor, Alan. 2021. *American Republics: A Continental History of the United States, 1783–1850.* W. W. Norton & Co. New York, N.Y.

Thompson, Christina A. 1997. "A Dangerous People Whose Only Occupation Is War: Maori and Pakeha in 19th-Century New Zealand." *Journal of Pacific History*, vol. 32, no. 1:109–119.

Tobey, R. B., and C. H. Pope. 1905. *Tobey Genealogy.* Charles Pope Publisher. Boston, Mass. 365 pgs. [https://archive.org/details/tobeytobietobyge00tobe/page/n389/mode/2up]

Townsend, Charles Haskins. 1925. "The Whaler and the Tortoise." *Scientific Monthly*, vol. 21, no. 2:166–172.

Townsend, Charles Haskins. 1926. "The Galapagos Tortoises in their Relation to the Whaling Industry." *Zoologica*, vol. IV, no. 3. The New York Aquarium Nature Series, New York Zoological Society. New York, N.Y. 137 pgs. [https://mysite.du.edu/~ttyler/ploughboy/townsendgaltort.htm]

True, Frederick W. 1904. "The Whalebone Whales of the Western North Atlantic." *Smithsonian Contributions to Knowledge*, vol. 33:27–464. Washington, D.C. (from the Library of the University of California)

Verheyden, Christophe, and Pierre Jouventin. 1994. "Olfactory Behavior of Foraging Procellariiforms." *The Auk*, vol. 111, no. 2:285–291. Accessed April 12, 2020. DOI:10.2307/4088593.

Wallis, Mary Davis. 1851. *Life in Feejee, or Five Years among the Cannibals.* William Heath, Publ. Boston, Mass. [https://www.google.com/books/edition/Life_in_Feejee/IE1LAAAAMAAJ?hl=en&gbpv=1&dq=inauthor:%22Mary+Davis+Wallis%22&printsec=frontcover]

Wallis, Mary. 1994. *The Fiji and New Caledonia Journals of Mary Wallis, 1851–1853.* Institute of Pacific Studies, Suva & Peabody Essex Museum, Salem, Mass. SNP Printing. ISBN 982-02-0095-4.

Ward, Alan. Donald McLean biography. First published in the *Dictionary of New Zealand Biography* in 1990; reprinted in the *Te Ara, Dictionary of New Zealand Biography*. [https://teara.govt.nz/en/biographies/1m38/mclean-donald]

Watson, Kevin. 2010. "The Expansion of Methodism in the Early 19th Century." *Methodist History* (June 15, 2010), reviewing: *America's God: From Jonathan Edwards to Abraham Lincoln* by Mark A. Noll.

Watwood, Stephanie, P. J. O. Miller, M. T. Johnson, P. T. Madsen, and P. L. Tyack. 2006. "Deep Diving Foraging Behavior of Sperm Whales." *Journal of Animal Ecology*, vol. 75, no. 3:814–825.

Webster, Steven. 1998. "Maori Hapu as a Whole Way of Struggle: 1840s–50s before the Land Wars." *Oceania*, vol. 69, no. 1, Anthropology, Maori Tradition and Colonial Process:4–35.

Weimerskirch, H., T. Guionnet, J. Martin, S. A. Shaffer, and D. P. Costa. "Fast and Fuel Efficient? Optimal Use of Wind by Flying Albatrosses." *Proceedings: Biological Sciences* 267, no. 1455 (2000):1869–1874. Accessed April 11, 2020. [www.jstor.org/stable/2665767]

Whalemen's Shipping List And Merchants' Transcript, 1843–1914. Provided by http://images.mysticseaport.org/images/, through the National Maritime Digital Library at https://nmdl.org/projects/wsl/.

Whitehead, Hal. 1996. "Variation in the Feeding Success of Sperm Whales: Temporal Scale, Spatial Scale and Relationship to Migrations." *Journal of Animal Ecology*, vol. 65, no. 4:429–438.

Whitehead, Hal, J. Christal, and S. Dufault. 1997. "Past and Distant Whaling and the Rapid Decline of Sperm Whales off the Galapagos Islands." *Conservation Biology*, vol. 11, no. 6: 1387–1396.

Whitehead, Hal, M. Dillon, S. Dufault, L. Weilgart, and J. Wright. 1998. "Non-Geographically Based Population Structure of South Pacific Sperm Whales; Dialects, Fluke-markings and Genetics. *Journal of Animal Ecology* 67:253–262.

Whitehead, Hal. 2001. "Analysis of Animal Movement Using Opportunistic Individual Identfications: Application to Sperm Whales." *Ecology*, vol. 82, no. 5:1417–1432. Wiley & Sons.

Whitehead, Hal, S. Gero, and D. Engelhaupt. 2008. "Heterogeneous Social Associations within a Sperm Whale Unit Reflect Pair-wise Relatedness." *Behavioral Ecology and Sociobiology*, vol. 63, no. 1:143–151.

Whitehead, Hal, and L. Rendell. 2004. "Movements, Habitat Use and Feeding Success of Cultural Clans of South Pacific Sperm Whales." *Journal of Animal Ecology* 73:190–196.

Whitman, Walt. "My Tribute to Four Poets." In *Rivulets of Prose*. Carolyn Wells and Alfred F. Goldsmith, eds. Philadelphia: Greenberg Press, 1928. Freeport, N.Y.: Books for Libraries Press, 1969, pgs. 31–33.

Whitridge, Peter. 1999. "The Prehistory of Inuit and Yupik Whale Use." *Revista De Arqueología Americana*, no. 16:99–154. Accessed April 10, 2020. [www.jstor.org/stable/27768424]

Wiley, David, Colin Ware, Alessandro Bocconcelli, Danielle Cholewiak, Ari Friedlaender, Michael Thompson, and Mason Weinrich. 2011. "Underwater Components of Humpback Whale Bubble-net Feeding Behaviour." *Behaviour*, vol. 148, no. 5/6:575–602.

Wilkes, Charles. 1845. *United States Exploring Expedition (1838–1842), Narrative of the United States Exploring Expedition during the Years 1838, 1839, 1840, 1841, 1842.* Philadelphia: Lea and Blanchard. [https://catalog.hathitrust.org/Record/001983708]

Wilmshurst, Janet M., Atholl J. Anderson, Thomas F. G. Higham, and Trevor H. Worthy. 2008. "Dating the Late Prehistoric Dispersal of Polynesians to New Zealand Using the Commensal Pacific Rat." *Proceedings of the National Academy of Sciences of the United States of America*, vol. 105, no. 22:7676–7680.

Wilson, J. G. 1951. *The Founding of Hawke's Bay.* The Daily Telegraph Co. Napier, New Zealand. 36 pgs.

Wollenberg, Ken R. 2000. *Bottom of the Map.* Xlibris Corp. ISBN # 978-0-7388-8866-8.

Wong, Kate. 2002. "The Mammals That Conquered the Seas." *Scientific American*, vol. 286, no. 5:70–79.

Woodford, C. M. 1895. "The Gilbert Islands." *The Geographical Journal*, vol. VI, no. 4:325–350. Royal Geographical Society. William Clowes & Sons, LTD. London.

Young, Peter T. 2017. *Triton. Polynesian* (Honolulu newspaper). March 25, 1848, pg. 2. In Images of Old Hawai'i. [https://imagesofoldhawaii.com/triton/]

Acknowledgments

Most importantly I would like to acknowledge and thank Robert W. Armstrong for being, surviving, and leaving behind a tale of his times. His grandson G. Franklin Ludington, who knew the whaler, cared enough to preserve the manuscript, his Bible, and other papers. Then, while never fulfilling his dream to publish them, G. Franklin at least handed them down to his daughter, my mother, Nancy Ludington Brash. My gratitude to her is boundless, on these and many other matters. While not always sure about my devotion to this project, my wife, Jane, love of my life, ultimately came fully aboard and cleaned up a late manuscript, contributing her meticulous grammar. Our children, Ian and Emily, my sister Diana Brash, and cousin Leland Ludington have all been incredibly interested and supportive through the long process. And in various places across our land are Armstrongs, Frees, Brueckners, Ruths, Flocks, Neals, Millers, Finns, and other cousins, and to them I say, "This is your story as much as mine."

This book would not be without Beth and Sam Gilliland. Beth is a great friend, a wonderful agent, and she had the brilliance to hand an early manuscript to her husband, Sam, who hails from Nantucket. He loved it; which helped garner Beth's full attention. An early editor, Holly Robinson, beautifully reimagined the book as a duet. Vicky Hunter Gohl, best friend since forever, stepped in to help with the illustrations. She has a great eye, and having worked for Ken Burns, she knew where to look and how to get all the permissions lined up. In addition, she read an early draft and suggested substantial and excellent changes. She and Beth together helped me keep my voice. The team at Lyons Press have been wonderful, with Brittany Stoner leading the way. From the manuscript's acquisition to the final production details, Brittany has been firm, thorough, and thoughtful. Also with Lyons, Melissa Baker prepared the map, Kate Hertzog brought style and standardization to the text, and Felicity Tucker shined as the production editor, then Alyssa Griffin led the charge on marketing and publicity. I brought in the talented Susie Strangland to build a social media presence for the book, which she and her daughter Caitlin did superbly. Lauren Beck crafted a beautiful author's website to let me shine, and good friend and consummate master of PR Joe Deplasco of DKC in NYC stepped in as deadlines approached to plot a marketing strategy and make a few key calls.

Off Cape Horn, Wings organized a wonderful trip, and Steve Howell and Luke Seitz were a pleasure to hang with, and giants among pelagicers. Kiwi thanks to Peter Panhuis and Larissa Pumipi at the Kauri Museum in Matakohe, the Kauri Bushman's Association for all that it does, Anne McDonald for hosting me in Wairoa, Ross Baker for finding me an elusive blue duck on the Tongariro, and Nicolas Dillon, wildlife artist extraordinaire, for his companionship as we explored the Southern Galapagos.

In my youth, my intrinsic love of birds was converted into a career in ornithology forged by Helen Hays—the Mother Hen of Great Gull Island. This broadened when I worked at the AMNH under John Farrand, Roger Pasquier, Robert Dickerman, and many others who populated its venerable Ornithology Department. At Connecticut College, Bill Niering, Dick Goodwin, William Barry, Robert Askins, and others taught the essential elements of ecology and "human ecology." Beginning a career at the World Wildlife Fund, Thomas E. Lovejoy was inspirational in conservation and philosophy, and he opened my eyes to the oubliette of inaction; Tom was a great friend and true mentor. I was then blessed to be a student at Yale SOE (then called F&ES), learning from Tom Siccama, Bill Burch, Chad Oliver, and Dean John Gordon, followed by several years at Rutgers with reknowned ecologists Ted Stiles, Stewart Pickett, and Peter Morin. All shared their knowledge with me and left me with a strong conservation ethic and an appreciation for "deep ecology." Shifting from academia to conservation I fell into creating and managing parks, and chronologically, Henry Stern, John Ciaffone, Betsy

Gotbaum, Ed Norris, Adrian Benepe, Tom Kiernan, Theresa Pierno, Tom Secunda, Gretchen Long, Norman Selby, Mike Kowalski, Sally Jewell, Bob Callahan, Oliver Spellman, Darcy Shiber-Knowles, April Mims, Rob Pirani, Ethan Carr, Michael Creasey, Sheridan Steele, Dennis Galvin, Destry Jarvis, John Reynolds, Michael Reynolds, Rolf Diamant, and many others who I worked with over more than three decades in New York City helped me appreciate and advocate for the multitude of the ecological, cultural, and philosophical values of our urban and national parks. Tom Kiernan, in particular, led a wonderful merry band at NPCA, fighting for our national parks with great zest, compassion, and inclusion. One of the best people I ever worked for, Tom also kindly wrote the beautiful and too gracious foreword of this book.

The New Bedford Whaling National Historical Park and New Bedford Whaling Museum are both fascinating and worth a visit any day. I first went there years ago as the northeast regional director for NPCA. While most Americans primarily think of our iconic western national parks when they talk about visiting our national treasures, there is a great array of unique and incredibly interesting urban and cultural national parks that capture the people and stories that forged our nation. The New Bedford Whaling National Historical Park is one. It preserves a historical New England townscape, highlights one of America's greatest industries, and illuminates whaling's role as one of the nation's first major steps toward multicultural inclusion. There is a reason Frederick Douglass settled there.

We should also all thank Ellis Howland, along with Henry Rogers and William Crapo, who helped establish what became the New Bedford Whaling Museum at the turn of the twentieth century. Inside that quiet gem today, I would especially note Mark Procknick, librarian, and Michael P. Dyer, maritime curator, who were incredibly gracious in showing me the institution's references and resources and unearthing Rob's logbooks, and later Michael even shared a draft of his manuscript entitled *A Pal of the World: The Observations and Illustrations of the American Whaleman at Home and Abroad, 1817–1900*. The Nantucket Whaling Museum, a part of the Nantucket Historical Association, also provided key assistance as Sara David, archive intern, and Amelia Holmes, the archivist, speeded up the scheduled digitization of Reuben Hobbs's log. A visit to that special island and the museum, though on a freezing winter's day, illuminated for me so many different facets of whaling.

Lastly, amid my research, I learned a lot from many great whalers, past and present, hunters and conservationists. Foremost, if I could, I would personally thank both Captain Rodolphus Tobey and Captain Reuben Hobbs for taking aboard, and returning, my great-great-grandfather. Others who took the time and made the effort to share their knowledge with us include: Clifford Ashley, Rev. Henry T. Cheever, Elmo Holman, John F. Martin, Scott McVay, Herman Melville, William Paddack, Horace Palmer, Roger Payne, Nathaniel Philbrick, Alexander Starbuck, Frederick True, and Hal Whitehead. And finally, no small nod to the others who "sailed" among the South Seas or lived in New Zealand so long ago and shared their recollections: Rev. Luther Gulick, W. H. Rossier, Mary Wallis, J. G. Wilson, C. M. Woodford, Joy Hippolite, Elsdon Best, T. Lambert, Te Rangi Hiroa (Peter H. Buck), H. E. Maude, and Donald McLean.

INDEX

150–51; by Europeans, 21–22; harvesting oil after, 151–53; by Native Americans, 20–22

whaling industry: disaster in Bering Strait, 23–24; final era of, 25–26; New Bedford fleet, 23; revival until War of 1812, 23; sailors and albatrosses, 249–50; second act after Civil War, 24–25; in twentieth century, 24–25; in United States, 21–25

whaling voyages: author's ship comparison, 252; burial services at sea, 57; employment after, 127–30; financial aspects, 93–94, 97, 125, 226; as manual labor, 56–57; mating of vessels, 90–91; natives on board, 70–71; news and letters, 82; oil barrels, 22, 23, 77–78, 82, 93; overboard, men falling, 48; punishments on board, 66–67, 76, 77; returning home from, 123–26; ship's signals for, 64–65; unhappiness of crew, 75–76. *See also Isaac Howland* of New Bedford; runaways; *Smyrna* whaling voyage;

weather; *specific other whaling ships*

Whitmarsh, William, 122, 124–26, 225

Whitney Hall of Oceanic Birds, 246, 270

Wilkes Exploring Expedition, 168–72

William (Hawaiian kanaka), 175, 176–77

William & Henry of Fairhaven, 84

William Penn, 89, 90, 138, 188

William Rotch, 143

Williams, Rev. Mr. John, 66, 119

William Thompson, 115, 230

Wills, Charles, 192–93

Winney, Payne "Winnie," 48, 67, 81, 190

Woodford, C. M., 162

Woodle Island, 71

World Wildlife Fund, 272

"worm of the sea" (sea slugs), 167

Worth, Captain Calvin, 177

wrecks, 76, 164–65, 178, 179–80, 190–95

Yupiks, 20–21

Zone of New Bedford, 114

About the Authors

ALEXANDER R. BRASH WAS BORN AND RAISED IN NEW YORK CITY, where an early love for birds evolved into a passion for quantitative community ecology and conservation. Along the way he graduated from Connecticut College, Yale School for the Environment, and worked in the Ornithology Department of the American Museum of Natural History. As he was nearly completing a PhD at Rutgers University, a hurricane leveled his study site, so he took a job with the New York City Department of Parks & Recreation (NYC Parks). Brash advanced to become the chief ranger, supervising the agency's uniformed officers, Natural Resource Group, Communications, Historic House Trust, and Special Events. He managed rock concerts while initiating the creation of forty-seven wilderness areas and launching the city's first program to reintroduce extirpated species. He was even a first responder on 9/11. He then spent nearly ten years with the National Parks Conservation Association as the northeast regional director, bringing attention to the system's urban parks, recreational areas, and historic sites, as well as instigating successful efforts to establish Katahdin Woods, Stonewall Inn, and Patterson Falls as new national parks. Alex then spent three years as president of Connecticut Audubon Society, which he reinvigorated by moving its finances into the black, tripling its endowment, and doubling the size of its nature preserves. He is happily married to Jane, with whom he has two children, Ian and Emily. He lives in Connecticut and spends his time consulting, writing, traveling, and birding.

Robert W. Armstrong was born in Baltimore, Maryland, in 1828, the only child of William and Rebecca Armstrong. After attending the esteemed Baltimore College of Dental Surgery, the world's first dental school, he served for a short while as a dentist in the midwestern and southern United States. He then spent ten years in the South Pacific as a whaler, pausing to log in New Zealand before returning to Baltimore and starting a second career as a store clerk. He rose to work at his uncle's millinery firm, Armstrong, Cator and Co. Soon after, he married Eudocia Muller, and together they opened their own successful millinery store on Lexington Street. The couple had eight children, and later in life Robert became more involved in church and community. Robert died peacefully in 1902 and lies with his family in Mount Olivet Cemetery.